MARY AND THE CHURCHES

Edited by Alberic Stacpoole OSB

Mary and the Churches

PAPERS OF THE CHICHESTER CONGRESS, 1986,
OF THE ECUMENICAL SOCIETY OF
THE BLESSED VIRGIN MARY

the columba press

the columba press
8 Lower Kilmacud Road, Blackrock, Co Dublin, Ireland

First edition 1987
Cover by Bill Bolger
Typesetting by Koinonia Ltd, Manchester
Printed in Ireland by
Genprint Limited, Dublin

ISBN 0 948183 41 1

Contents

Dedicated to
George Kennedy Allen Bell

Priest of the Church of England and Ecumenist
Dean of Canterbury, 1924-29
Bishop of Chichester, 1929-58
Chairman, Council for Foreign Relations, 1945-58
Honorary President, World Council of Churches
Joint-Chairman, Anglican-Methodist Conversations
Editor, *Documents on Christian Unity*, 1924-58
Author, *Christian Unity: the Anglican position*, 1946-48

and in recent remembrance of
Archbishop Kevin MacNamara, 1926-87

Primate of Ireland since 1984
Consultor to the Secretariat for Christian Unity
Patron of the Irish Branch, ESBVM
Author, *Mother of the Redeemer*
and of *Christian Unity*

ST BERNARD'S PRAYER TO THE BLESSED VIRGIN MARY

FROM DANTE'S *PARADISO* XXXIII 1-45 LINES

Virgin Mother, daughter of thy Son,
humble and high more than (any) creature,
fixed term of the eternal counsel

Thou are she who didst so ennoble human nature
that its Maker
did not disdain to be made his own making.

In thy womb was re-kindled the love
by whose warmth in the eternal peace
thus has been germinated this flower (i.e. the Celestial Rose)

Here (in heaven) thou art for us a meridian flame
of charity, and below (on earth) among mortal men
thou art a living fountain of hope.

Lady, who art so great and so availing
that whoso wants grace and does not run to thee –
his desire wants to fly without wings.

Thy loving kindness not only succours
him who asks, but many a time
freely runs ahead of the asking.

In thee pity, in thee holiness
in thee the magnanimity, in thee is gathered into one
whatever goodness is in any creature.

And now this man, who from the deepest pit
of the universe right up to here has seen
the spirit-lives one by one

beseeches thee, by grace, for such power
that he may with his eyes be raised
yet higher towards the last salvation.

And I who never burned for my own vision
more than I do for his, put forth to thee
all my prayers, and I pray they may not fall short,

that thou mayest disperse every cloud
of his mortality with thy prayers
so that the supreme joy may be disclosed to him.

Also I beseech thee, Queen, who canst do
whatsoever thou willest, that thou keep healthy
after so great a vision his affections.

Let thy protection rule his human passions:
see Beatrice with so many saints
putting their hands together for my prayers.'

The eyes loved and revered by God,
fixed on the supplicant, made plain to us
how welcome to her are holy prayers.

Thence they were directed to the eternal light,
into which one must believe
that no eye of creature penetrates so deeply.

Translation: Rev. Max Saint (Oxford 1983)

Introduction

Alberic Stacpoole, OSB

The last three International Congresses of the Ecumenical Society of the Blessed Virgin Mary (ESBVM) having been held at Westminster, Canterbury and Dublin for reasons that were fairly evident, Chichester proved a good location but for less evident reasons. It had been the home of the great ecumenist, Bishop Bell; and it is the home of one of the Society's three Executive Co-Chairmen, Bishop Eric Kemp (who had been a member of both the Anglican-Methodist Conversations and the Preparatory Commission to ARCIC I). Adjacent is Arundel, with its Catholic cathedral of the diocese whose Bishop is Cormac Murphy-O'Connor, Co-Chairman of ARCIC II; and with its Castle, whose seigneur is the Duke of Norfolk (a leading Catholic). At the time of selection, the Vice Principal of Chichester Theological College was John Cosmo de Satgé (d. 1984), a founder member of ESBVM. At the Cathedral of Chichester, the Chancellor was and is Canon Roger Greenacre, a Council member of ESBVM. And of the Society's dozen scattered branches, one of the most active is that of West Sussex, based in Chichester.

This was our first two-cathedral site, the VIIth International Congress (15-20 September 1986) being housed at Bishop Otter College, which two years earlier had housed the Bishop Bell Centenary Colloquium, ten minutes away from the Cathedral close. Those present – mostly members – numbered about two hundred; they came from Canada and the United States, from Rome and Uppsala, from England and Ireland. They came prepared for work (7 main papers, 15 Communications), for prayer (morning and evening offices, and daily eucharist) and for various degrees of play (from a cathedral concert to a mayoral tea-party). In the work of the Society there is a policy phrase, that we should achieve the balance between *say – pray – play*, eliciting at least two of these at all events. After a Congress, however well planned the balance of these, there is always a regret that there was not more time for unofficial prayer groups (in this case, Rosary groups especially), and for more relaxed discussion. But a Congress, uncommon as it is, needs to retain its own impetus: it needs to achieve much within the allotted week.

This VIIth Congress had moments which recalled the first at

Coloma in Kent in the summer of 1971. There Cardinal Suenens, the Archbishop of Malines (Belgium), had been joined by seven Catholic and five Anglican bishops, a Greek Orthodox and other denominational leaders. Here in Chichester a frailer Cardinal Suenens, now a Patron, past 80 and semi-retired, gave us that same sense of the presence of the Holy Spirit from what he said and did, surrounded again by bishops, Anglican, Catholic and Orthodox (see Appendix I). Some of the same speakers were present: Fr John McHugh from Durham, now England's representative on the Biblical Commission, Dr Donal Flanagan, and Fr William Burridge WF (still our principal reporter). Where Dr Eric Mascall was participant in 1971, this time he was the subject of prayers for his health. Mgr Delhaye spoke from the Vatican in Coloma , Fr Kevin McDonald in Chichester; J. Neville Ward from the Methodists in 1971, Norman Wallwork in 1986 – and the English Benedictines were not unrepresented at both. What had changed was the former mood of criticism and limitation. In his paper on 'The reticence of the biblical tradition as to the BVM', Alan Richardson, Dean of York, had given the impression of extreme 'de-mythologising': indeed there were even murmurs of dissent at the degree of dismissal of marian historicity. That is now a thing of the past, without loss of scholarly sharpness: at Chichester, as at all Congresses in the 1980s, the search for the truth has been generous.

On the opening evening we received signals of prayer and blessing from high and far places. To our amusement, Bishop Murphy-O'Connor left on his mantlepiece the cable from the Secretary of State, Cardinal Casaroli, and it came to us later:

> His Holiness Pope John Paul II sends cordial greetings to participants. He hopes that Congress may be instrumental in deepening knowledge and fostering veneration of Mary Mother of God and Mother of the Church. It is his prayer that her intercession may bring all Christians together in unity of faith and love so that with one voice and one heart we may all proclaim the glory of God for the salvation of the world.

From Lambeth Palace came a message from our Co-President, who wrote:

> I firmly believe that the importance of the work of the Society in its study of the place of Mary in the Church and the promotion of ecumenical devotion cannot be over-estimated. Your programme at Chichester is clearly wide ranging and challenging, and I assure you all of my prayers for your deliberations.

From Archbishop's House, Westminster came a message from our other Co-President:

Although we must never forget that Church unity is a gift which we have to receive, there is nonetheless a part that we Christians have to play. Increasingly I believe in the part which Our Lady must play. Our study of her part in the redeeming work of Christ and the invoking of her aid seem to me to be of enormous importance. This has always been the view of ESBVM, and if people like me think along the lines stated above, it is thanks to the work done by all of you.

From our Free Church Patron, Dr John A. Newton (Chairman of the Liverpool District of the Methodist Church) came this warm message:

You meet in the Sussex of Hilaire Belloc, that doughty warrior for the Christian Faith, who wrote and sang so often in praise of our Lady. You will no doubt give thanks for the life and work of Bishop George Bell, that committed ecumenist and Christian patron of the arts. His patronage may well serve to underline the central place of our Lady as an icon of the Church.

I pray that the Congress may be a fruitful and inspiring one; and that, as you ponder the mystery of Mary's place in the economy of salvation, you may pray more fervently the prayer of St Richard of Chichester:
O most merciful Redeemer, Friend and Brother,
May we know Thee more clearly, love Thee more dearly,
and follow Thee more nearly; for Thine own sake. Amen
If you take Mary as an exemplar, I am sure you will.

From our Methodist Executive Co-Chairman (the Anglican and Catholic both being present), Dr Gordon Wakefield (Principal, The Queen's College, Birmingham) came this equally warm message:

I am particularly anxious to assure you of my good wishes for the Congress, since I would especially like to have been with you, and am distressed that an August spent in Nigeria, and the attendant accumulation of tasks, makes it impossible. No programme of any of our Congresses has so much interested and intrigued me, and I shall feel very deprived by my enforced absence. But 'inseparably bound in heart the friends of Jesus are'; and that goes too for those to whom he has given his Mother also. May God bless you in everything, and make us ever closer in the Communion of Saints.

From the Patron of the Dublin Branch, and indeed the Dublin Congress of 1984 (who had there given the opening address), Kevin McNamara, Archbishop of Dublin, came words of encouragement which included this: 'I look forward to continuing my association with the Society's work, which – I am convinced – has a great contribution to make to the cause of Christian unity and to the Christian life of our respective Churches.' Other signals were received, notably one from Archpriest Dimitry Grigorieff of St Nicholas Orthodox Cathedral, Washington: 'Sorry to be unable to participate in the Congress, in thoughts and prayers with you.' And perhaps the most heartening of the messages came from the President of the Secretariat for Promoting Christian Unity, Cardinal Johannes Willebrands: it included these words to us:

> It seems to me as time goes by that it is increasingly fitting for ecumenical discussion and indeed ecumenical prayer to embrace the figure of Mary, *Theotokos*, Mother of God. When Mary figures in ecumenical debate she usually does so against the background of thorny problems, be they about authority in the Church, or the proper understanding of the unique role of Christ in redemption. But precisely because Mary pinpoints and focusses theological differences, she is able also to clarify the issues and to point to their resolution. For this reason I submit that the work done by your Society can be and already has been a vital source for the whole ecumenical endeavour.

That great ecumenist, Cardinal Willebrands, successor of Cardinal Augustin Bea SJ in his Secretariat, had begun by thanking us 'for your gracious invitation' to be present, and assured us of his continued interest and support. The English staff member of SPCU, Fr Kevin McDonald, was present in his stead and gave a valuable communication.

St Benedict's *Rule* of *c.* 540 ends (with an afterthought) in these words: *Christo omnino nihil praeponant, qui nos pariter ad vitam aeternam perducat.* 'Let (monks) prefer nothing whatever to Christ; and may he bring us all alike to life everlasting.' That is a good principal of mariology, and might have been uttered by the Mother of God. It is the principle the Protestant tradition waits for, before it can accept any claims for the *Theotokos*. For the monks it has a second and more practical meaning, coming in a chapter on the good zeal which monks ought to have' (c. 72). And so we should begin by discussing prayer – in the Spirit, through Christ (the one Mediator) to the Father.

Our days began privately in the chapel of Bishop Otter College with silent prayer, some making up the *Opus Dei*, while others prayed the rosary or meditated. Some of those who could not communicate later on joined the eucharist of a particular denomination. The first public prayer was before the main morning lecture, in the lecture hall at 09.15; and the last public prayer was after all work at *c.* 22.00 in the chapel. 'Orders for Morning and Evening Prayer' had been printed for issue to all members, the service for the evening being a modification of the Office of the Society. Daily at 12.00 the whole Congress met for the conventual eucharist, regretting that intercommunion was not as yet possible. There were other prayerful moments, perhaps the best being *Musica in honorem Beatae Virginis Mariae* one evening in the floodlit cathedral. Rev David Clark of Leicester, a tenor (see his communication, below) had designed the programme with the St Richard Singers (directed by Michael Walsh). It was all Marian music, drawn from the works of Hildegard Abbess of Bingen, Josquin des Près, Robert Whyte, John Dowland, Claudio Monteverdi, William Byrd and Stanford. Perhaps the best of it was the *Ave Maris Stella* taken from Monteverdi's 1610 Vespers, a setting conceived on the grandest scale in the full tradition of the Italian Baroque and needing a double choir. Sound and stone mingled marvellously.

Of the conventual eucharists, centre of our day, a little should be said. On the Tuesday it was led in Bishop Otter College by Bishop Edward Knapp-Fisher, Archdeacon and recent acting Dean of Westminster Abbey. Professor Donald G. Dawe of Union Theological Seminary (Richmond, Virginia) preached to the text: 'His mother said to the servants, "Do whatever he tells you".' He affirmed the ecumenical meaning of these words of Mary for all of us who are servants in God's house to this day. Following Mary's admonition, servants of God encounter the transforming power of Jesus her Son: the water of mundane life becomes the wine of the Kingdom. This transformation renews Mary's words, bringing us closer to one another as we are bound in obedience to her Son Jesus. On the Wednesday in College, Rev Sister Mary Holliday, Methodist minister in the Guildford circuit and head of the Farncombe Community (ecumenical), Godalming, led the Free Church Eucharist, the preacher being Rev Brian Pickett, Methodist minister in Winchester.

On the Thursday the Congress took itself some miles down the road to Arundel Cathedral, where Bishop Cormac Murphy-O'Connor led the concelebrants in Mass of the Assumption: 'All-powerful God, You raised the sinless Virgin Mary body and soul to the glory of heaven. May we see heaven as our final goal and come to share her glory.' The cathedral cantor, Paul Inwood, excellently led the singing. The frail but lively Cardinal preached the homily, speaking again of the Holy Spirit. The *Magnificat* was sung as a communion antiphon, first in plain chant Latin and then in hymnal English – 'Tell out, my soul, the greatness of the Lord / To children's children and for evermore!' Present among us was the Duke of Norfolk, and he took us on to Arundel Castle for a splendid lunch party (with fitting speeches that amused us all), before he confessed that he had appointed himself guide for the afternoon for all save those who preferred the professional guides. . . and the amusement continued; and we were shown the rosary of Mary Queen of Scots.

On the Friday the college chapel was used for an Orthodox liturgy led by Bishop Kallistos of Diokleia, aided by a single chanter in the pulpit, Peter Lascelles. With preparations and explanations – and it was most clearly performed – the liturgy took an hour an a half. Finally on the Saturday the Congress repaired to Chichester Cathedral for an episcopally led eucharist (ASB, Rite A), the choir being from Chichester Theological College. The organist played Marian music beforehand, notably Boëllmann's 'Prière à Notre Dame' (Suite Gothique). Bishop Eric Kemp himself preached, and his text is provided (see Appendix II). He then invited the Congress to his episcopal palace for a farewell wine party, to a room filled with the portraits of himself and his predecessors (notably Bishop Bell); and to a chapel in which was painted on the wall 'the Chichester roundel' of Madonna and Child with censing angels (c. 1250) which reminded one of a later artist, Donatello. It was very completing to see this at the end, devotional evidence from before the Reformation separation.

A word should be said about the element of *play*. Afternoons took us on foot around the ancient sights/sites of Chichester, including the unique Hospital of Blessed Mary, of which, on his retirement from Westminster Abbey, Bishop Knapp-Fisher is to become Custos in 1987; out to Fishbourne Roman Palace, and to a tea party given by the mayor (a former tutor in religion at Bishop Otter College) in the Assembly Rooms – more words of welcome. On one after-lunch hour Patricia M. Wharton brought over her players from Gosport to stage a Christian pantomime, *Ave Eva*, a kind of modern-day Marian Gloriana, inspired by medieval mystery plays, half real and half ritualistic. One evening Malcolm Miller, a guide-lecturer to Chartres Cathedral (twinned with Chichester), gave a slide-illustrated talk on Our Lady and the iconography of Chartres, a colourful tour around just some of the stained glass of that ancient church. The talk stemmed from his work on television in Britain and the USA.

Of the seven main lectures (each taking about an hour, with a half-hour of chaired discussion), two were by Orthodox, one Church of England, one Presbyterian; two were by bishops, one by an abbot, two by laymen and one by a woman; two were by Americans, one by a Swede and one by an Irishman. One was the John de Satgé Memorial Lecture delivered under the auspices of Chichester Theological College, and will be printed elsewhere. One was a dialectic between Orthodox Bishop and Jesuit, which leaves no written text but an account for the record (in short, below). One, that by the American Orthodox lay woman (married to an Orthodox priest), is here given in contracted form. Four are texts as delivered. Space also allows publication of the reserve paper (by the General Secretary and Editor), available at the Congress though in the event undelivered.

Of the fifteen Communications (each taking about fifteen minutes, with no subsequent discussion), three were by members of the Church of England, one each were Presbyterian, Congregationalist and Church of Ireland; three were by Religious, one was by a layman and four were by women (including an ordained minister); two were by Americans, one Irish, and two from Rome. In written form, a few have been slightly expanded, given footnotes and/or a bibliography: most texts are as delivered, where possible grouped together according to common subject-interest.

The debate or dialectic – what the speakers emphasised as 'a search for agreement' – took its origin in a lecture delivered at the previous Congress in Dublin in 1984: Bishop Kallistos of Diokleia had spoken on 'The sanctity and the glory of the Mother of God', and Dr Edward Yarnold SJ proposed a discussion in public on issues pertaining to the Immaculate Conception touched therein. Bishop Kallistos began with the phrase 'Forgive us our sins. . .' from the *Pater Noster*, arguing that there is a solidarity in the matter, men sharing the responsibility for each other, for everyone, for everything. So the Mother of God is in the same way involved in mutual co-responsibility within the human race. To this Dr Yarnold replied: Mary was subject to *singularis gratia*, to unique and unparallelled grace; her role in fulfilling the redemption was unique. It would be wrong to suggest that her own holy parents were 'a degree below her', for it was a quantum leap in grace effect when the Virgin was conceived. To this Bishop Kallistos replied: yes indeed, Mary was uniquely *mater Dei*, and in that she was given unique grace for a unique vocation. But then, each of us has a unique vocation; as Martin Buber has said, God never does the same thing twice, God has need, in his economy of salvation, of every single person. Do we need to express this in relation to Our Lady by excluding her from the effects of original sin? The Eastern Orthodox liturgy celebrates the feasts of the conception of Mary and of John the Baptist on an equal footing: for both come as the last of the Old Covenant, each heralding the Messiah.

To this Dr Yarnold replied: The theology of original sin has never been entirely clear either in the east or in the western Church. The term was not used by the patristic scholars until St Augustine coined it. When we ask 'what is original sin?', what are we focusing upon – a concept? As with the hunting of the Snark, we ask what it is we are hunting. Why do we baptise babies, who – we know – have no personal sin attaching to them? 'Because of original sin!' Why is it that (as St Paul so graphically described in Romans 7) it is so difficult for us to do what we know we should do? Why did Mary need *healing* grace? To save her in advance from original sin? There are levels of understanding of original sin: physical, juridical, spiritual. The first sees suffering and death as consequence of original sin – but should we suppose that otherwise there would be no suffering, no death? We can say no more than that such physical events are to fallen man spiritual problems. He may become subject to events pertaining to fallen nature. As the Son of Man was tempted, so may Mary be tempted in suffering and dying, so sharing our nature; and she may be liable to ordinary temptations and to weakness of will – for holiness requires growth, requires fruitful reaction to challenge. The juridical level of understanding perceives the solidarity of the whole human race in what Aquinas calls 'a lack of original justice'.Where grace is not present, where the Spirit is not indwelling, man's obediential capacity (his 'God-shaped hole in the heart') is gnawing unfulfilled – and therefore it is said that mankind has inherited a spiritual defect. But Mary has never experienced such a heart-ache, in that she has never in her life lacked original justice. So is Mary filled with grace for the part she has to play; is she thus equipped for her role in the whole of redemption?

To this Bishop Kallistos replied: Reject the concept of original sin, and rather look to the Fall. We ask, did Christ in his incarnation take fallen or unfallen human nature? If fallen, then Mary possessed fallen nature too. Did Christ perhaps take both (and we remember Newman's insight, that theology may be saying and unsaying to a positive effect)? We know that Christ is the true mirror of what it is to be human in the way God had meant it; he was and is the first such. We may say that Christ was fallen, in the aspect of his involvement in our salvation through sharing our predicament. He shares in our poverty, and we in his riches: he as us, so we as him: 'He has lavished his gifts on the needy. . .' (2 Cor 9.9). 'For ours is not a high priest unable to sympathise with our weaknesses, but one who, because of his likeness to us, has been tested in every way, only without sin' (Heb 4.15). Juliana put it thus: 'When Adam fell, Christ fell too; because *one-ing* with all mankind'. And in our time Karl Barth said of Christ: 'His situation, inwardly and outwardly, was as a sinful man. He freely associated with our sinful existence', so to save us. Since the Orthodox Church does not accept Augustine's view of original sin, it finds such doctrines and dogmas as that of 1854 unnecessary. Believing with Occam that one should not multiply dogmas, the Orthodox find both 1854 and 1950 superfluous. But for the Orthodox Mary was indeed filled with grace in her conception, and given a fuller degree of grace at the moment of the Annunciation. So, in a word, Christ was subject to original sin, and therefore so was

Mary. As grace perfects nature, the fulness of her grace can occur only in a perfect nature. As man in solidarity with Christ must respond to temptation, so God had need to make Mary capable of that response in a total way – and so she was made wholly whole, i.e. holy.

APPENDIX I

A note on Cardinal Léon-Josef Suenens of Belgium

This great churchman still in our midst was born on 16 July 1904; so that he was past eighty-two when he travelled over to the Chichester Congress. Afterwards he wrote to the General Secretary of ESBVM (AJS): 'Do you know that I went on to Walsingham and prayed in the chapel where Martin Gillett's ashes are, and I blessed these ashes in the name of the Ecumenical Society of Our Blessed Mary, with implicit delegation from his successor? . . . I asked the Lord to give you all courage, inspiration and perseverance.' A protegé of Cardinal Mercier of Malines (he of the Malines conversations of 1921-6), Suenens became Vice-Rector of the University of Louvain in the dark hours of 1940, standing in for his Nazi-imprisoned Rector for the remainder of the War. In 1945 he was consecrated Auxiliary Bishop to Cardinal van Roey. During the following years he discovered that international movement which emanated from Dublin, the Legion of Mary; and at once he saw the apostolic potential of such a movement for the laity. So on several occasions he journeyed to Dublin to the headquarters of the Legion, there to confer with its founder, Frank Duff, and to study the implications of the movement throughout the world. He then wrote a commentary upon its promise, *The theology of the apostolate of the Legion of Mary*; and later he wrote a biography of one of the Legion's outstanding early members, Edel Quinn. In 1957, at the request of Henri Daniel-Rops (editor of *The Twentieth Century Encyclopedia*), he contributed a book designed as a synthesis of Catholic marian theology, *Mary, the Mother of God* (in French, *Quelle est celle-ci?*; in German, *Maria im Plan Gottes*). After the Council it was revised in an Italian edition, *Chi è Costei?* (Paoline 1980).

From the earliest days Cardinal Suenens has taken an active part in the work of the Society. Twice at International Congresses he has spoken on the role of Mary as overshadowed by the power of the Holy Spirit. At Chichester his intervention was focussed on the mystery of the annunciation as expressed in a new 'Fiat Rosary'. These are his own words upon it: 'Full of ecumenical and apostolic meaning, it concentrates upon nine mysteries of the Lord – three joyful, three sorrowful, three glorious. The Rosary is introduced by a prayer to the Holy Spirit, asking for his active presence in our life. It is meant as a prayer for all Christians as a means for visible unity in living together in the mystery of the Annunciation and Mary's *fiat* to the Spirit and His overshadowing.'

This pastoral initiative, introduced by the present Cardinal of Malines, is now spreading over the world. Cardinal Suenens' explanation of it at the Congress was sympathetically received, and taken up by some.

APPENDIX II

Sermon by Eric Kemp, Bishop of Chichester
Executive Co-Chairman of ESBVM, at the final eucharist
of the Chichester International Congress, 20 September 1986

If you have ever watched a great waterfall, such as High Force in Teesdale, you will have seen how, at the bottom of the fall, the foam gathers itself into patches of various sizes, continues for a distance and then breaks up and parts of it reform in larger or smaller clusters, and so it goes on collecting and dispersing until it finally disappears into the smoother flow of the stream.

So is our life on earth – a coming together in groups, a dispersing and reforming into different groups, and so on until we disappear from the sight of men. For these last five days there has been a large cluster of people formed here in Chichester, a cluster of smaller clusters, one which breaks up today as we go back to our homes and our communities.

It has been good to be here – good to renew old friendships and make new ones, good to have pleasure in the beauty of the scenery, to have our imagination enlarged by the dimensions of history and art from ancient Rome to modern Germany, to be uplifted by beautiful singing and music. The theme of joy runs through the scriptures, it opens our Lady's hymn – My soul magnifies. . . my spirit rejoices. And so this morning we say Thankyou to God our Father for this week.

We go back home. The big cluster is broken up into smaller ones – with our branches, our local groupings. What are we going to take with us? Each of us will probably have some special thing, some special memory, some fresh understanding, some new friendship. But I hope that for all of us this week has renewed the vision of our founder.

As I remember Martin, two things stand out. The first is his determination to meet difficulties head-on. Who but Martin would have thought of an *Ecumenical* Society of the Blessed Virgin Mary? Marian Societies of one sort or another abound in the various churches, but an Ecumenical Society, that was something different, for was not Mary a major cause of division? But precisely because she was a major cause of division Martin thought it important to bring people together to talk about this; and that is a pointer to the right form of ecumenism which does not avoid the difficult questions but faces them directly – and Christians meet to talk with frankness and charity and in a search for truth.

The second characteristic of Martin that I recall was his persistence. There must be many of us here who are involved in the Society because Martin cajoled and pushed us into it, and are now grateful that he did. We do not all have the temperament which makes it impossible for people to say 'No' to us, but we must persist in telling people about the Society and in persuading them that it is not a piece of exotic fringe religion, but is concerned with important questions which touch the heart of the Christian faith. And not only concerned with them, but has in its publications a substantial record of teaching and enlightenment, and evidence of success in bringing Christians of differing allegiances together. The experience of this week should strengthen us in our conviction and in our determination to bring many others to join the Society.

The reason above all is, of course, because Mary is at the heart of the creed, at the very beginning of the Gospel. She said 'Yes', and because of that yes we are here as Christians today. She said yes on our behalf; and inspired, impelled by her we say yes to God. I like to dwell on the contrast between Mary and that other figure in the centre of the creed, Pilate, who cared for himself, who feared and who sentenced Jesus to death. Mary trusted in God alone, hoped in him alone; and through her Jesus was born. And we have to be like one or the other. In all our choices we are Mary or Pilate.

But there is another biblical figure I like to contrast with Mary, Lot's wife. She set out with her family following God's call, but she was afraid and hesitant, the pull of the old ways and the familiar things was strong. She could not keep her face towards the future, but looked back hankering after what she had left, and so she became stuck, a pillar of bitter useless salt. And that too is a choice that we always have to make – to go on and not to turn back, to go on in faith even though going on brings us, as it brought Mary, to the foot of the cross. But because she was at the cross and the grave she was also a witness to the risen Lord. How we would love to know the first words of the Son to his mother at the first Eastertide.

Like those clusters of foam we go now down the stream. We

carry with us what we found this week – we carry it to share with others, to witness to Mary's love and obedience which led to our salvation and will bring us closer to our saviour and our creator.

APPENDIX III

Officers of the VIIIth International Congress, Ecumenical Society of the Blessed Virgin Mary (ESBVM), at Bishop Otter College, Chichester, West Sussex

Patrons present:
His Eminence Cardinal Léon-Joseph Suenens, former Archbishop of Malines (RC).
The Rt Rev. Kallistos, Bishop of Diokleia (Dr K. T. Ware) (Orthodox).

Patrons of the Chichester Congress
The Rt Rev. Dr Eric Kemp, Bishop of Chichester (Anglican).
The Rt Rev. Cormac Murphy-O'Connor, Bishop of Arundel and Brighton (RC).

Congress Committee
Dom Alberic Stacpoole, St Benet's Hall, Oxford: General Secretary.
Rev. Dr E. J. Yarnold, SJ, Campion Hall, Oxford: Co-General Secr.
Mr Joseph P. Farrelly, 11 Belmont Rd, Wallington, Surrey: Membership Secretary.
Mr Peter McQuirk: Congress Treasurer.
Canon Roger Greenacre: Chichester Committee.
Mrs Molly Corbally: Chichester Committee.
Rev. Norman Wallwork, The Birches, Crosthwaite Rd, Keswick: Liturgical Secretary.
Rev. & Mrs Geoffrey Pinnock, 11 Drove Acre Rd, Oxford: Minute/Publication Secretary.
Mrs Linda Rice, Bishop Otter College, Chichester: Conference Secretary of College.
Rev. William Burridge, WF, 15 Corfton Rd, London W4: Press Secretary.

'This Virgin for a Good Understanding': reflections on intercessors

Rev. J. A. Ross Mackenzie
Minister, First Presbyterian Church, Florida

Devotion to the Blessed Virgin

In the winter of 1973 Father Thomas celebrated the twenty-fifth anniversary of his ordination. He was then a priest, and is now a bishop, in the Orthodox Syrian Church of the East, a church which traces its lineage to the mission of the apostle Thomas, who, according to tradition, landed near Cranganore in south India in the year 52. I had known Father Thomas for five or six years as a student and a friend. His silver jubilee as a priest was celebrated in his family church in a country district in Kerala State. He had been baptised in that church, confirmed there and ordained there. That day was also a Marian feast, and in the holy qurbana (or holy communion) the congregation sang in Aramaic, the language of Jesus, to commemorate

> her who is worthy of being called blessed, and extolled of all generations of the earth, holy, glorious and blessed, ever virgin and blissful, Mary the Mother of God. . . Let us remember, at the same tme, the whole company of the saints, both men and women.

When the service was ended, and in the usual place for preaching, Father Thomas introduced me, with the invitation to preach the sermon on Mary. Between rising to come forward and speaking before the congregation, I remember thinking about three things. First, there was a question: what on earth is a Presbyterian minister doing preaching about the Mother of God? Then I remembered the statue done by Jacob Lipschitz that stands in the cloisters of St Mary's Abbey on Iona, and especially its inscription. 'I have made this Virgin,' it says, 'for a better understanding to spread among all people.' That helped. I needed a better understanding of Mary to spread to me right then. Finally, I put myself in mind again of what Mary had said at Cana: 'Do whatever he tells you' – good words for servants at a wedding feast, as recorded by John; good words for a serving priest and his congregation, who speak in Malayalam but still sing the language of Jesus in their liturgy; and good words for all God's servants here and everywhere who speak to one another in Catholic, or Orthodox, or Presbyterian, or Methodist, or Episcopalian, but who are learning to sing in ecumenical devotion to the Blessed Virgin Mary in the Church, under Christ.

Protestant repudiation of such devotion

It is far from clear, however, that such a language or such a song has as yet any general ecumenical assent. In the year 1877, one Charles Chiniquy wrote – the very title is a giveaway – *Fifty Years in the Church of Rome*. The apostate priest (or zealous champion of Protestantism; the judgment was formed according to which side of the divide you stood) records half-way through the book the slow fragmentation of his formerly unbounded confidence in the intercession of the blessed Virgin Mary. He finally consulted his bishop, who (he confides, with words sufficient to the wise) shortly after the interview became insane. The doctrine of Mary's intercession, he blurted out to the presumably not yet insane bishop:

> was a blasphemous lie, and I have been nearly convinced that you and I, nay that our whole Church, are preaching a blasphemous falsehood every time we proclaim the doctrine of the worship of Mary as the gospel truth.

If as a priest he had ever learned to worship Mary, he got it wrong from someone. No one ever taught that in good Catholic teaching, A dozen years later, in 1899, another Protestant tub was being thumped with the publication of Walter Walsh's *Secret History of the Oxford Movement*. After a mild tut-tutting at Frederick Faber for kissing the Pope's foot in Rome, the author castigated E. B. Pusey for his folly and superstition in wearing a hair shirt *every night* (in italics: horrors are always in italics in this book). But the gloves (if not the hair shirt) were really off with the infamous disclosure that some priests in the Church of England were *preaching the doctrine of the immaculate conception of our Lady*. The Roman cat was finally out of the bag when it was revealed in the appendix that Arthur Henry Stanton, curate of St Alban's, Holborn, prayed to the Virgin like this:

> Remember, O most loving Virgin Mary, that never was it known that any who fled to thy protection, implored thy help and sought thy intercession, was left unaided.

It is one thing to misapply evidence. But something was wrong when a hit man from the Protestant underworld attacked Fr Stanton. Stanton had gone, aged twenty-three, to help Mackonochie at St Alban's, Holborn, and stayed there fifty years neither expecting, wanting nor getting anything other than the satisfaction of pastoral and priestly work in one of the toughest areas in London, 'Do you know Jesus?' a well-intentioned missionary asked one of Fr Stanton's young toughs. 'No, sir,' replied the boy, 'but I know a friend of his who lives up our way – Father Stanton.' If one of the helps young toughs needed to go straight was Fr Stanton, then all I can say is, 'God bless all go-betweens like him'. And if one of the helps A. H. Stanton, one of the gentlest of men, needed to keep going at all was the intercession of Mary, all I can say is 'May God bless you, Mary, for your intercession.' (In the words of the Hebrew blessing, spoken over daughters, *Y'simeych Elohim k'sara, rivka, rachel, v'leya* – May God bless you as he blessed Sarah, Rebecca, Rachel and Leah.)

Loving intercessors

God certainly blessed Sarah, and had a purpose for her even if she laughed. In fulfilment of that calling to Sarah, God told Abraham, 'Whatever Sarah says to you, do as she tells you' (Gen 21:12). So a long time later when Mary said almost the same thing at Cana, words out of Israel's history came back with power. And God had a purpose in choosing Rebecca (Gen 21:24), whom Philo of Alexandria regarded as a symbol of the joy of God. God also heard Rachel weeping for her children (Mt 2:18), as God hears every mother who feels the desolation of the land in her soul. And Leah – dear Leah, one of the plain folk, one of those you never look at – God opened her womb, scripture says (Gen 29:31). God heard her too, and she became the mother of many, including Judah, that Judah who is first to be named in Matthew's Gospel under Christ, and after only the patriarchs Abraham, Isaac and Jacob. At the end of the line of loving intercessors, Sarah, Rebecca, Rachel and Leah, mothers all, comes another of the plain folk, one of the *anawim*, Mary, 'of whom Jesus was born'. Mary was the daughter of Israel. In solidarity with her people she recapitulated their hope and history. Through her co-operation, echoing and fulfilling that of the other loving intercessors, the whole course of human history was caught up in redemptive history.

Sarah and Mary

So may God bless you, Mary, as he blessed Sarah, *Y'simeych Elohim k'sara*, first in the list of women who prayed for those they loved. Sarah is therefore the first from whom we learn the meaning of intercession. God blessed her, the pioneer who was willing to leave the security that she knew for the risks attendant on becoming a stranger in a strange land. When God put Abraham to the ultimate test, and when Abraham did not withhold his son, Sarah herself was torn to the heart, for she saw her only son led off to God knows what sacrifice. But in that willingness to trust she learned the supreme value of self-surrender and obedience to the divine will. You can count on it that she prayed that day, interceding for her son.

And Mary? The line of loving intercessors soars to the heights in her. Mary recapitulated Sarah's hope and history. If we bless God for Sarah, we bless God even more for Mary. She is never more the daughter of Israel than when she said 'amen' to God. 'I am the handmaid of the Lord; let it be to me according to your word.' To say amen like that to God means to confess that God is true, true absolutely, true to his nature in holiness and goodness. That is what Mary said about God. To Abraham and Sarah the promise had been given by God that by them all the nations of the earth would be blessed (Gen 12:31). But a nation does not produce a child. Only a particular mother does. So Mary in saying 'yes' to God became the concrete embodiment of Israel, as uniquely she became the mother of Jesus. To disallow her the designation *Theotokos*, Mother of God, God-bearer, and not to call on her as such in the communion of saints is to deny that she was the daughter of Abraham and Sarah. It is to deny that the Messiah was born in Israel.

From Mary we therefore learn the meaning of intercession. Jim Wallis of the Sojourners community in Washington DC, describes how Henri Nouwen shared with the community how the desert fathers regarded prayer as an act of 'unhooking' from the world's securities. Such prayer, Wallis says, 'may be the only action powerful enough to free us from our spiritual bondage to property, money, power, ideas, and causes.'[1] That is surely how Sarah prayed when, like Abraham, she went out, not knowing where she was to go. She was looking for the city which has foundations, whose builder and maker is God (Heb 11:8-12). And that, with no less doubt, is how Mary prayed, when she left with Joseph to live like a refugee in Egypt. She prayed for the child in her arms.

Another Sarah whom I know is Sarah Matheson, our church visitor. She was assaulted late one night by an intruder who raped her: Sarah was then 80. When I went to her hospital bed later, we prayed, and Sarah prayed for the man who had assaulted her. How did Mary pray when she saw her Son, her only·Son, when he was nailed to a Roman gibbet? The evangelist records the words of Jesus: 'Woman, behold your son.' The reference is clearly to the beloved disciple. Or was Jesus asking her also to look at each of the Roman soldiers at the foot of his cross? And was Mary praying only for her Son, or for every mother's son on that garbage dump? When we encounter her again, it is in the upper room in Acts, and she is still praying fervently. If we look at Jesus as Mary looked at him on the hill of Golgotha, we see what money, power, ideas and causes can do to make people assault and destroy. But if we attend to Mary, we shall learn from her that those who find security in God take up in prayer the most powerful political weapon that can be used in spiritual warfare against principalities and powers.

What would happen – and the question is Jim Wallis's – if the churches made prayer for our enemies a regular part of the eucharist? 'Prayer for our enemies,' he says, 'takes them into our hearts. It would bring the Russian people and other potential adversaries into our daily consciousness... As we pray, we begin to see people as God sees them.'[2] That is Mary's intercession. She said amen to God, when, like Sarah, she showed she was ready at the cross to part with what was dearest to her. Joseph was dead. Jesus was all she had that was bone of her bone and flesh of her flesh. He was the one on whom all her own hopes for the future depended.

Rebecca and Mary

May God bless you, Mary, also as he also blessed Rebecca, *Y'simeych Elohim k'rivka*. Rebecca is second in our line of loving intercessors, Rebecca the modest and hospitable, the friend of animals and the framer of her family. Philo in his writings speaks often of Rebecca, who was a symbol and a reminder for him that 'the Creator of all continually rejoices... and plays and is joyful, finding pleasure in accordance with the divine play.' The divine play – what a powerful, even dangerous, phrase! 'Primitive religion,' said Arthur Darby Nock, 'is not believed. It is danced.' There is a time for words. But the Church only too often deserves the castigation of the Scottish poet, Edwin Muir: 'the word made flesh is here made word again.' It is time to rediscover the enfleshed word, the incarnate word, the word carried in Mary's womb. It was hard for her to believe: 'How shall this be?'

The divine play is always hard to believe. Some years ago we adopted in Richmond, Virginia, a Cambodian family, Buddhists all. They came to church with us their first Christmas. Their English was faltering at best. Never one to take the impossible seriously, my wife Flora sat down with them before they went to church and explained the Christmas story. She reported later how their eyes expressed stunned incomprehension as she told them about a virgin, shepherds seeing angels in the heights, and kings coming from distant lands. 'When you come to think about it,' Flora said, 'it is ridiculous.' Yet she believes it all. So now do the Cambodians. *Credo quia absurdum*. That was Rebecca. When servants of Abraham came to arrange a marriage with Isaac, they asked Rebecca, 'Will you go with this man?' and she said, 'I will' (Gen 24:58). She was ready to carry forward the divine promise. She too said, 'Amen: Yes I will.' And they blessed her. And she became Isaac's wife, and he loved her. The act of trust and then the discovery of the love that is diffusive of itself and multi-plies itself into a myriad forms of love: that was Rebecca's trust and love. To the divine initiative she said, 'I will.'

That is also what Mary said. Mary recapitulated the delight that Rebecca took in the divine play. Was it any wonder that as Rebecca danced at her wedding with Isaac, Mary danced when she was espoused to the Lord? 'My soul magnifies the Lord, and my spirit rejoices in God my saviour.' These are not words to be chanted but to be choreographed. Girls not out of their teens may not know much theology. They do know how to sing and dance. Theologians would put it differently: Mary, they would say, was not a separate channel for God's grace, but the channel through which the grace of God is mediated. That is why John Ruusbroec,[3] a giant in an age of spiritual giants, called Mary 'the dawn and daybreak of all the graces in which we are to rejoice eternally'. There is the joy again. Mariology is not a heresy; it is the choreography of our joy. The angel said it: *'Chaire kecharitomene.'* That does not mean 'How do you do?' It means, 'Be glad, because the favour of God had come to you.' L. P. Jacks, who was the editor of *The Hibbert Journal,* wrote about sixty years ago in *The Lost Radiance of the Christian Religion*:

> Christianity is the most encouraging, the most joyous, the least repressive, the least forbidding of all the religions of mankind. There is no religion which throws off the burden of life so com-pletely, which escapes so swiftly from our moods, which gives so large a scope for the high spirits of the soul, and welcomes to its bosom with so warm an embrace those things of beauty which are joys for ever. . . Christianity does not brood upon the sorrows of mankind. It is always music you hear, and sometimes dancing as well.

That is the authentic note. What Mary still prays for is surely that we shall enter into that kind of joy. Such joy is not a naïve cheerfulness. It knows the storms, the hurts, the assaults. It is Julian of Norwich's kind of joy: 'God did not say you will not be assailed, you will not be belaboured, you will not be disquieted, but he said: "You will not be overcome."' To live like that, like Julian, or Mary, or Rachel, is to live with the joy that (as Jesus says) no one takes from us.

Rachel and Mary

Then there is Rachel. May God bless you, Mary, as he blessed Rachel, *Y'simeych Elohim k'rachel*, third in the line of loving intercessors. John Calvin has an interesting comment on the text of Gen 29:11, 'Then Jacob kissed Rachel.' Calvin was quite sure Moses must have made an error in editing the Torah, because strangers (at least in Calvin's Geneva) did not kiss one another. But a girl that could steal objects of worship from her father's house (Gen 31:19) was presumably quite capable of kissing strangers. Rachel was a young woman who knew her mind, and quite willing, if need be, to take the law into her own hands. She is not the best moral example, that is obvious. Headstrong and impetuous, charming and jealous, she is the only woman of the four not buried beside the other matriarchs and patriarchs at Mechpelah. She was not much of a saint, perhaps. Yet in one of the most tender passages in Jeremiah, the voice that the prophet heard was Rachel weeping for her children. The prophet personified the nation as Rachel, the bride of God, who wept for her exiled son (Jer 31:15). In Jeremiah, Rachel weeps for her children.[4] Yahweh responds and brings Ephraim back from exile. In Matthew Mary weeps, and Yahweh brings Jesus back from exile. And in both Jeremiah and Matthew the restoration is Yahweh's work. The consolation Yahweh brings in Jesus is a universal consolation, bringing every child of Rachel release.

Go to Haddington in Scotland, the birthplace of John Knox, to see what this means. The sick are coming again in pilgrimage to the parish church of St Mary's. The parish minister blesses them with a simple prayer, that they may be holy in every part. The laying on of hands is given to all who desire it. In the church of her name Mary is still observant of their need, still saying, 'They have no wine.' And Jesus is still showing the signs of the new age. So Rachel's children come from all over Scotland, and beyond, for a blessing. When they come, they still remember the good news brought by the angel, 'Blessed are you among women, Mary, full of grace.' 'Prayers,' says the Earl of Lauderdale in whose family aisle many of them pray, 'have been bountifully answered.' And Mary can no more stop praying for them than Rachel can stop weeping for them. May God bless us as he blessed Mary, through whom he brought us the restoration in Christ.

Leah and Mary

Then there is Leah, fourth of the loving intercessors. May God bless you, Mary, as he also blessed Leah, *Y'simeych Elohim k'leya*. She blinked a lot, or was it a tic she had in her eyes? Jacob had contracted with Laban to marry Rachel, but at the wedding feast the veiled Leah was put in her place, at least for a week. Leah is the old-fashioned wallflower, the one who does not get invited, the rejected, the less than desirable. But two things in scripture will strike us. First, Leah taught her son Judah to pray. Martin Luther said he would have given anything if he could pray to God as Judah prayed to Joseph. Where did Judah get that gift of prayer, if not from his mother? Mary recapitulated Leah's patience and gift of prayer. The gospels uniformly attest to Christ's deep range of feelings and emotions, especially his joy and capacity for love. And when Jesus interceded – for the sick and suffering, for Judas at the betrayal, for the disciples at the Mount of Olives, for the crook on the gibbet beside him – where had he first learned the art of prayer, if not from Mary?

A second reference to Leah in scripture comes in the account of her burial. At Hebron Abraham had purchased ground for a family tomb. But who is buried there? Abraham and Sarah, of course: Isaac and Rebecca, of course. And – this is the surprise – Jacob and Leah (Gen 23, 25:9, 49:31). Rachel is not there. She was buried near Ephrath and Ramah. In her death Leah was honoured. Here too one of the loving intercessors points to her own fulfilment in Mary. If God took such care over the body of Moses that he charged the archangel Michael with guarding the body, perhaps even (and this is Jewish tradition) with carrying Moses up to heaven, why would it seem strange that God should show similar care for the Virgin Mary after her death? Why should not the idea of the falling asleep of the Virgin (as in Orthodoxy) or her assumption (as in Catholicism) be for us – with all the needed translation of language and removal of mythic elements – a sign of God's intention to transfigure the whole creation – to transfigure not just the Virgin, but you and me also in all our need and sinfulness? Why not? John Calvin himself insisted that by faith we are sharers of Christ's ascension: 'By his ascension into heaven,' he said, 'the Lord has opened up access to the heavenly kingdom. . . We are in a manner now seated in the heavenly places, not entertaining a mere hope of heaven, but possessing it in our Head' (*Inst* 2:16:16). The assumption of Mary can well be regarded as one of the signs of the new age – a sign that through Christ, whose own body was transfigured on the mountain before Peter and James and John, the whole creation, which has been groaning for so long, will in the end be made whole.

Our intercession and Mary's

God listened to Sarah, Rebecca, Rachel and Leah. Scripture so teaches. They all offered their aid to those who fled to their protection, implored their help, or sought their intercession. What, after all, is it to intercede? To intercede means to pray for others. Literally, it means to go between, to mediate, to intervene between contending parties with a view to reconciling them. Intercession is based on a loving concern for one another. To ask someone to intercede for us is to ask to be taken to that person's heart in a special way. When those who were out on a limb, or out in the cold, or left unaided, asked these four intercessors to pray for them, they were not asking that the women should try to wheedle God, because God (like Zeus with Hera) responds to women's wiles and pleas. To ask someone to intercede for us is the very opposite of manipulating God. It is to ask that God will visit us with grace and blessing, to ask that God will act upon us.

This is the meaning of Mary's intercession. Go back to the story of the wedding at Cana. There is great embarrassment in the feast when the wine runs out. There is an odd, almost panic-stricken conversation. Mary says, 'They have no wine.' Jesus responds, 'Woman, what have you to do with me?' Then he says, 'My hour is not yet come.' We know he means the hour of the kingdom, the hour of his messianic triumph. She seems to be on the edge of saying, 'The hour of kindness and courtesy is always at hand.' In fact, she says, 'Do whatever he tells you.' And Jesus, contrary to all expectations – grace is always contrary to expectation – turns the water used for washing hands and feet into wine that makes the heart glad and every meal a mystery of the kingdom.

What Jesus' question to Mary means has something to do with seeing or not seeing the signs of the kingdom. 'How are you approaching me? On what basis? Are you asking for a gift because you are my natural mother, the woman who gave me birth? If that is how you come to me, I can do nothing. Then we are not on the same level.' But Mary does not come like that. She does not approach Jesus on a human level. She has pondered this day, or a day like it, for years. She does discern the signs of the new age. So she shows that she has perfect faith in him. She sees him for what he is. The conditions are exactly right for a manifestation of the kingdom.

To intercede is to do what Mary did. I would say, it is to do what Mary still does, it is to come to God, wherever we are, and stand on behalf of people, even if they don't believe, even if they don't see what we see, even if they are blind to the signs of the kingdom. However gloomy or hopeless the situation seems, the fact that we are there, standing beside people, changes the situation because through our faith in Christ, God is present. 'Where two or three are present,' Jesus says, 'I am in your midst.' When we pray for someone, there are the necessary two or three. So Christ is present, God is present.

Christ's intercession for us, in the lovely phrase of Peter Taylor Forsyth, is 'God's soliloquy on our behalf'. Christ's priestly atonement was once and for all, but it was final in the sense that it goes on and on, forever releasing for us the opportunities and powers of the kingdom of heaven. That is why, in turn, we properly pray for the world. The Church is never truer to Christ than when it stands before God, praying that the world may be reconciled to God. And that, no less properly, is why we ask the saints to pray for us: because Christ is never alone. 'To enter Christ,' as Forsyth put it, well conveying Augustine's sense of the *totus Christus*, 'is in the same act to enter the Church which is in Christ.' Our union with others who share that life together in Christ is not a matter of choice but of spiritual necessity.

We ask the saints to pray for our sake, but they are also praying for Christ's sake. Christ prays for us and they pray for us. Their prayer flows from the Holy Spirit. And if that is true of them, it is supremely true of Mary. She is the intercessor *par excellence*, meaning, in the excellence of her humility. I can understand the enthusiasm that has led some to call her 'queen of heaven', but the imperialism of queens like Catherine the Great or Victoria are far gone. If Mary is a queen, her royalty can only be one of service, after the example of Jesus, whose most royal act was that of a servant. Knowing that he had come from God and was going to God, at this apex he took a towel and began to wash the disciples' feet (Jn 13:2-6). Christ's majesty is revealed in his most glorious servanthood. We can seek no other place. John Ruusbroec wrote: 'What is higher than the mother of God, yet what is lower than the handmaid of God and of all the world, Mary herself?' Mary is never more royal than when she sees the need of the hungry or thirsty and brings their need to her Son.

To invoke Mary and to ask her to pray for us is simply to ask that she, because we know she loves God, will also include us in her love, and through the energising powers of her own love stir us up and make us ready to receive whatever God gives us by way of grace and blessing. This is Mary's intercession. The range of Sarah's love, and Rebecca's and Rachel's and Leah's, was bounded by their time and place. The range of Mary's love is all-embracing. In love she made herself wholly available to God as the channel of God's grace. In that same love she cares that all who come to her Son will do what he tells them.

God grant that we can get beyond Reformations and condemnations and narrownesses when bad polemicists and even good reformed ministers preached against love songs that call on the saints to lend their aid. I will never know how it slipped into the Presbyterian Hymnbook, but it is there, Athelstan Riley's hymn calling on the saints to join us in our praises. In it Mary is addressed like this:

O higher than the cherubim,
More glorious than the seraphim.
Lead their praises, Allelujah!
Thou bearer of the eternal Word,
Most gracious, magnify the Lord,
Allelujah, Allelujah, Allelujah.

If we lose the prayers of the saints, above all those of the bearer of the eternal Word, we lose all sense of belonging to Christ who alone, as Calvin says, 'has all the parts of blessedness and eternal life included in him.'

Notes

1. Jim Wallis, *The call to conversion* (Harper & Row, San Francisco 1981), 95.
2. *Ibid.*, 97.
3. Otherwise Jan van Rysbroeck (1293-1381).
4. St Matthew uses these words in the typical sense, referring to the sorrow of mothers over the loss of their children murdered by Herod (Mt 2:18).

St Aelred of Rievaulx on the Imitation of Mary

Dr Alf Härdelin
Roman Catholic, Lecturer Uppsala University

The last decades have witnessed a rediscovery of the medieval monks, not only as spiritual guides but also, in many cases, as theologians. Not the least important among them is Aelred, or Ailred, of Rievaulx, who stands out as a good representative of that 'monastic theology', which, following the Fathers, was cultivated in the monasteries and which experienced a 'second spring' during the twelfth century, among the black monks as well as among the Cistercians.[1] Born in Hexham in 1110 as the son of a priest, educated at the school of his native town and serving in his youth at the court of the Scottish king David, Aelred was the beloved abbot of Rievaulx during almost twenty years, until his death in 1167.[2]

It seems convenient to introduce him and his thoughts on the blessed Virgin as a type, or model to be imitated by every Christian, by reminding ourselves of the kind and style of life that the author lived, for without such a background we shall have difficulties in rightly understanding what he is saying in the works he has left to posterity. Many literary works can indeed be read and understood properly, even if the reader knows very little about the writer's times and the circumstances and specific purposes for his writing. Such sources may presuppose that the readers have a certain knowledge of the matter beforehand, but the argument itself requires only an ordinary intelligence, a sense for logic and, perhaps, a certain amount of general human experience, in order to be understood.

Other texts are more definitely bound to their times, or to the specific way of life they are reflecting, or to the purpose for their being written. They are not intended for the general public, but for people who share something at least of the writer's own experiences and who are in accord with him with regard to certain basic moral and spiritual values. For these texts are not written down so much to convince you of the truth of certain theoretical statements as to provoke you to *act* on the affirmations you are already sharing, or professing, with the writer. They are speaking not only to your head, but to your heart and your will, to your entire person.

What I have expressed here in rather general terms, can in a more specific sense be applied to the two main forms of theological thought and writing in the high middle ages. At the same time as the Cistercian order was born in France with the intent, as the first leaders saw it, to restore the old Benedictine monasticism to its pristine purity, a new institution was taking form: the schools of the great cities in Italy and France were developing into what we call universities. But schoolmen and monks thought and wrote, as a rule, differently. The schools were above all concerned with the purely intellectual, or rational, aspects of things, their method of reaching truth was the disputation and the questioning, their language abstract and technical, or philosophical. The monasteries, on the other hand, had a different goal and cultivated therefore another style of thought and writing. They were built as secluded places for the quest of God; as St Benedict said: as 'schools for the service of the Lord'. For that purpose a clear intellectual grasp of revealed doctrine was certainly of the greatest importance, but it didn't suffice; only divinely illuminated wisdom and the affections of a willing heart could transform men of this world into ardent followers of Christ and of his saints. Whereas the theology of the schools, i.e. scholasticism, is of a speculative kind, monastic theology, then, is a practical one born out of, and nourished by, religious and liturgical practice, and meant to inform and stimulate this same practical exercise of a spiritual life. Therefore, when the monks studied the scriptures, the aim was not so much to solve its real, or supposed 'difficulties', but to take and receive it as God's living bread, to digest it mentally and to 'taste, how sweet the Lord is'. No language could be more congenial, or natural to the monks than the poetical, concrete, affective language, which is the bible's own and which was the food of their continual meditative reading and prayer.

Due to the purpose of their life, it is quite natural, then, that monks, with a few remarkable exceptions, such as Anselm and Lanfranc, have contributed little to the development of dogma, or to its speculative penetration. Monastic theology is meant to be a personal challenge to the reader, it invites him to become a participator in the sacred drama that the bible tells. For monastic theology is essentially a biblical theology, finding expression most congenially in sermons and biblical commentaries. It is true that more than one of the Cistercian fathers, and Aelred too among them, also have written tracts, for instance 'on the soul' (*de anima*). Nevertheless I think that it would be misleading to us, imbued as we are with the ideas of modern psychology, to say that these monks were interested in the psychological rather than in the doctrinal side of Christian teaching. As I have said, it is rather the question of a different kind of theology than that dogmatic, 'objective' one, which is scholastic in origin and which we find today also in most textbooks on theology. For, to try to say it again, what the monks are offering us is not merely a timeless, systematically well-organized doctrine about God and his deeds of salvation. There is, as in the bible itself, truly the question of God's revelation, but also of men's answer; of his deeds of salvation through Christ, but also of the individual Christian's response in faith and hope and love, and of the imitation and following of Christ, the head, through mortification, virtue and sanctification.

Of course there are differences between individual monastic writers, even within the same order and at the same time. Our Aelred has been called the 'St Bernard of the North', which is a fair expression of high esteem. And they have, indeed, much in common. Both are ardent lovers of God, both are zealous pastors for their flocks, both are eloquent preachers. However, Aelred is, in the best sense of the word, more simple and obviously less complicated than the great abbot of Clairvaux. He has less of that penetrative mind that was Bernard's. Aelred seems to have had no need to be theologically 'wise above what is written'. What was important to him was that loving response and that obedience to God's calling and that desire of the heart for the face of God, which prepares man on the pilgrimage for the heavenly Jerusalem and its peace.

We find a very characteristic example of this typically monastic attitude in Aelred's tract *De puero Jesu*, which is a meditation on the text in St Luke about Jesus at the age of twelve going up with Joseph and Mary to Jerusalem. In discussing the difficult words, saying that Jesus 'grew in wisdom and grace', he refers to the different interpretations that are currently given to these words. He himself, however, wants to leave the solution of the problems involved to those who are wiser; *they* may judge. This can be taken as a humble admittance from Aelred's side of his own intellectual limitations. I think, however, that they also contain a slight criticism of the dialecticians of the schools. These were often criticized by the monks for their undue curiosity *(curiositas)*, for their proud desire to pry into mysteries that God had not deigned to reveal. Thus, Aelred concludes this section with the following request to his disciple: 'But you, my son, don't look for questions but for devotion'.[3] We would seriously misunderstand the abbot, if we took words like these as a disregard for doctrinal truth, or as an argument for a merely private, emotional devotionalism. No, I think the opposite comes nearer to the truth: It is precisely because you cannot base your devotion on anything but the truth that Aelred refuses to take the road of uncertain speculations. It is safer to keep to what the church teaches as revealed truth.

Thus, even in his marian doctrine he abstains from taking sides in controversial matters. He confines himself to profess the traditional, received doctrines concerning Mary, but dogmatic questions which are under dispute he is always inclined to leave open. He seems to believe in the sinlessness of Mary, at least from the moment of the annunciation, but it is doubtful, whether he held the 'full' doctrine of the immaculate conception. There are, in his sermons for the old feast of the assumption, beautiful hymns to, and glowing praisings of, the Mother of God, reigning with her Son in heaven. But still, in one at least of these sermons, he explicitly admits his ignorance in the question, whether Mary was taken into heaven with her body and soul, or with her soul only (*PL* 315B).

This was a long but perhaps a useful prelude, which will help us to understand a monastic writer like Aelred. But now to our proper theme: his teaching on the imitation of Mary. The expression itself *(imitatio Mariae)*, or similar forms of it, can be found in several of his sermons for the different liturgical feasts related to the blessed Virgin.[4] Or, in other instances, he can speak about Mary as an example for his hearers, or as their *form*; he can encourage them to follow *(sequere)* her, who is their mother.[5] The same thought can also be expressed simply by using the subjunctive form of a verb: e.g. 'let us enter into our inner chamber together with the blessed Virgin', or, let us, 'like her', do this or that.[6] Or, the admonition to imitate Mary may be implicit in the text only. So, for instance, when Aelred, in one of the sermons for the feast of the assumption, referring to St Paul, analyzes Mary's way from a 'carnal' to a 'spiritual' understanding of Christ, or, in another variation, referring to a passage in the Song of Songs, when he describes how the blessed Mother first searched for the one she loved during the night, without finding him,and in the end found him in the eternal day (*PL* 310B-C). Nothing here is explicitly said about the Church, or the Christians. But, clearly, Mary is pictured, not merely as an individual finding the goal of her life, but she is put forth as a type, or a pattern, for the whole Church.

The idea of imitation and the vocabulary used by Aelred to express it, is, as everybody well knows, of biblical origin. And not only is there in the New Testament a question of imitating Christ and of following in his footsteps. Even the Mother of Jesus is, at least according to some biblical scholars, clearly pictured as a pattern, particularly in the Gospels of Luke and John.[7] There is also an imitation of Paul *(imitatio Pauli)*. 'I admonish you', as the apostle says in 1 Cor: 'be my imitators, as I myself imitate Christ'. And we can also remind ourselves of the Letter to the Hebrews, in which a long series of saints and fathers in the old covenant are presented, in order that you, as the writer says, 'might imitate those, who through faith and patience inherited what was promised' (Heb 6:12).

Some of these biblical ideas and expressions are brought together in one of Aelred's sermons for the feast of Mary's nativity. He is expounding the words in Ecclesiasticus 24, 26, which formed a part of the feast's first reading and where the divine Wisdom is speaking: 'Pass over to me, all ye who desire for me.' After having explained to his monks what it means for them to pass over to Christ, who is the Wisdom of God, he continues by applying the text to Mary. The words have, says the abbot, a special meaning, when read today. For certainly Mary listened to the call of the Wisdom and followed its voice. From her early infancy she desired for Christ, and so passed over to him. But how was that possible, as Christ was not yet born to the world? This is the sum of Aelred's answer: 'Moses lived very long before the birth of Christ, and nevertheless did he, looking forward to Christ's passion, choose to sustain passion rather than to reign in Egypt'. This is an echo from the Letter to the Hebrews. Similarly, Aelred goes on, 'the blessed Mary began to imitate Christ's life, although his life was not yet to be seen on earth, because she knew that he was going to be born. As Moses imitated his passion, although it had not yet occurred, so did the blessed Mary: in her heart she passed over perfectly to Christ, so that he should pass over to her and take up his abode in her body'. And so, further on in the sermon, comes the abbot's admonition: 'Let us, my dear brethren, as much as we can, imitate our Lady. Let us desire for the Wisdom, let us pass over to the Wisdom' (*PL* 318B-319B). But, as the preacher says in another place, only those who imitate her virtues, as well as they can, can worthily praise her. For the praise of her sounds false in the mouth of those who are not willing to be her imitators in humility, chastity and love (*PL* 324C-D).

So much generally on the imitation theme in Aelred's sermons. Let me now be a little more specific, by going into two or three particular points. This will give us, at the same time, a broader view of the abbot's theological and spiritual teaching. The first point takes us to what I consider to be the basic structure of thought in monastic theology generally, and in Aelred in particular. For though it is not the question here of a systematic theology in a scholastic, or later sense, Aelred and his fellow-monks are not therefore devoid of order, theological organisation and structure in their thought. As a careful analysis can often demonstrate, even in their sermons they are offering more than merely loosely connected associations. They are not expounding biblical texts simply 'vers-by-vers', as it is sometimes said, but they can be shown to have had a full control over their composition.

The structure, or pattern, I have in mind, and which is so very clearly discernable in Aelred's sermons, is that of history, conceived of as salvation history, as we would say today. They abound in different kinds of formulas to express the stages of that history, or to denote its development in time. There is the series: creation, re-creation – or restoration – and glorification;[8] there are the different tenses: past, present and future tense;[9] there are the stations of Israel's exodus, often used by the monks to picture mankind's history, or the history of the individual Christian in the Church: we were once in the Egypt of darkness, we are now in the desert and we are expecting to enter into Jerusalem, the eternal city.[10]

This historical concept becomes evident also in Aelred's handling of the imitation theme, for in a couple of sermons he expounds this admonition, which is as it were their sum: 'Be an imitator, not of Eve but of Mary.' At the beginning there is Eve, who through her pride and sensuality became the 'mother of misery', and there is Mary, the second Eve, who through her humility, obedience and love of God became the mother of mercy and grace (*SI* 84-88). Thus, the two can be taken as examples; the one of vice and the other of virtue, Eve as the morally weak one and Mary as the strong one. If Eve ought to be taken as a warning, Mary stands out as an example of virtues, of virtues, that is, which are the opposites to Eve's weakness and vice (*FD* 178-9). However, Aelred doesn't dwell so much upon the latter, for he prefers to exalt and praise Mary. But when she is presented as the contrast to Eve, the abbot in particular stresses, as is to be expected, the humility and the obedience and the love of Mary.

However, faithful to the historical perspective which is so important to him, Aelred does not treat the two women merely as two timeless figures, in order to illustrate opposite characters, one worthy of blame and the other worthy of praise. No, the meaning he gives to them is closely connected with the phases of history they are inaugurating. Both are for Aelred historical persons, not only in the simple sense that they have existed in history and are not merely the inventions of fiction. They are historical in the sense that they represent – like Adam and Christ – old, fallen mankind, on the one hand, and new, restored mankind, on the other. That this is what Aelred really means, can be noticed clearly in the abbot's manner of talking on the matter. Thus, he says, when Mary received benediction from the Lord, she took away the malediction brought on the world by Eve's disobedience (*PL* 326D). Similarly, Mary's virtue of obedience is with preference described by him in terms which put her in contrast to Eve, for Mary is, he says a cause of 'the world's redemption, of mankind's reparation, of the paradise's re-opening, of the hell's harrowing, of heaven's restoration, of the dead's resurrection' (*SI* 80). Mary is indeed 'the mirror', or 'the form of obedience', worthy to be imitated and honoured by all her sons and daughters (*SI* 81).

In a sermon, in which Aelred dwells particularly on the Virgin being the Mother, not only of Christ but also of every Christian, the contrast to Eve is again evident. Through Eve we were all in the state of death, and darkness, and misery. But, Aelred goes on, we are indeed not only born as sons of Eve, for through Mary we have a better birth, as Christ was born of her. So she has become our second mother, who for the old nature has given to us the new life, for corruption has gained for us incorruption and for darkness light. And Aelred concludes by repeating his admonition: follow your Mother; grow in purity, in charity and in humility, by taking her as your example (*PL* 323B-D).

These virtues in Mary and in those who imitate her are, of course, good in themselves, but Aelred takes us a step further, it seems to me, by demonstrating that they are only a pre-requisite for something greater: they are the soil for 'spiritual fecundity'. What is most marvellous of all: Mary's virginity, being in a sense akin to sterility, proved to be the opposite. She took on herself what in men's eyes was the curse of virginal sterility, he says, but thus she deserved that fecundity which gave Christ to the world (*PL* 253A-C). What is important to Aelred here is, of course, not physical virginity in itself, or by itself. There is nothing great to preserve physical chastity without the inner virtues, which alone make it fruitful (*PL* 255B-C). It is true: Eve is not mentioned explicitly in this connection, but it is obvious that Aelred is describing Mary's spiritual fecundity in contrast to Eve, the mother of misery. As he does say in one of his sermons for the feast of the annunciation: the fecundity and fruitfulness of Nazareth is greater than that of the paradise; and 'paradise' in Aelred's mind recalls here, not happiness and goodness, but perdition and ruin (*SI* 89).

In order to understand even better the capital importance that our abbot attaches to our taking Mary as our example instead of Eve, another sentence by him might be added as a conclusion to this section. If Mary hadn't prepared herself by listening to and by keeping the word of God, he says, the Lord would not have taken up his abode in her soul and in her body. The abbot is aware himself of being audacious in maintaining this, for he introduces the sentence by saying: *Audacter enim dico*, I speak audaciously (*PL* 303D). A scholastic preacher might have felt the need to be a little less audacious, for it could be asked, can a man's virtue, or lack of virtue, really have such a decisive importance with regard to God's eternal plans? Aelred, however, dared to be audacious, and I think it is not difficult to understand his motive: if Eve through her weakness could draw such a curse on God's creation, it is nothing strange to presuppose that, in some sense, he was dependent on the new Eve's free consent and willing obedience, when he wanted to restore that same creation. Under no circumstances had Aelred the intention to deny the power and sovereignty of the Almighty.

It should by all this be quite clear, why it is so important to imitate Mary, and not Eve. By imitating Mary you are not only following an example of virtue generally and, in so doing, turning your back to other, all too 'human' ideals and values. It is far more important: by following Mary you are faithful to the mother of the new race and to the privileges of being a member of the new mankind, the head of which is Christ, the second Adam. To imitate Eve would, on the other hand, be equal to falling back into the misery which belonged to the fallen race, before the advent of Christ. To imitate Mary is to open oneself for those forces that alone are spiritually fruitful, for what to the world looks like sterility and weakness, is for God a means of blessing. This is, for Aelred, one of Mary's lessons to the Church.

The second point I would like to select for special treatment refers to the abbot's teaching on the active and the contemplative life, because even with regard to this theme Aelred has interesting things to say; even in this respect Mary is presented by the abbot as a model to be imitated. Most of what he has to say about this matter is to be found in a couple of sermons for the feast of the assumption. As the Gospel reading on that day, the Cistercian liturgy, like many other liturgical traditions, used the narrative from St Luke about the Lord's visit to the two sisters in Bethany, Martha and Mary. As it is the question there, not about that Mary who is the Mother of the Lord, you might ask, why this text was selected for one of the marian feasts. Let me give you Aelred's answer, by relating the relevant parts of his commentary (*PL* 303A-309A).

Aelred starts by speaking about the blessing of receiving the Lord. Martha and Mary were blessed by Christ's coming to them in person, but even more blessed are those, who, like the Virgin in Nazareth, receive him in their minds and hearts also. And if we have within us a room ready to receive him, the abbot says to his monks, he will no doubt enter even into us. But even in the mansion of our hearts, he continues, the two women, Martha and Mary, ought to live together: one sitting at the feet of Jesus, listening to his words, and another ministering to him. For if Mary alone were there, no one would be there to give to the Lord what he needed, and if Martha alone were there, no one would take delight in his words and his presence. Thus, Martha signifies that action, by which man labours for Christ, and Mary that leisure, or rest, in which a man, through holy reading, prayer and contemplatin, makes himself free from the works of the body, in order to enjoy the sweetness of God.

Thus, as long as Christ is in this humble state, starving and thirsting, it is necessary that the *two* women, i.e. the two kinds of action, are present in one and the same soul. For Christ is indeed in this humble state on earth, as long as I, and you, or anybody else of Christ's members are on earth, starving and thirsting, because it is Christ who is starving and thirsting in them as the Gospel lays down. As long then as this miserable life remains, Martha in our souls has to take trouble with bodily actions. But these ought not to fill all our time. Even Mary, i.e. the spiritual action, must be there, ready to listen to the Lord's words and ponder them. As long then as this age is still going on, it is dangerous to separate the two women in our soul.

So far Aelred has only made clear that the active and the contemplative life ought not to be divorced from each other on this earth, not even in a monastery. There is, in the sense that Aelred is using the terms, no solely contemplative monastic life, and he also refers to St Benedict for his support. In holding this opinion Aelred shows himself to be a good Cistercian, for, as Fr Charles Dumont, one of the leading experts on Aelred, has written, one of the most characteristic traits in the reform of Cîteaux is precisely 'the reconciliation of contemplation with action, of spirituality with asceticism, of theory' – taken in its original Greek sense – 'with practice'.[12]

But, to go on, what has all this to do with the Lord's Mother? In other words: why was this biblical narrative chosen for a marian feast? Aelred's answer is definite and quite clear: action and contemplation were perfectly united in our Lady, and in this respect also is she a model for our imitation. In all her humble service of her Son she fulfilled the part of Martha, and in her listening to and meditation on the divine word in her soul she fulfilled the part of Mary.

There is no time now to analyse the text, that I have related, in all its details. However, a few remarks might be appropriate. First, we ought to observe that even here Aelred remains faithful to that historical concept of which I have spoken earlier and which is so characteristic for his thought. For when speaking about the two lives, we could notice, first, how the active one was described as that life, which belongs to the present state of salvation history, that stage in which we are, as long as we are on pilgrimage to the heavenly Jerusalem. This is the age, not only of hunger and thirst, but also of different kinds of temptations, for we are still in the desert. Thus, not only service to our neighbours but also asceticism is' considered by Aelred, as by the monastic tradition before him, to be a part of the active life, for which there will be no need in heaven, when the spirit has won complete victory over the flesh. And, consequently, the contemplative life is to Aelred that part of the spiritual life, which is an anticipation, or a foretaste, of the coming, eternal life, the life of heavenly rest and peace.

Mary had, as the Lord says in the Gospel, 'chosen the better part, and that will not be taken from her'. The meaning of these words are quite clear to Aelred. The 'better part' is the heavenly life, which will remain when all troubles are gone and all misery is definitely ended. Thus interpreted, the Lord's words to Mary can be taken as a ground for estimating a contemplative life as 'higher' or 'better' than the active, *only* in the strictly eschatological sense that it represents that being with God, that will remain for ever. But, as Aelred insists, Mary, the Mother of God, is a model of a full, genuine, spiritual life by perfectly *uniting* attention to God with compassion for others.

Aelred spoke and wrote primarily for monks, and not for people living in the world. And more than once he insisted on the active side of the monastic life. However, while not forgetting that, let me briefly point to his manner of portraying the blessed Virgin from her contemplative side. It is nothing strange that he does this by giving her traits borrowed from the meditative practice within the monasteries. I suppose you have all seen medieval pictorial representations of the scene of the annunciation, where Mary is sitting with a book on her knee, or on the reading-desk in front of her. This iconographic form has, I think, its background in the biblical words, telling how Mary kept all the words, said to her by the angel, and pondered them in her heart. And this is how Aelred relates these words: *Memoria conservabat, meditatione ruminabat,*[13] she kept them in her memory, like a monk or nun, endeavouring to learn a passage of scripture by heart, and in her meditation she ruminated them, in order to taste their flavour and assimilate their spiritual nourishment.

It is clear to medieval preachers in general that Mary's attention to God's word was not confined to the single moment of the annunciation. She was considered to be amongst the blessed ones, 'who hear God's word and keep it'. As a contemplative she continually devoted herself to divine reading, meditation and prayer. So even, according to Aelred, at the moment of the angel's visit. In that moment she had withdrawn from the vanities of the world, he says, and hidden herself in the secret chamber of prayer. There she was attentively reading the bible, and Aelred cannot but help imagining that at the moment the object of her study and meditation was the words of the prophet: 'Lo, the virgin will conceive and bear a child, and he shall be called Emmanuel' (*PL* 254C-D). No wonder, then, if there was a struggle within her soul between the loving devotion, saying: am *I* that virgin? and a humility mingled with fear, saying: I am not worthy (*SI* 85).

It ought to have become clear that the abbot of Rievaulx considered the Blessed Virgin to be in a quite special sense an example for imitation. She was singular and unique with regard to the grace bestowed upon her, but she was nevertheless a pattern for every follower of the Gospel. In her obedience, humility and love of God, she was the very opposite of Eve. In her attention to the voice of God speaking through the angel and through the scriptures, as well as by her compassion, she was set forth by Aelred as a pattern for his hearers.

Two newly discovered collections of sermons by Abbot St Aelred of Rievaulx [Ed]

More is known of St Aelred than of any other early Cistercian monk except St Bernard of Clairvaux himself. Walter Daniel's *Vita Aelredi*, to take only that work, was one of the first biographies worthy of that description in our historical literature – coming so soon after Eadmer's *Vita Anselmi*, almost the first. It is heartening then to hear of new material discoveries, which (if established) can only deepen our understanding in a most valuable area, where understanding is already abundantly present. And it should included an understanding of Aelred's mariology.

Gaetano Raciti, Monk of Orval in Belgium, has described his finds made in 1981 and 1982, in *Collectanea Cisterciensia* 45, fasc 3 (1983), 165-84. They are two sermon collections lurking in well known twelfth-century – i.e. virtually contemporary with Aelred – manuscripts (Paris BN nouv acq lat 294, and Troyes bibl Munic 868). Abbot Hugh of Reading (Cluniac) brought the first over to Cluny in 1199 when he was elected Abbot there. Raciti judges that the collection is a copy of a personal dossier once belonging to Aelred himself, compiled for his preaching outside his own Rievaulx Abbey. Of the sermons therein, several were directed to black monk houses, such as Westminster; 37 follow the liturgical year: 58 commemorate feasts of saints. There are 95 in all in this Paris collection, providing new insights into monastic and broader theology; and into Aelred as the 'messenger of a kind of ecumenical dialogue among the Benedictine families' (thus Raciti).

The second collection is traceable to Clairvaux, notes taken by a monk listening to Aelred preaching, some 18 sermons on the liturgical year and saints' feasts. Raciti says of them: *leur lecture. . . est saisissante et touchante*; and he places them 'among the most beautiful pages of Aelred's work' because of their 'extraordinary simplicity'. They appear to come from a pre-literary and unartificial age, an age at the heart of the primitive Cistercian inspiration when there was perfect agreement between monastic experience and doctrine.

Walter Daniel attributed 200 sermons to Aelred; and now most of them seem so lately to be coming into our ken. If Raciti can validate his claim, we then have a mirror into twelfth century historical and homiletic thinking, not to say Cistercian spirituality and doctrinal catagories. Raciti publishes, *per exemplum*, one of these new sermons, that for the feast of All Saints. The language is in harmony with all that we already know of Aelredian spiritual expression. Perhaps we shall have a feast of it to follow, some surely marian.

Notes

1. For a general introduction to 'monastic theology', see Jean Leclercq, *The Love of Learning and the Desire for God*, London 1974 and other editions.
2. For a good modern life, see Aelred Squire, *Aelred of Rievaulx: A Study*, London 1969.
3. Aelred, *De Jesu puero*, 1, 10: ed A Hoste, *Sources chrétiennes* 60, Paris 1958, 68. – For references I shall below use the following abbreviations: *PL*, followed by page number, for the sermons printed in Migne, *Patrologia Latina*, vol 195, *SI*, followed by page number, for the *Sermones inediti*, ed by C.H. Talbot, Rome 1952, and *FD*, followed by page number, for the same editor's 'Aelred's Sermons: Some First Drafts', in *Sacris Erudire*, vol 13, 1962.
4. See e.g. *PL* 304D, *PL* 318D-319A, *PL* 324D, *PL* 326A.
5. See e.g. *PL* 323D, *SI* 80, *SI* 138, *SI* 140.
6. See e.g. *PL* 258C.
7. See e.g. *Mary in the New Testament*, ed by R. E. Brown, London 1978, passim.
8. See e.g. *SI* 31, *SI* 34, *SI* 105-6, *FD* 186.
9. See e.g. *PL* 209A-B, *PL* 251A-D, *SI* 52-5.
10. See e.g. *PL* 239B-C, 247C-251A, *SI* 41-2, *SI* 94-5.
11. *PL* 303A-309A. See also A. Squire, 'Aelred of Rievaulx and the Monastic Tradition Concerning Action and Contemplation, *Downside Review* 72 (1954), 289-303.
12. Charles Dumont, 'Aspects de la dévotion du Bienheureux Aelred à Notre Dame', *Collectanea Ord Cist Ref* 20 (1958), 322.
13. Aelred, *De Jesu puero*, 1, 11: ed Hoste, 66.

Mary, model for the Church and so for all of us

Mrs Mary Ann De Trana
Orthdox, Richmond, Virginia

In looking at Mary as model for the Church, it is important to remember that when we speak of 'the Church' we refer to the institution as well as to its members, the people of God. There is no doubt that Mary has been held up as a model throughout history for both. She has been seen by the faithful as the first member of the Church of which we are all now members.

However, our task is to attempt to take the pulse of our world, to look at it critically and to ask whether Mary, the Mother of God (or *Theotokos*, as she is called by Orthodox), her life and all it implies, has anything to say to us today. Is she a model for us today?

I believe the answer is an emphatic 'yes' for all of us and I shall show what I mean by describing her role in the piety of Orthodox Christians. In the words of the late Orthodox theologian, Fr Alexander Schmemann, 'Something is expressed in mariology which is fundamental to the Christian experience of the world and of human life.'[1]

Let us look for a moment at some selected examples of how Mary has been seen as a model.

Jean Daniélou, in his work on Genesis, points out that Mary '. . . is the first fruit of the Church', that in her, the Church was already present.[2]

In the seventh century the Venerable Bede commented on this verse from the *Magnificat*, 'for he that is mighty hath done great things for me and holy is his name' (Lk 1:49). He wrote:

> Mary attributes nothing to her own merits. She refers all her greatness to the gift of the one whose essence and power and whose nature is greatness, for he fills with greatness and strength the small and weak who believe in him. . . it is an excellent and fruitful custom of holy Church that we should sing Mary's hymn at the time of prayer. By meditating upon the incarnation, our devotion is kindled, and by remembering the example of God's Mother, we are encouraged to lead a life of virtue.[3]

André Feuillet, the Roman Catholic scripture scholar, says:

> Through her maternity and her mediation Mary appears as the archetype of the Church. . . She is the perfect model of the Church.

Only by becoming more and more like Mary, does the Church realize more and more fully the intention of her Founder.[4]

Mary is sometimes spoken of as the symbol of the Church. Edith Stein, the Carmelite nun who was a Jewish convert to Christianity, wrote, 'Mary is the most perfect symbol, because [she is the] type and origin of the Church. She is also a unique organ of the Church, for she is the organ from which was formed not only the whole mystical body, but the head itself.' She also said, 'The Virgin, who kept every God-sent word in her heart, is the pattern of those listening souls in whom the high-priestly prayer of Jesus is for ever renewed.'[5]

The Orthodox theologian, Nikos Nissiotis aptly states that in

. . . Orthodox hymnology and iconography, Mary is always praised or presented with Christ and at the centre of the saints as a *representation of the worshipping and praying community*. She is always the Mother-of-God together with the incarnate Word as well as the centre of the intercessory prayers of the gathered community as the person who represents its striving towards personal sharing in the holiness operated by the Spirit in the Church.[6]

This connection between Mary and the Church is described by the Orthodox priest, Fr Lev Gillet, when he discusses the significance of Mary's presence at Pentecost for the Church today. This is mentioned in Acts (1:14), 'All these with one accord devoted themselves to prayer, together with the women and Mary the Mother of Jesus. . .' Gillet stresses the importance of the continuity between that group in the upper room and the Church today. He says, 'Nobody can today be a real member of the Church if he does not feel that he has an unbroken connection and a spiritual communion with all them that were gathered together in the days of Pentecost.' Gillet also points out that they pray 'with one accord'. He wrote, 'This "one accord" can only mean a harmony and agreement between Mary's intentions and our own; we know that Mary has no intention but a perfect assent to the will of God; therefore, it is only the conformity of our will to the divine will that can effectively unite us with Mary.'[7]

The identification of the *Theotokos* with the Church is a most visible aspect of Orthodox belief about her. In iconography, which reveals the Church's understanding of a feast or event in the history of Christianity, the icons of the ascension and of Pentecost show her as the central figure. In each case, the event is crucially associated with the foundation of the Church following Christ's death and resurrection. In the ascension icon Mary stands in the centre of the apostles who remain on earth after Christ has returned to heaven. This assembly is the future Church who are waiting in Jerusalem for the coming of the Holy Spirit. In some icons of Pentecost she is surrounded by the twelve apostles, but she clearly is the centre of the composition.

As a final example of how Mary has been seen as a model, we turn to another Orthodox theologian, Vladimir Lossky, who commented on the verse which is stated twice in the second chapter of Luke, first at Christ's birth, and later, when Mary and Joseph found him in the temple, 'Mary kept all these things pondering them in her heart' (Lk 2:19,51). Lossky wrote that we have a hint of her as personification of the Church's Tradition before the Church was. He said, '. . . it is already possible to see the connection between the Mother of God, as she keeps and collects the prophetic sayings, and the Church, the guardian of Tradition.'[8]

At this point I would like to touch on a related issue. There is an inner tension which an honest discussion of Mary as model must mention. This tension is her use at some times in the past as an unrealistic model for women and the extreme reaction to that by some of our contemporaries, especially women, who have discarded Mary as irrelevant and even as harmful. I believe that both of these positions are wrong and result from an erroneous view of Mary as model.[9]

Before I return to my theme, Mary as model, I must make some introductory comments about our world today and about Orthodox theology of Mary.

It is not difficult to provide an analysis of one of the basic faults of our world today. It clearly is an abuse of freedom. Never have men and women had such freedom to choose how to spend their lives as in the Western world today; and yet, has all that freedom resulted in our choosing wisely, in our freely using everything we have to live a better life, a happier life? I do not think we would say that our world today is a happy one.

Although the reality of Mary, the person who lived in Nazareth and was the Mother of Jesus has not changed throughout history, those aspects of her life which have been emphasised undoubtedly have varied according to the climate of the times, and the needs of the people. Our age, with its emphasis on freedom, independence, personal success, and individuality, has ignored Mary, and in some cases, has moved her to a back closet as a symbol of an outmoded piety. She is seen as irrelevant on the one hand, and on the other, as an embarrassment in these times of heightened ecumenical contact and sensitivity. We might ask, what does the example of this poor and humble girl have to say to us about freedom.?

It is important in a gathering such as this to understand something about the origin of ideas or the presuppositions of the speakers, and of the church tradition represented. Failure to do this can sabotage any goodwill we may have towards the subject as we inwardly gasp at statements which are radically different from our experience or belief.

It is clear that the same set of facts in Christian history have been the occasion for very different focuses and this is true particularly with reference to Mary. The scriptural references to Mary, if judged by their length and frequency alone, or their specific content have led to two very different results in the West. On the one hand, her importance was greatly diminished; on the other, it was deemed necessary to make dogmatic statements explaining beliefs not made specific or clear in scripture.

The Orthodox approach to Mary has been quite different. First of all, it '. . . followed the development of Christology; it was a part of the Church's contemplation of the mystery of the Incarnation.'[10]

Also, remembering that I am viewing this from a focus perhaps different from others, Orthodox would say, '. . . if nothing else were revealed in the Gospel than the mere fact of Mary's existence, i.e. that Christ, God and man, had a mother and that her name was Mary, it would have been enough for the Church to love her, to think of her relationship with her son, and to draw theological conclusions from this contemplation. It is the ultimate meaning of these events that the Church contemplates, not the poetical elaboration of Byzantine hymnographies.'[11]

The product of that contemplation is a vast body of liturgical treatises about Mary. The texts, which are hymns used throughout the annual cycle of worship in Orthodox churches worldwide, number in the hundreds. Since Orthodox mariology is primarily liturgical, the teachings of the Church about Mary must be extracted by reading the services, or as is the case with an Orthodox Christian, hearing them sung during a lifetime.

In search of the answer to my question, is Mary a model for us today, especially as regards the contemporary world and its abuse of freedom, I set out to read all of the verses to Mary. There are hundreds of them, maybe even thousands.

At one point in this very serious endeavour, I was beset with an overwhelming fear, really a terror – how can I do this, is it possible to put all of these things into words, to try to explain them in an organised and analytical way? Is it possible to make ourselves understood by each other at this conference? I had reached a real crisis.

I had written in my notes, 'I am overwhelmed with fear and trembling by this task 1) because it is too difficult to put into words all that the Orthodox Church believes about Mary, and 2) because of the extremely serious nature of it.

A few days later I received by mail the taped lectures of a course on mariology given at St Vladimir's Orthodox Theological Seminary in New York by Fr Alexander Schmemann. I ran to the tape recorder and prepared to listen to the first tape. At last, I would be pulled out of my dilemma by this Orthodox theologian with his many years of teaching, lecturing and pastoral experience. This would give me the information I needed.

In the first thirty seconds of the introductory lecture Fr Schmemann said, 'I never approach Mariology without great fear and trembling because of the great difficulty of the subject and because of the seriousness of it.' The message was clear, I had to pull myself out of my own dilemma. And, more significantly for us here today, there clearly is something about the Orthodox approach to, and understanding of, Mary which does not lend itself to easy analysis.

I have said that my focus on the contemporary world is its abuse of freedom, so my search through the texts of the feasts was with a view to answering the question, 'What does Mary as a model for the Church and for us have to do with freedom?'

To answer the question whether and how the Church presents Mary as a model I have studied the texts of the major marian feast days and several of the minor ones. When I say 'studied', it is necessary to explain that those hundreds of hymns to the *Theotokos* are sung each year in the cycle of marian feasts as well as in the daily services of the Church. They are always sung, not read, and it is a very difficult thing to read them all at one time, as it was necessary for me to do. There was a point in my work where I felt like I was drowning in a pond of treacle.

It must be understood that Mary has never been a part of the external, preaching aspect of the Orthodox Church. She is a part of the inner life of the Church. As was stated by the Orthodox theologian, Vladimir Lossky, 'While Christ was preached on the house tops and proclaimed for all to know in a catechesis address to the whole universe the mystery of the Mother of God was only revealed to those within the Church. . .'[12] So, all those verses, that poetry, those exaggerations, are not presented in such a way that makes them a subject of analysis. They are not meant to be didactic, nor are they apologetical.

Now, having said that the hymns are not meant to be analysed, I will proceed with my analysis. There was a recurring frustration in attempting to do this, for the more I tried to zero in on the attributes of Mary, the harder I tried to listen to all that poetry, the more illusive it seemed to become. I went through a period of thinking it was my fault for not being able to penetrate the message in those texts. However, I am convinced now that the illusive quality of that information about the *Theotokos* is related to the reality which is presented. It is very much like quicksilver which shows itself bright, shining, and lustrous, and when we grab it to put it into a container, it escapes our grasp, eludes confinement, multiplies and scatters in all directions. It is for this reason that someone who attends a single Orthodox service, particularly one of the marian feasts, will not obtain the same impression of the hymns as someone who participates in that service in the context of the Church's annual cycle.

So, this is not a computer analysed graphic, but an attempt to convey the impression of Mary which might be left on any ordinary Orthodox Christian who is attempting to live a life of prayer and is a regular participant in the services, sacraments, and life of the Orthodox Church.

It is useful to note what Fr Georges Florovsky wrote about the hymns to the *Theotokos*:

> The intimate experience of the Mother of the Lord is hidden from us. Nobody was ever able to share this unique experience, by the very nature of the case. It is the mystery of the person. This accounts for the dogmatic reticence of the Church in Mariological doctrine. The Church speaks of her rather in the language of devotional poetry, in the language of antinomical metaphors and images.[13]

At first I tried to extract a picture of the *Theotokos* as model by analysing the focus of the hymns for each of the four major marian feasts. Those feasts are the nativity of the *Theotokos* on 8 September, the entry of the *Theotokos* into the temple on 21 November, the annunciation on 25 March, and the dormition or assumption on 15 August. I began by actually ticking off the number of times she is referred to as 'light', 'joy', 'hope', and the dozens of other titles given her. However, I reached a point when I jettisoned the specific references to Mary in search of the deeper and underlying message placed by the Church in those four marian feasts, and looked instead at the scripture readings.

It was here, in the Gospel readings for matins and divine liturgy that I discovered a dramatic statement about the *Theotokos* as model. The Gospel for matins in all four of those feasts is identical; it is the story from Luke (1:39-49, 56), when Mary visits her cousin Elizabeth, after they both are pregnant. Mary greets Elizabeth, who is then '. . . filled with the Holy Spirit'. Elizabeth says to Mary, 'Blessed are you among women, and blessed is the fruit of your womb!' Then she says, and this is what is important for our discussion, 'And blessed is she who believed that there would be a fulfilment of what was spoken to her from the Lord.'

I also discovered that the Gospel for the divine liturgy is the same reading for three of the four marian feasts. The one exception, the annunciation, has its own reading from Luke 1:24-38, the story of the annunciation. The reading for the other three feasts is the story from Luke when Jesus visits Martha and Mary, the sisters of Lazarus

10:38-42 with the addition of two verses from later on in the next chapter, 11:27-28:

> Now as they went on their way, he entered a village and a woman named Martha received him into her house. And she had a sister called Mary, who sat at the Lord's feet and listened to his teaching. But Martha was distracted with much serving; and she went to him and said, 'Lord, do you not care that my sister has left me to serve alone? Tell her then to help me.' But the Lord answered her, 'Martha, Martha, you are anxious and troubled about many things; one thing is needful. Mary has chosen the good portion, which shall not be taken away from her.'
>
> As he said this, a woman in the crowd raised her voice and said to him, 'Blessed is the womb that bore you and the breasts that you sucked!' But he said, 'Blessed rather are those who hear the word of God and keep it!'

It is significant that the Church underscores the essential truth which Jesus tells to Martha, that Mary has chosen the one thing needful. By selecting the Martha/Mary Gospel for three of the marian feasts, the Church has pointed out an extremely important lesson about how we all should live. Mary, Jesus' Mother, provides a model for us in the focus of her life, which was completely centred on God. She had the ability to be still, to listen, to contemplate. That is why, I believe, the Church has given us that specific reading for the marian feasts. The purpose is to point out that the *Theotokos* was able to achieve that balance and to reconcile those roles of Martha and Mary because she had the perfect vision of what life is about.

It is important to notice that the reading for those feasts does not end with Jesus's rebuke to Martha. Remember, the two verses from the middle of the next chapter of Luke are the conclusion of that reading. When the woman in the crowd praises Jesus' Mother because of her motherhood, he corrects her by saying, 'Blessed, rather, are those who hear the word of God and keep it!' (Lk 11:28).

In light of the exalted role given to Mary by the definition of the dogma of her divine maternity as God-bearer, or *Theotokos*, this verse from Luke is extremely important. Scripture says that Mary's glory is not merely in that physical maternity, but also in her freely choosing to 'hear the word of God and keep it'. None of us can be the Virgin-Mother of God, but all of us can hear the word of God and keep it.[14]

It is also important to note that the concluding phrase which Elizabeth uses in her praise of Jesus' Mother in the reading for matins, 'Blessed is she who believed. . .', is echoed in the closing line of the reading for divine liturgy, '. . . rather, blessed are they that hear the word of God and keep it'. It seems that the Church is careful to underscore the role which the *Theotokos*'s own faith and faithfulness had in her holiness, especially in light of all the poetry in those feasts which appears to exalt her because she was chosen to be the Mother of God.

In the one exception, the feast of the annunciation, whose primary theme is obedience, there is a surprising dialogue between Mary and Gabriel in the canon for matins which is a reflection or meditation on the Gospel reading in the divine liturgy for that feast (Lk 1:24-38). It lasts for a number of verses, and leaves no doubt that in the mind of the Church, Mary's (the *Theotokos*'s) choice to obey God was done freely, and only after questioning Gabriel about the impossible nature of his request. It is even slightly amusing when she tells him that she is afraid of him, and a few verses later, he says, why should you be afraid of me, for it is I who am afraid of you.

We have two significant points which are made about the *Theotokos* and which are reinforced by their repetition. These are the necessity of choosing the 'one thing needful', and the importance of believing and of hearing the word of God and keeping it. It is in this way that I believe Mary is a model for all of us.

There is a tendency, or, I should say, I have a tendency to be a bit rankled by that apparent rebuke which Jesus gave Martha, for I always think, 'Yes, it is wonderful that Mary could sit there and listen to Jesus; somebody had to do all the work for the guest who was visiting them.' But the truth of that remark made by Jesus is much deeper than that. He said that Mary had chosen the 'one thing needful', and he points out that Martha is anxious about many things. He does not simply say that she is *doing* many things. Also, it is significant that Jesus says Mary had *chosen* the better part. For someone to have chosen one thing means that there were other choices which might have been made. There is also the implication that an action was freely taken.

Of course someone has to do the work. There are very few of us whose life allows us to be only Mary. But, the point is, hers is the better part, and our world with its misuse of freedom, has missed the point, abandoned the quiet, prayerful, contemplative part for the pursuit of the active, doing, acquiring, busy part, When in fact, only a firm hold on the quiet, prayerful part gives us the inner peace to go through all those busy, busy days with a proper perspective.

It is extremely hard to be Mary as opposed to Martha. There are so many worthwhile things to do, and so many things which must be done each day simply to keep a family or church or school or a business or a farm going. However, and this is why it is important to understand the significance of those readings in the marian feasts, it is also necessary to be quiet, to listen to God, to pursue the truth which is, I believe, only the will of God for each one of us in our daily lives. The one thing needful is truth, and God will give it to us in prayer if we will only be quiet and listen long enough to hear it.

In appointing the Martha/Mary reading for those feasts the Church is saying something very specific about the *Theotokos* and her life on earth and her use of freedom. This is especially important today, for it seems our frantically busy, achieving, acquiring society has forgotten Mary's part and chosen to pursue Martha's part exclusively.

It is not possible to separate life into different compartments. They overlap, you cannot have one without the other. I believe that we are all called by God to live on two levels, that of the daily tasks of our station in life which include the obligations of loving and caring for those around us, and the life of the Spirit of God, that of quiet, prayer, study, contemplation, withdrawal from the world. These two levels are not separate, they cannot and should not be separated, and this results in a tension which is extremely difficult to live with unless we have an authentic understanding of God and creation and our place in it.

It is encouraging to see this idea being echoed by some contemporary writers. Matthew the Poor, a Coptic monk who lives in the desert in Egypt has written revealingly about the need for spiritual understanding gained through prayer. He says:

> He [man] can no longer perceive anything but the passage of time sweeping past him and overpowering him till he falls dead beneath it. . . it is the knowledge of God that saves man from falling under the dominion of time and its illusory finality in death. The knowledge of God inevitably causes us to rise above the passage of time and death till we sense that we are greater than time, higher than events, and truer and more lasting than death.[15]

It seems to me that this knowledge of God, given to us in prayer, is the only thing which can give us an inner peace, so necessary to maintain a balance in this hectic world. It is necessary to make the effort to choose the one thing needful.

Evelyn Underhill, the Anglican theologian, wrote, 'It is the special function of prayer to turn the self away from the time-series and towards the eternal order; away from the apparent and towards the significant; away from succession and towards adoration and adherence.'[16]

A similar remark was made recently by the Roman Catholic priest Fr Henri Nouwen. Speaking about the deep tensions we experience in life, he said that he believes that the American Christian community as a whole is deeply affected by what he sees as the problems of the Western world: alienation, segregation, separation, loneliness. He also said,

> If you have a family where the father, the mother and the children have a deep life of prayer, there is a greater chance that they can sustain a life together. Because they acknowledge the loving presence of God in their lives – not only intellectually but by prayer in their hearts – they don't make each other into gods and therefore can forgive each other their limitations and weaknesses. When people have no experience of God, they start demanding more of each other than human beings can give.[17]

We live with the Martha/Mary tension all the time. God is greatly generous and merciful, even in the hard things he gives us, especially in the hard things he gives us, if only we will let go of our own wills, and believe it. We may not always see the point of doing what we have to do; in fact, we may never see it. Everything in our lives is a gift from God – the adversity which makes us pray, the suffering which turns us towards God, a devastating loss which makes us wake up, realise the true purpose, the value, the worth of our life, and the relative unimportance of the things of this world.

However, the immediacy of the pressures of time keeps us busy in a whirlwind of tasks which can smother the inclination we have for prayer, exhaust us, and deceive us into believing that if we fill our lives up with worthwhile activities, we can somehow avoid or be excused from the difficult labour of prayer. This is very far from the truth; in fact, I believe that the need for prayer and quiet increase in direct proportion to the pace of life. This is true, I think, because it is so easy to lose perspective, to become discouraged, and to miss the right focus, if we do not have a firm rooting in a daily encounter with God.

There are times when that tension between the Martha/Mary roles cannot be resolved, and must simply be accepted and gotten through as best we can by seeing it as the cross which it is. I will illustrate this by a personal reference.

A few years ago, in the middle of Holy Week, the busiest week of the year, the new winding sheet arrived. A winding sheet is an icon depicting the burial of Christ which is used in Orthodox services during Holy Week. It had been ordered months earlier, and I had almost forgotten about it.

The icon on canvas had to be finished with fabric and trim. I drove to five different fabric stores in search of the appropriate velvet, lining and trim, and was greatly annoyed at having to spend so much time and energy in such a hectic week. I was also irritated at the curious looks and outright stares as I walked from store to store carrying the winding sheet. Some people clearly thought I was crazy.

When I had collected all of the velvet border, the satin lining, the brocade trim and the right colour thread, I began looking for a tailor who would put all this together in only a few days. I got the name of a prosperous sounding establishment from the telephone book and drove there, taking the children with me.

It was obvious when I first entered the door of the tailor shop, that I had made the wrong choice. Although the man was polite and tried to be friendly, he was Moslem, and clearly was horrified by this colourful depiction of a dead Christ. I drove down the street, thinking that I recalled another tailor shop nearby. By this time, the youngest child, a baby, was crying. We parked, collected all our materials, and walked across the busy parking lot. I was trying to quiet the baby and keep the two older boys from fighting while avoiding wrinkling the icon and all the fabric, which was getting heavier by the minute. This time the tailor feigned interest in the project, and I was encouraged. However, when he told me how much he would charge, it was clearly a cynical gesture, for the amount was at least five times what it was worth.

Dejected and discouraged, I drove home, not knowing what to do. The next day I got a sitter for the children and drove into the city, taking one last chance on a tailor in a large department store.

I arrived at the store irritated, tired, angry and hostile. I was angry at my husband because his being a priest had gotten me into this job, angry at God because he was responsible also. I was ready to punch this tailor for the slightest provocation.

I asked directions to the tailor shop, and was shown to a narrow stairway in the back of the gentlemen's dressing rooms. I was embarrassed to go through there, and getting more miserable by the minute. As I ascended the stairs and opened the heavy steel door into the workshop, my nose was assaulted by the smell of wet wool and slightly burned fabric. I asked for the chief tailor, ready to explain what the Orthodox Church was, why our Easter was so late that year, what a winding sheet was and why I needed all that fabric sewn onto it.

When the tailor walked up to me and saw the canvas icon which I had gingerly unrolled onto his large cutting table, he said, 'I recognise your winding sheet, you must be Eastern Orthodox. I grew up on a small village in Poland ·where a third of my classmates were Jewish, a third were Roman Catholic, and a third were Orthodox, not like in Richmond, where you are not well known.' He recognised the icon, knew what it was used for, and in fact had often seen the Holy Friday procession in which it was carried.

He said, 'You are very fortunate in being able to have the time to do something as important as getting beautiful things ready for church. All my life I have wanted to be able to do things directly for the Church, and I have not been able to because of having to work long hours for a living as a tailor.' I was totally taken aback, chagrined, and not a little embarrassed at myself after he finished.

So, there are times when that Martha/Mary tension melts away, even in the crosses God gives us, if we will only be open and aware of the 'one thing needful'.

The theme for the feast of the annunciation is obedience. There is also another important aspect of the verses for this feast. It is clear that Mary's assent to Gabriel was made only after realising the seriousness of the request, its impossibility, in the world's terms, and the suffering it would bring her. It says as much about freedom as about obedience, if looked at in the manner which Mary questioned Gabriel before saying 'yes'.

We live in a time of unparalleled interest in freedom – freedom of thought, speech, movement, way of life, opportunity. Newspapers are filled with reports about places all over the world where people are struggling for freedom to believe in God, freedom from oppression, freedom from poverty.

Freedom is good, it is in the bible: 'You will know the truth and the truth will make you free' (Jn 8:32). But freedom is tied to truth. There is, then, a true freedom and a false freedom. I believe we have somtimes chosen the false freedom. Perhaps we 'modern' men and women really have misunderstood our freedom. We think that to be free is to be completely on our own, to be free to do what we wish, when we wish, and then, with our weak will, we quickly become, more often than not, not free, responsible and mature servants of Christ, but slaves to our own wills, to the pursuit of pleasure, money, power, possessions. We have substituted license for freedom and that license has become a tyranny. We are now, it seems, slaves to our own passions instead of masters over them, we serve them instead of using them to serve God. We have given away the freedom to be truly human. George Herbert's poem, 'The Collar', deals with this. The speaker is rebelling against service to God, when he suddenly realises that the freedom he is seeking is to be found in that service to God which he had been trying to escape.

What is it about today's world which makes it so difficult to live in, specifically to be Christian in? Are we any busier, or more tempted than those who have lived before us? If we have read accounts of people who have lived through the sufferings of war, the torture of unjust imprisonment, the deprivations of the depression, or if we have lived through them ourselves, then we may be sensitive to the levels of heroic suffering endured throughout history. There has always been extreme suffering in the world and there always will be. There are large portions of the world today in the third world and under totalitarian regimes, where such extreme conditions of life still prevail. But the afflictions of us in the so-called modern world, though not so physically difficult or painful are, I believe, much more dangerous and difficult to survive. It is the affliction of soul, the spiritual boredom from which our enlightened, urbane technocrats suffer, and the worst part is, that we do not even realise it.

We certainly have seen this in the United States where the distortion of the sense of our laws which were written to safeguard the freedom of speech and the rights of those accused of crimes have led to a level of pornography and drug use which threaten to enslave us.

Another distortion of the concept of freedom is, in my opinion, the so-called sexual liberation of women. Rather than using its force, influence, momentum to remove the sexual double standard by upholding the value of virginity for the single life and fidelity and chastity in marriage, for both men and women, it has instead taken the opposite approach of encouraging women to pursue sex outside of marriage and unfaithfulness in marriage.

No one would think of asking a man to work full time in a profession and manage a small farm or business in the late afternoon and evening. No one would think of asking a man to go back to work three or four weeks following major surgery and to continue to manage a small farm or business with small amounts of broken sleep. And yet that is what we women have done to ourselves with our new freedom when we return to fulltime jobs only a few days or few weeks after childbearing.

Edith Stein, when speaking of the status of women in Germany following World War II, might have been speaking of us today when she said:

> Many of the best [women] are almost crushed by the double burden of professional and family duties; they are always on the go, worn out, nervy [sic] and irritable. Where can they go to find the interior calm and serenity in order to be a support and guide for others.?

She answers this by saying that the solution lies only in finding a balance which is founded on a spiritual life rooted in the eucharist[18] – all that implies, of course, actively pursuing the better part, Mary's part of the one thing needful.

I am struck by the contrast of emphasis today on our physical well being and lack of emphasis on our spiritual well being. There is a nearly fanatical preoccupation with what we eat, how much we eat, what we breathe. We are all aware of the importance of exercise in our largely sedentary lives. Assuming this concern with fitness does extend our lives a few years and give us more energy each day, do we use this extra time and energy to serve God better with the life he has given us? Do we use it to pray with more attention, to suffer more faithfully, more silently, to serve the poor?

However, this preoccupation with our physical health sometimes overlooks our spiritual health. In the name of intellectual freedom we permit the showing in prime time television of facts about the most sordid kinds of sexual perversion, murder, drug and alcohol abuse. It is a fact that I cannot even let my children watch the evening news without my being there to explain the assortment of mayhem which is shown to keep us informed.

It is really an abuse of freedom to be human, to choose to serve God. In the words of the collect for peace in the Anglican Book of Common Prayer, the service of God. . . 'whose service is perfect freedom.' Only when we do this do we become truly human, truly sons and daughters of God. It seems to me that Mary, the *Theotokos*, by humbly saying 'yes' to God's will, gives us the supreme example of how to behave.

Remember, we are talking about the freedom to choose the better part. True freedom can only be realised in submitting ourselves, our bodies, our minds, our wills, all of our talents and possessions to do God's will. We must accept our cross with Christ and live this life in a way that will draw us close to God and ultimately to eternity with him. Truly the only real freedom is complete and absolute submission to God's will, as the *Theotokos* did.

Matthew the Poor, quoted earlier, says, in a chapter on Mary:

The Virgin is here a fine model of the person to whom the Holy Spirit has granted the indwelling of the Word of God. Servitude to God is our joyful gift to God, for those who enter into the freedom of the children of God cannot but offer that freedom back to God once more as a sacrifice of love. . . Servitude here is the servitude of love for God and it is a fruit of freedom.[19]

There is even a parallel to this in the world's terms. Alexander Solzhenitzyn states in *The Gulag Archipelago* that he was never so free as when he was in prison. He made this statement as well as a comment on one of the dangers of living in the affluent West. He pointed out the subtle beguilement of the freedom to choose where to live, what to do, what to believe, what to eat, which easily becomes a full-time endeavour, diverting our attention from the truly important things in life.

By using our freedom to choose to follow God's will, we must remember that we have to let go of our own will. To do God's will is on the one hand, ridiculously simple, and on the other hand, impossibly difficult, for it requires great humility. We must submit our-selves totally to God, as Mary the *Theotokos* did.

How is it possible to 'let go' of our own will? Something hap-pened to me which might shed some light on the difficulty of 'letting go' of our will and accepting God's will. Some years ago, when preg-nant with one of our children, I was at the shore with our first child, who was then two years old. Suddenly I was hit from behind by a large wave, knocked down, and pulled under the water and away from the shore. I am a strong swimmer, and my automatic response was to struggle to swim to the top. My attempts failed. There was nothing else to do but relax, and that is what saved me. The waves were no less turbulent, in fact, they were worse. However, by ceasing to struggle with them, they quickly brought me to the top where I was able to clear my head, determine that I was really quite far out from the shore, and to swim back.

Since then, I have often thought of that terrifying experience, how close I came to tragedy, and of the application of that lesson in the desperate times in life. Sometimes, when life closes in, the best thing to do is to 'let go', to stop fighting so hard against the things in life over which we have no control and to let God take care of us.

Mary 'let go' at the annunciation. What was told her was imposs-ible, ridiculous, even crazy in the world's terms, and she showed that she was aware of this when she questioned Gabriel. However, in his reply, when he told her it would be done by the Holy Spirit, she believed in God, gave herself to God, and let him use her as his instrument. So, too, we today must believe, we must pray and be open to him and look for his providence in our lives.

It is at this point, where Mary's use of her freedom to choose to do God's will also touches her freedom to choose the cross that she shows herself clearly as a model for us today. This aspect of the *Theotokos* standing beneath the cross of Christ, her Son, is central to Orthodox understanding of her.

The Church has two aspects, the visible part which is formal, structural, and ordered, and the hidden part which is its inner life of joy. It is in that second aspect, the inner life, the joy, that the *Theotokos* may be seen as our model. For if we concentrate only on that structure of the Church, we will be rooted in the things of this world, even though our whole life is given to working in the Church, and we will of necessity be 'anxious about many things'.

However, if we use our freedom to choose the better part, the 'one thing needful' and if we are faithful in prayer, in a constant and unremitting attention to God and to doing his will, we will find joy, even in this life filled with crosses.

The inner life of the Church cannot be developed without regard for its structure, and it is only in the light of the cross that we can truly accept that constant tension which will always be present if we choose the 'one thing needful'. It is only in the light of the cross that we can believe, that we can 'hear the word of God and keep it'.

The place which the Orthodox Church accords to the *Theotokos*, the constant awareness of her as a real person, her frequent and recurring mention in all the services, serves to create an awareness of the unity of creation, and of the responsibility each of us bears for each other. This continuity extends from the beginning of creation, through the lives of all those who have gone before us, to all the living and dead, all of those in the kingdom of God. It is only in that kingdom which we hope to enter at the end of this earthly life, and which we enter each time we receive the eucharist, that the dual and apparently contradictory role of Martha/Mary is understandable. Therefore the *Theotokos*, since she already is in the kingdom, has resolved that tension for us.

For it is only by abandoning our agendas, and conforming our will to the will of God, as Mary, his Mother did, that we truly can become transformed as bearers of Christ, and his truth to the world.

Notes

1. Alexander Schmemann, 'On Mariology in Orthodoxy', *Marian Library Studies 2* (1970), 26.
2. Jean Daniélou, SJ, *In the Beginning, Genesis 1-111* (Baltimore, Maryland: Helicon Press 1965), 65f.
3. *Homily* (Lib 1, 4: CCL 122, 25).
4. André Feuillet, *Jesus and His Mother*, transl. Leonard Maluf (Still River, Massachusetts: St Bede's Publications 1984), 117.
5. Hilda Graef, *The Scholar and the Cross* (London: Longmans, Green 1955), 85.
6. Nikos Nissiotis, 'Mary in Orthodox Theology', in *Mary in the Churches*, ed. Hans Küng and Jürgen Moltmann, (New York: Seabury Press 1983), 270. Italics are the author's.
7. Lev Gillet, 'The Veneration of the Blessed Virgin Mary, Mother of God', in *Mother of God*, ed. E. L. Mascall (Westminster: Dacre Press, n.d. [? 1949]), 79f.
8. Vladimir Lossky, *In the Image and Likeness of God* (New York: St Vladimir's Seminary Press 1974), 199f.
9. For a succinct discussion of this debate, see Anthony J. Tambasco, *What Are They Saying About Mary?* (New York/Ramsey: Paulist Press 1984), 77-82, and Rita Crowley Turner, *The Mary Dimension* (London: Sheed and Ward 1985), especially Chapter 7.
10. Schmemann, 'On Mariology in Orthodoxy', 27.
11. *Ibid*, 26f.
12. Lossky, 209.
13. Georges Florovsky, 'The Ever-Virgin Mother of God', in *The Mother of*

God, ed. E. L. Mascall (Westminster: Dacre Press, n.d. [? 1949]), 183.

14. Lossky, 197f.

15. Matthew the Poor, *The Communion of Love* (New York: St Vladimir's Seminary Press 1984), 42.

16. Evelyn Underhill, *An Anthology of the Love of God*, ed. Right Rev. Lumsden Barkway, DD and Lucy Menzies, DD (London & Oxford: Mowbray 1984), 126.

17. Henri Nouwen, 'Living the Spiritual Life: An Interview With Henri Nouwen', *St Anthony Messenger*, April 1986, article by Catherine Walsh, 12.

18. Hilda Graef, 80.

19. Matthew the Poor, 207.

Men, Women and Ministry

Rt Rev. Edward Knapp-Fisher
Anglican, Archdeacon of Westminster

Whether we realise it or not, we are all influenced by the prevailing
ideas, trends and tendencies of the age in which we live. So I begin
with a reminder of the sexual revolution – the turmoil into which
relations between men and women have been thrown – which is a
marked characteristic of contemporary life. Women's liberation is
primarily, but not exclusively, a Western development. It has meant
that there has been an insistent demand from women in all walks of
life for equal rights, equal opportunities, equal status; and this has
naturally incuded a mounting demand for every office in the Church
to be open to women as well as to men.

The movement for women's liberation – of which the Movement
for the Ordination of Women is, as it were, the ecclesiastical arm –
is the product of a society which has become excessively secularised.
In consequence its promoters and protagonists have, for the most
part, had no interest in theology; they have been activated by pragmatic considerations. The only question at issue has been whether or
not any job could be done equally well by a man or a woman. The
assumption commonly made by many feminists is that women are
equally competent to fill most, if not all, the posts hitherto monopolised
by men. This has produced an egalitarianism which implies that the
only differences between the sexes are physiological. Symbols of this
attempt to obscure all differences between male and female are, for
example, unisex hairstyles and clothes.

This development is, however, a perversion and its consequences
are frequently absurd. 'What has tended to happen in practice,' writes
Dr Eric Mascall, 'is that women have simply been allowed or encouraged to enter into structures designed for men, and this has largely
resulted in women becoming defeminised. G. K. Chesterton (he continues) once characteristically commented on the admission of women
into the business world with the remark that "twenty million young
women rose to their feet with the cry, *We will not be dictated to*; and
proceeded to become stenographers".'[1]

When we consider the nature of men and women and relations
between them we have (as in other less important matters) to be on
our guard against simply and uncritically going the way of secular

society and accepting its assumptions. 'It might seem clear,' says Dr Mascall again, 'that the extraordinary confusion concerning all matters involving sex into which the contemporary world has got itself, now that it has emancipated itself from any kind of Christian control, makes it a very unsure and dangerous guide indeed.'[2]

The false assumption that men and women are in most respects interchangeable appears to be modern; that the sexes are different but complementary was until recently accepted as self-evident:

> As unto the bow the cord is
> So unto the man is woman;
> Though she bends him, she obeys him,
> Though she draws him, yet she follows,
> Useless each without the other.[3]

Or, as an English contemporary of Longfellow put it more briefly and prosaically: 'God created men and women different – then let them remain each in their own position.'[4]

Obviously in these post-Freudian days we accept that *every* human being possesses both male and female constituents and characteristics; nevertheless equally obviously men and women are recognisably distinct. They differ not only in respect of their physical organs and capabilities, but also in temper, temperament and psychology; they act and react in different ways to situations and stimuli. To try to conceal or suppress their differences is likely to produce a kind of hermaphrodite. Precisely *because* men and women, are, by God's design, different they are necessary to one another. Neither is more important nor more valuable in God's eyes than the other. 'Women have a fundamental difference from men. . . albeit with an identical nature'(Paul VI).[5]

In spite of the emergence in public life of such women leaders as Margaret Thatcher or Benazir Bhutto, the mode in which men and women exercise influence and authority is different. In general men are better equipped for formal positions, for sitting on committees or walking the corridors of power. Women, on the other hand, wield their influence in less obtrusive, more subtle, but equally effective ways by, for instance, suggestions made quietly behind the scenes. It is true that in the past, and still frequently today, women were regarded – to the shame of us men – as little more than chattels or toys. Thus Jacques Maritain, among others, rightly insists on the importance of recognising women as persons of equal value and significance to men. In the case of a woman, however, he writes: 'It is in the order of private life, and in the domain of all the humanity, the vigilance and firmness implied by. . . private personal relations, that she will exercise her primacy'.[6] And Mary Ann Evans, who was far from being a downtrodden housewife, makes the same point: 'I should like to know what is the proper function of women, if it is not to make reasons for husbands to stay at home and still stronger reasons for bachelors to go out!'[7]

When the complementarity of the sexes is obscured women ask for, or are required to attempt, tasks for which they are not adequately equipped. When women police began to be recruited in this country they were at first sent out on the beat alone. In practice it speedily became apparent that this was impracticable and each policewoman had to be accompanied by a policeman.

More important by far, however, than such relatively trivial examples is the fact that society as a whole is impoverished if it is deprived of the distinctive contributions which each sex is designed and equipped to make to its life, happiness, health and stability. The difference between the sexes is ontologically rooted in the order of *creation* and is consistently maintained from the opening chapters of Genesis throughout the scriptures. It is a truth reaffirmed in the order of *redemption* when God became flesh in the man Jesus Christ, the supreme miracle made possible only through the willing response of a woman, his Mother.

If women are to be given full opportunities for exercising their own proper and distinctive ministry in the Church, these are theological considerations with important implications which must be borne in mind. Men and women are designed by their Creator to be not competitors but collaborators, to their mutual advantage and well-being and in the interests of the whole human race.

Women and Priesthood

It cannot be denied that women form the majority of the worshippers in our pews, of those who pray privately in our churches, and of the volunteers who assiduously do the many and various chores which in every parish have to be done. In all this there is nothing new. Six centuries before Christ Pythagoras had observed that women as a sex are much more religious than men. It is significant that a recent study of the contribution made by women to the life of the Church is entitled *First among the Faithful*.[8] Quantitatively and qualitatively (so to speak) women, by their devotion and self-sacrifice, put to shame the male-minority practising members of Christ.

This fact, which few if any would dispute, seems to constitute a powerful argument in favour of admitting women to *any* office in the Church, including the ordained priesthood and the episcopate. It is the apparent injustice of excluding women from responsible posts in the Church that provokes such comments as 'the Church is the Stag Party supreme' (Rosemary Sheed).[9] There can be no denying, either, that authority in the Church has been generally regarded as the monopoly of the ordained clergy who are male. It is also clear that women have been given inadequate opportunities and scope for developing and using their distinctive ministerial gifts in the service of Christ for the extension of God's kingdom. In this connection there is certainly some truth in the allegation that male clergy have been anxious through jealousy to retain their exclusive hold on the higher ranks of the ordained ministry:

> For take my word for it, there is no libel
> On women that the Clergy will not point,
> Except when writing of a woman saint,
> But never good of other women, though.[10]

Such discrimination must, of course, be acknowledged, repented and corrected. We shall later on be considering some ways in which women's opportunities for ministry can and should be greatly extended. Nevertheless it does not follow that the only way of putting right this wrong is or should be the ordination of women to the priesthood and episcopate. There are arguments against such ordination which cannot be as lightly dismissed as some suppose; personally I believe it to be simply untrue to claim (as did the General Synod of the Church of England) that there are *no* theological objections to the ordination of women to the priesthood. There *are* theological objections to this course; whether or not they are strong enough to be *conclusive* may be still open to question. It is, however, a question which can be convincingly or authoritatively answered only by a Church substantially more united than at present it is, when the great Catholic Churches of West and East (constituting some two-thirds of all Christendom) still refuse to admit that such ordination is a possibility.

Theological arguments against the ordination of women to the priesthood are familiar and it would be tedious and unnecessary to do more here than to refer briefly to those which seem to be more weighty.

In the bible female priests are associated invariably with paganism and never with the people of God, whether under the old covenant or the new. It is significant that there was no corresponding exclusion of women from the role and ministry of prophetess fulfilled, for example, by Miriam, Deborah and Anna.[11]

The gospels make it clear that, so far from being conditioned by the influence of contemporary culture, Christ was revolutionary in his attitude to women. Yet one who was in many ways no respecter of traditional practices still excluded women from the band of his apostles. 'One cannot deny the fact that Our Lord chose only men as his apostles though he broke with tradition·in his relations with women in many respects' (Graham Leonard).[12] In this our Lord inaugurated a tradition which the great majority of his members has been careful to preserve unbroken by remaining opposed to the ordination of women for almost two thousand years. Such adherence to tradition is not to be dismissed as the last refuge of those whose minds are not only closed but locked, and who are irrevocably committed in all circumstances and at any price to policies of preserving the *status quo*. 'Authentic traditionalism,' writes Kallistos Ware, 'is not a slavish imitation of the past but a courageous effort to discriminate between the transitory and the essential. . . If there is a dynamism in Holy Tradition there is also continuity.'[13]

It is, however, in the context of the theology of *redemption*, in the respective and complementary vocations of Our Lord and his mother, that the most cogent argument against the ordination of women to the priesthood is to be found. For the salvation of the world, and to reveal the infinity of his love, God became flesh in the person of the man Jesus Christ. Yet the incarnation was made possible only by the humility and obedience of the blessed Virgin Mary, his Mother. If the distinctive identities and functions of the Son and his Mother are confused we fall into error and heresy. The Son is the only mediator between God and humanity, and the term 'mediatrix' applied to his Mother, if susceptible of orthodox interpretation, is liable to misunderstanding.

Again, the Son alone is *priest* and from him all priesthood derives. In virtue of our creation in God's image and likeness, and of our baptism into Christ's Church, the company of the redeemed, we are *all* partakers of his priesthood, *a royal priesthood, a holy people*.[14] 'The human person who expresses most perfectly this royal and universal priesthood,' writes Kallistos Ware, 'is not in fact a man but a woman, the blessed Virgin Mary. . . "Behold the handmaid of the Lord." At the annunciation, as throughout her life, the Mother of God exemplifies that priestly act of self-offering which is the true vocation of *us all*.' (italics mine)[15]

This is one level of priesthood in which by baptism into Christ, the only saviour of mankind and womankind, we are every one of us partakers. But there is also another and distinct level of priesthood, the ministerial priesthood of *order*. 'Nevertheless,' as Anglicans and Roman Catholics have agreed, 'this ministry is not an extension of the common Christian priesthood, but belongs to another realm of the gifts of the Spirit.'[16]

An argument sometimes claimed in support of the ordination of women, on the basis of a text in the Epistle to the Galatians, is based on a confusion of these two levels of priesthood. It is of course, true that *there is neither Jew nor Greek, there is neither slave nor free, there is neither male nor female: for all are one in Christ Jesus.* But this passage is set in the context not of *ordination* but of *baptism*, as the preceding verse makes clear: *For as many of you as were baptised into Christ have put on Christ.*[17]

Of the privileges and responsibilities to which an *ordained* priest is called none is greater than that of presiding at the eucharist. This is the characteristic activity of the whole body of Christ, head and members, in intimate union with him and one another. Christ the risen Lord, ever present in his Church through the Holy Spirit, our one high priest, is himself the celebrant of this as of every sacrament. The priest can neither replace nor displace Christ. Yet, in presiding at the eucharist, he in a unique manner represents Christ; he is a visible symbol of the invisible Lord whose agent and instrument he has been commissioned and empowered to be. Hence, in the West, a priest has been described as *alter Christus*, a term liable to give rise to misunderstandings. In this respect the usage of the Eastern Church in speaking of the priest as an *ikon* of Christ is therefore perhaps to be preferred. 'Our Lord and God Jesus Christ,' wrote St Cyprian, 'is himself the high priest of God the Father: he offered himself as a sacrifice to the Father and commanded that this should be done in memory of him; thus the priest truly acts in the place of Christ.' And St John Chrysostom: 'It is the Father, the Son and the Holy Spirit who performs everything, but the priest lends his tongue and supplies his hands. It is not man who causes the bread and the wine to became Christ's body and blood: this is done by Christ himself, crucified for our sakes. The priest stands before us doing what Christ did and speaking the words which he spoke; but the power and grace are from God.'[18] If the priest presiding at the altar were not invariably male, the powerful and pregnant symbolism denoted by the terms, *alter Christus* and *ikon of Christ* would be destroyed.

It is noteworthy that the movement for the ordination of women to the priesthood was born in churches where our Lady's unique place in the divine scheme of redemption was neglected and devotion to her regarded with suspicion. They were also communities which tended to place more stress on the priesthood of all believers than on ministerial priesthood, and to set more store by the ministry of the word than the administration of the sacraments. 'The Protestant rejection of the veneration of Mary,' writes Fr John Meyendorff, 'and its various consequences (such as, for example, the really *male-dominated* Protestant worship, deprived of sentiment, poetry and intuitive mystery-perception) is one of the *psychological* reasons which explains the recent emergence of institutional feminism.'[19] Although this remains true of the genesis of the movement, the statement would require some qualification today when the demand for the ordination of women is supported by some Catholics, including members of women's religious communities. In their case it may be that pragmatic considerations are sometimes more influential than theological conviction. As convents, for instance, have greater difficulties in securing the services of chaplains, the demands of nuns to be able to celebrate for themselves will understandably become more insistent.

It seems likely, however, that many, perhaps most, of those women who seek ordination to the priesthood do so for primarily *psychological* reasons rather than on theological grounds. They feel with justification (as we have already noticed) that authority in the Church has been and is still vested largely in high-ranking ordained ministers. They believe that the only way in which they can gain their proper share of authority and influence in ecclesiastical affairs is by their ordination to those offices. Discussions with such women suggest that many of them are ignorant of the nature of the priesthood which they seek and of the sacraments which priests alone are ordained to administer. This ignorance is even more pronounced in members of non-episcopal churches which already 'ordain' women: and it is indeed understandable that they should fail to appreciate the real difference between priests ordained in the Catholic and Orthodox churches and their own 'ordained' ministers. It therefore appears that, whether they are aware of it or not, for many would-be women ordinands theological considerations are secondary if not irrelevant. But, as Kallistos Ware aptly remarks, 'the ministry is not to be envisaged in *professional* terms as a job that a woman can carry out as competently as a man, and which she has an equal right to perform. Still less is it to be conceived in terms of power and domination; as a *privilege* from which woman is being excluded. *It shall not be so among you* (Mt 20:26).'[20]

It is difficult to doubt that a primary responsibility for all Christians today is to participate in promoting that visible unity in truth and love which is Christ's will and prayer for his Church. To this all other considerations should at present be subordinated. Only when our own divisions are healed can we with genuine conviction proclaim the gospel of reconciliation in and to our warring world: for until we are obviously *one* a sceptical world can say to us with justification, *Physician, heal thyself.* In these circumstances any issue which is likely to diminish or postpone Christian unity ought to be deferred. Such a matter is the possibility of ordaining women to the priesthood. Whether or not this be the will of God can (as has been already suggested) be clearly known only when unity between Christians is far more advanced than at present it is.

Meanwhile great sympathy and understanding is due to the women who are unable to proceed to the ordination to which they sincerely believe that they are called. (We must not forget that equal consideration and sensitivity is to be extended to the not inconsiderable number of men whose personal conviction of their vocation to priesthood has not been endorsed by the Church.) If they can be enabled to meet their frustration and disappointment with humility, dignity and patience, they will bear effective and faithful witness to the crucified Lord by so clearly sharing in his redemptive suffering. It may also be a great encouragement to them to be reminded that, in a secularised society ordered with little or no reference to God and his purposes, most men and women are square pegs in round holes who have been forced into occupations which they would not have chosen, and for which they are not necessarily equipped. With all such persons disappointed would-be ordinands of either sex are closely identified; through sharing their experience they are well equipped to minister to them. After all, vocation to the *ordained* ministry is only one among many vocations, all of which are necessary if Christ's redemptive work is to be done and God's kingdom advanced. If women cannot (at any rate as yet) be priests, there are many other ministries which they are particularly equipped to fulfil, for which more scope should be offered, and to which appropriate honour and status should be accorded.

The Ministry of Women

There is no dispute about the wide variety of ministries open to women. 'It is common ground,' write a man and a woman, in a joint essay, 'that the discussion is not about women as preachers, pastors, teachers and prophets: they are these already and have long been so. The question is whether *womanhood* is an appropriate carrier of the sacramental and symbolic role of the priest.'[21]

We have already noticed that from Old Testament times God has called and equipped women to be *prophets*. A prophet's vocation is only rarely to foretell the future; more usually he or she is given inspired insight into the significance of historical events, together with an understanding of God's will for those who are involved in them. This is a role which women may be peculiarly qualified to play since they are often gifted with an intuitive sense and perceptiveness denied to men. Whether in the providence of God or (more probably) because of human obtuseness, prophets appear today to be in short supply. It is to be hoped that many more men and women may find and respond to this vocation.

Preachers are called to proclaim and expound God's word in the course of the public worship of the Church. Recognition that women as well as men may share this ministry seems to be relatively recent. The Pauline prohibition against allowing women to preach was for centuries regarded as decisive and in some quarters is still so regarded.[22] Understandably, it is within the churches of the Reformation, which stressed the importance of the long-neglected practice of public preaching, that opening the pulpit to women first occurred. Since, however, the Reformers attached equal importance to literal obedience to the scriptures, it took some centuries for this development to take place. Yet, even if it lacks explicit scriptural authorisation, the practice of allowing women to preach involves no point of principle; and those who possess obvious gifts for doing so should surely be encouraged to develop and exercise them.

Nor can there be any grounds of objection, theological or other, for excluding women from the Church's *pastoral* ministry, which can only be enriched by the inclusion of shepherdesses as well as shepherds![23] To this ministry, with the responsibility for counselling which it involves, women can contribute conspicuous gifts of sympathy, compassion and understanding.

In an age when pluralism is accounted a virtue and ignorance of our religion is widespread, it is more important than ever that Christians should be able and ready to give an answer to all who seek a reason for the hope that is in us.[24] In consequence, a heavy burden of responsibility is imposed upon the ministry of *teaching* in the Church. This is a sphere in which women are extensively involved at many different levels: but they have not received either the training or the recognition they deserve. At the highest level the Western Church, at any rate, has been slow to recognise women as Doctors of the Church. St Teresa of Avila, for example, although canonised in 1622 was not accorded this distinction until 1970. It is encouraging to know that today many more women are taking degrees in Theology or Religious Studies; but they must be given scope for making good use of the qualifications they acquire, not only in universities and schools, but also as Sunday school teachers (often in the past inadequately trained for this responsibility), convenors of the parochial study groups, and conductors of confirmation classes. Instruction, by example and word, cannot begin too early; unless it starts in infancy at home it is unlikely to start at all, Since, as we have seen, women are more faithful than men, it is they who are usually, under God, the most powerful influence for good upon the young in their formative years.

Since women form the majority of our congregations, it would seem only right that they should be allowed also to participate more formally in the Church's liturgical worship. There would again seem to be no objections in principle to their participation in public worship in such various capacities as readers, servers, acolytes or administrants at the eucharist. It is unfortunate, if understandable, that any attempt to transfer women from the pew to the sanctuary is viewed with suspicion by those opposed to their ordination to the priesthood, as the thin end of the wedge. This seems to be the explanation for the attitude of those who refuse to permit girls as well as boys to act as servers. And, more strongly, it fuels the misgivings of those opposed to the admission of women to the diaconate, a practice recently sanctioned by the Church of England, and other Anglican provinces. In this case apprehensions *are* justifiable. In the West, deacons have long been regarded as little more than probationary priests who proceed virtually automatically, after a year or so, to the higher office. In these circumstances, when women are made deacons, they naturally regard this as being a stage on the way to priesthood. Even though, as I believe, there is no theological objection to making women deacons, the expectations which this step arouses have a powerful psychological effect upon them as well as upon their sympathisers. This situation would be eased if the diaconate could be regarded as a ministry in its own right, with its own distinctive privileges and responsibilities, instead of as a means to an end. It may well be that the establishment of a permanent diaconate (open to married men) in the Roman Catholic Church will help us all towards a deeper understanding of this ministry.

The call to serve God in the religious life has always been open to men and women alike. The debt of the universal Church to these communities is incalculable. All Christians must then be alarmed by the present sharp decline in vocations to join them; unless this trend is arrested and reversed the Church's impact upon the world it is called to serve will be grievously diminished.

In the case of the enclosed communities this dangerous decline may not be apparent to the outside world because their life of sustained prayer and worship is necessarily hidden. The rapidly dwindling resources of the active orders are, however, evident as they are compelled to withdraw from, for example, hospitals and schools for which – in some cases for centuries – they have been responsible. Yet the demand for their services is greater then ever, and is often made most vociferously by those who would be horrified if one of their own sons or daughters contemplated becoming a monk or nun.

There are some works of mercy which possibly only women can do, such as the care of the mentally handicapped, the dying, and orphans – requiring sacrifical dedication to a degree infrequently found outside a religious community. The worship of God and the service of humanity will in many places go by default unless large numbers of novices come forward to replace elderly sisters struggling to carry burdens beyond their capacity. Within the Church every woman – and every man – not called to marriage should at least give careful consideration to the possibility of being called to serve God in the shared ministry of a religious community. And Christian parents ought to emulate their ancestors, who, in Catholic countries, put before their children the possibility of this vocation, and regarded it as an honour if one of them responded to it.

Finally, let me turn to a particular ministry, long suspect but now widely accepted, to which some women are called. In the Anglican Communion, as in the Orthodox Church, many priests are married: and the vocation of their wives is distinct from and complementary to that of their husbands. Although they are not themselves priests, they are united with a priest by a skein of the closest possible bonds, physical, spiritual and psychological; and such wives cannot fail to be intimately associated with their husbands' ministry. The priest's wife can and should be a most regular member of his congregation, alert to discern and correct any liturgical idiosyncracies which distract his people but of which he would otherwise be unaware. An assiduous listener to his sermons, she should be their sternest critic. She can be the trusted confidante on whose discretion he can completely depend: hers is the ear to which he can disclose his own perplexities, and the voice which can comfort, reassure, and suggest solutions to problems which, unassisted, he knows himself to be powerless to solve.

In his pastoral work the wife of a priest can have, and is expected to have, an active share. 'The fact that the parish priest has a wife is not to be seen as accidental or peripheral to his pastoral work; nor should the priest's wife merely be someone who happens to have married a [future] clergyman. Her status is indicated by her title: in the Greek Church the priest is called *presbyteros* or *pappa*, and his wife *presbytera* or *pappadia*; in the Russian Church the priest is "little father", *patushka*, and his wife "little mother", *matushka*.'[25] In my own former diocese in Africa visits to scattered village congregations were regarded as incomplete unless I was accompanied by my wife – who was enthusiastically welcomed as 'our mother' even by many who were twice her age.

The vocation to be a priest's wife is in some respects more demanding than that of her husband. If *her* ministry is to bear fruit it has almost invariably to be exercised unobtrusively in the shadow of limelight and prominence enjoyed by her husband in virtue of his formal office and position. It is essential that any woman, wondering whether to accept the proposal of marriage of an ordinand or priest, should regard the matter as one of *vocation*: she must, before committing herself, be convinced that God is calling her to such a marriage and that he will give her strength and grace to meet the demands it will make upon her. Only if *both* are called will they be enabled together to find joy and fulfilment in sharing a ministry which neither could exercise alone.

If the Church is to recognise more widely and to make full use of married priests, it has realistically to face the financial implications. This is something which Anglicans have hitherto largely failed to do. Many priests' wives are compelled, whether or not they wish to do so, to undertake full-time work in order to supplement the inadequacy of their husbands' stipends, to feed and clothe their families. In consequence most clergy wives so engaged, and with young children to look after, can find neither time nor energy to fulfil their distinctive ministry. The tragic breakdown of some clerical marriages, and the inability of many priests' wives to be and do what is expected of them, is largely due to the inadequacy of clerical stipends. Priests and their wives cannot together do the work God calls them to share unless they are provided with reasonable financial security for themselves and their dependents.

Conclusion

Mary, in whose honour this Society is dedicated to the glory and service of God, is in truth *Blessed among women* – as all Christians throughout history have agreed in acclaiming her. But it is to her that women of every age and condition who seek God's will for their lives have particularly looked for inspiration and illumination. She is unique, *alone of all her sex*, mother and virgin, 'in whom all opposites are reconciled'.[26] In her, more clearly than in any other creature, are displayed those distinctive virtues of humility and obedience revealed in their perfection in her incarnate Son. In humility she accepted her vocation:

Behold the handmaid of the Lord.

In humility through his childhood she ministered to her Son, providing the background of a loving home in which he prepared for his ministry. In humility she *pondered in her heart* the meaning of behaviour she sometimes could not understand:

Son, why have you treated us so?
O woman, what have you to do with me? . . .
Do whatever he tells you.

What, by grace, her presence and quiet influence did in him and his disciples only God can know. Quietly, unobstrusively, in the background, she was *there* throughout his earthly life.

Your mother and your brothers are outside, asking for you. . . Here are my mother my mother and my brothers! Whoever does the will of God is my brother and sister and mother.

No other woman has done the will of God as Mary did it, nor paid a greater price for obedience given from the moment of her Son's conception to the day of his death, and beyond.

Be it unto me according to thy word. . .
A sword will pierce through your own soul also. . .
Standing by the cross of Jesus were his mother and his mother's sister. . .

For Mary we thank God: to her we look, united in Christ and redeemed, as she was, by him our only mediator and saviour: in him and through him we implore her prayers that we, each one, may be enabled to follow the example of her humility and obedience, and to seek, find and respond to our vocations.

Hail Mary, full of grace,
The Lord is with thee.
Blessed art thou among women
And blessed is the fruit of thy womb, Jesus.
Holy Mary, Mother of God,
Pray for us sinners
Now and at the hour of our death.
Amen.

Notes

1. E. L. Mascall: *Whatever happened to the Human Mind?*, (SPCK 1980), 135-6.
2. Ed. Peter Moore, *Man, Woman and Priesthood*, (SPCK 1978), 17.
3. Longfellow, *Hiawatha's Wooing*.
4. Queen Victoria: *Letter on 'this mad wicked folly of Women's Rights' to Sir Theodore Martin*, 29 May 1870.
5. *Address to Jurists*, 11 July 1974.
6. *True Humanism*, (Bles 2nd English edition, 1939), 191f.
7. George Eliot, *The Mill on the Floss*, chapter VI.
8. Francis Moloney, (Darton, Longman and Todd, 1985).
9. *The Way*, January 1970, 23.
10. Chaucer, *Wife of Bath's Prologue*, trans N. Coghill, (Penguin), 295.
11. Exodus 15:20; Judges 4:4; Luke 2:36.
12. *Bishop of London's Newsletter*, November 1985.
13. Ed. K. Ware, *Women and the Priesthood*, (St Vladimir's Press 1983), 13. The editor is Bishop of Diokleia and a Fellow of Pembroke College, Oxford.
14. 1 Peter 2:9.
15. *Op cit*, 21
16. ARCIC I, *Final Report*, (1981) 'Ministry and Ordination', para. 13.
17. Galatians 3:27,28.
18. Ware, *op cit*, 23.
19. *The Orthodox Church*, September 1975, 4. Quoted Ware, *op cit*, 22.
20. Ware, *op cit*, 22.
21. Gilbert Russell and Margaret Dewey: in Ed. Peter Moore, *Man, Woman*

and Priesthood, 91.

22. 1 Timothy 2:11,12.

23. It would be absurd to maintain that a pastor is an *ikon* of Christ, the good shepherd, in the same way as a priest at the altar is the *ikon* of Christ, the high priest.

24. 1 Peter 3:15.

25. Ware, *op cit*, 31f. In the Orthodox Church ordinands must marry *before* they are ordained. Hence the 'future' in this quotation.

26. Marina Warner, *Alone of all her Sex*, (Quartet Books 1978), 336.

Mary: some problems in ambivalance

Donal Flanagan
Roman Catholic, at Radio Telefís Éireann, Dublin

There was a time not so long ago when the word ambivalence was unlikely to be found in the title of a lecture on the blessed Virgin Mary. This was so, quite simply, because within the Christian community there were two broad certainties about Mary – mutually opposed certainties to be sure – but certainties none the less – the first that she had a significant and effective role in the salvation which is in Christ and the second, that she had not.

There was no ambivalence then about Mary but there is now, and the strange thing is that we are not talking about an ambivalence in one Christian community and a certainty in another. We are talking about an ambivalence that runs through many, maybe even all Christian churches.

1. Why speak of ambivalence

The title 'Mary: Some problems in ambivalence' is chosen to focus how many Christians feel because both the ecumenical movement and the feminist movement have called into question some old rigid clear lines of demarcation, with which all of us were too satisfied. I see ambivalence here as a stage of growth as Christians move away from the mutually exclusive portraits of the Mother of God which the West inherited from the Reformation and the controversial Christianities to which it gave birth and also from the totally male-drawn pictures of Mary which have come down to us.

Both Reformation Christians and Roman Christians have to pass through stages of ambivalence to reach a new and more real and more profound grasp of the Marian dimension of the mystery of Christ.

There are marian certainties called in question by feminism rather than by ecumenism. The male-centred orientation of human thinking about women (including Mary) has been with us throughout history and exists also within Christian theological thought. These male certainties and modes of thinking are now under attack by feminists. Their breakdown leaves us again in a situation of ambivalence. The old certainties are gone, but a new and clear vision has not emerged yet. The ambivalence within Christian thinking on the subject of women, necessarily spills over into Christian thinking about the

Virgin Mary. This ambivalence is at a very profound level. It is of great ecumenical significance because here we Christians are *all* called in question together. This is a problem older than our historical divisions and tends to unite rather than divide us if we grapple honestly with it to seek a common solution.

Just recently I was reading again an issue of *Concilium*, (168, October 1983) on the subject 'Mary in the Churches'. It was edited by Hans Küng and Jürgen Moltmann who contribute two separate editorials by way of introduction to the various articles. I would like to quote one or two remarks from each of those editorials.

Hans Küng writes (vii-xi):

> An ecumenical issue of *Concilium* devoted to Mary: not the easiest of undertakings. Has not Mary been largely left aside in the ecumenical discussions of recent decades? 'Mary in the Churches' – (the subject of the issue of *Concilium*) – surely a topic to cause embarrassment?
>
> 1. An ecumenical mariology? Apart from a few exceptions the evangelical Churches have lost practically all interest in mariology; Martin Luther's famous commentary on the *Magnificat* had more or less no lasting theological or spiritual effect; for many people, as a result of their reaction against the Catholic Church and their christocentrism mariology has in fact become 'mariolatry' – a 'negative symbol of ecclesial faith'. *Orthodox* theology on the other hand has kept the classical mariology of the ancient Church, embodying it in its liturgy and hagiography. But it is the *Catholic* Church which has heightened the figure of Mary theologically and 'used' her in the service of a particular doctrine of salvation; moreover with the proclamation of the 1854 and 1950 dogmas, Mary has got into the ambience of papalism and triumphalism.

Thus Hans Küng.

Jürgen Moltmann writes – somewhat more profoundly, I feel – (xii-xv):

> An ecumenical dialogue about mariology if it is carried on in all sincerity, with a readiness to understand the deeper roots both of marian devotion and of the resistance to it, is bound to be difficult. That is why mariology has been largely excluded from the official ecumenical dialogue. Where mariological conversations did occur, they often resulted in a mere consensus of specialists, which was of not great importance to the Churches represented. If we want to see what an ecumenically compelling mariology would look like we must dig deeper and be prepared to face the anti-ecumenical factors at work in mariology as cultivated by the Church.

Thus the challenge as seen by ecumenical theologian, Jürgen Moltmann.

These quotations show I believe that the subject we are looking at is not an easy one. It is notable also that it took *Concilium* a journal which has had, since its foundation, an express commitment to ecumenism, so long to get around to the topic of Mary as an ecumenical problem.

The problem of Mary and the Churches is a complex and difficult one, a problem which operates at many levels. It is not, as Moltmann emphasises a purely theological one. It is a much more deep seated crisis existing in the worlds of sensibility and feeling. Because of this very fact it generates a whole range of feelings, even hostility and a whole range of emotional responses. Not all of these, by any means, are consciously understood by the people in whom they occur.

When therefore I speak of ambivalence in regard to Mary as a phenomenon in many Christian groupings today I am not simply saying that there is an unfinished reconsideration of doctrines going on in the Churches. Nor am I simply saying that people are worried about theological or doctrinal truths about Mary and are not sure where they stand. This is only part of it. What I am really trying to indicate with the term ambivalence is an attitude shift. I am saying that some people in many Churches are engaged in a questioning of the way they looked at – felt about, acted towards the Virgin Mary, that at the moment they are experiencing unsureness in how to relate to her, that they have not moved beyond the stage of ambivalence towards her. In other words, they know the attitudes they come from and are trying to leave behind, they do not know clearly, where they are or more important, perhaps, where they are going.

I am not saying that this ambivalence is widespread in different Churches. I only say that some people are for better for worse moving into it. I think it must be admitted as a fact of the ecumenical scene that there are solid blocks of people in all the Churches committed to what they understand to be the tradition (and therefore I am afraid for some the unchangeable) position of their Church on the Virgin Mary. When I speak of ambivalence I am speaking of something that only affects some people, leaving others unchanged. But personally I see it as a sign of hope.

2. *The secure past of Roman Catholicism and its mirror image.*

The emergence of a more general ambivalence about Mary in Roman Catholicism in the modern period can be dated to the period of the Second Vatican Council which began in 1962. Before that date there as an unquestioned unbroken acceptance of a very large role for Mary in the life of the Church and of the individual Christian.

Mary was the dominant figure in Roman Catholic devotion. Her role as intercessor, refuge of sinners, mediatrix of graces was constantly emphasised in sermons and in popular writings.

In the generation which preceded the sixties the Roman Catholic world was bestridden like a colossus, by Pius XII who became Pope in 1939. It is interesting, in the light of the extremely important role he played in encouraging marian devotion all through his papacy, to look at his life and to see how it parallels for a lot of its length the growth of a very powerful marian devotional movement in the Roman Catholic Church. Pius XII was over eighty years old when he died in 1958, this means he was born and grew up in the immediate aftermath of the definition of the Immaculate Conception by Pius IX in 1854. The devotional atmosphere of his childhood would have been that of the newly encouraged marianism of Pius IX. He was ordained priest in 1899 under Leo XIII – another pope who put a mighty emphasis on popular marian devotion particularly on the rosary. Pius XII was made a bishop in 1917. He was ordained bishop, in fact on 13 May 1917 – the day of the first Apparition of Mary at Fatima, in Portugal. Who knows how this strange coincidence affected him? At any rate, his pontificate was characterised by a huge emphasis on marian devotion, which he forwarded with every means at his disposal. And he was not just a devotional encourager. He was also concerned to ensure that people's devotional approach to Mary would be firmly founded in theology.

Pius XII was the creator or certainly the shaper of a certain style of Catholic sensibility about Mary. This sensibility which the Catholics of the time imbibed would tolerate no other approach but that that of Pius XII as the way in which Mary should be seen, talked about, venerated, presented to people. It represented a severe narrowing in of the tradition of the Church on Mary and an emphasis on her glory, her heavenly status and her relationship to Christ which was to need subsequent correction. This style of marian theology and the kind of marian devotion in which it issued was unintelligible to many other Christians as a devotional form. It appeared to obscure Christ, even to import pagan values into the heart of Christianity.

Pius XII the principal architect and the chief reinforcer of the modern Catholic marian sensibility presented his teaching on Mary, which was always theologically nuanced, in a strongly devotional context. In this he was at one with the Churches' marian past in which marian doctrine and devotion were always very closely intertwined. He was also the recognisable heir of this past in another way. The overall shape of his marian presentation was strongly traditional in style and reflected closely the outline of marian doctrine and devotion which had emerged in the Counter Reformation. This was a presentation of Mary, born in the fires of controversy for although Mary was not a specific focal point of attack by the first reformers at the theological level, the implications of some of their fundamental and new positions in areas like justification and the invocation of saints could not but make themselves felt in regard to Mary. It might, indeed, be suggested that the march forward of the doctrine of the Immaculate Conception which was proceeding with giant steps already in the early seventeenth century, represented some kind of response to theories advocated by Christians of the Reform on sin, grace and justification.

It seems equally clear that the Reformers' assault on the invocation of saints, including Mary produced a reaction of equal and opposite force from Catholics of the Counter-Reformation. This reation seems to have been particularly strong in regard to Mary. In effect, it is from this period that marian devotion began to be conceived in the West as something archetypally Roman Catholic, a process which continued without interruption right down to our own time.

The mariology and marian devotional stance of Pius XII was no more and no less than a more developed version of the mariology and marian devotion of the Counter-Reformation. It was shaped by an unacknowledged polemical bias and had no ears to hear the faint queries emanating from less strident voices within the Roman Catholic Church. Pius XII, was in fact presenting to the twentieth century world a global marian position which had developed even within the Roman Catholic Church in isolation from other theological currents, which had a strongly devotional element in it, and which in its development never called in question the ultimately Counter-Reformation framework within which it had grown.

This Counter-Reformation picture of Mary would eventually be called in question by the movement associated with Vatican II, a movement which we remember generated considerable surprise and great joy on the part of other Christians. It was understandably unexpected by them. For they had regarded the position and style of Pius XII as the only possible Roman Catholic one and had seen it as merely the twentieth century confirmation of a theological and devotional position which their forefathers had rejected.

If the effect of Pius XII on the Catholic world was to confirm and enhance a marian spirituality of Mary's power and glory, his effect on the world of other Christians, by and large, was to reinforce an inherited negativity towards Mary. This can be very clearly seen in two publications dating from the fifties, one originating in Italy, the other in Ireland. I refer to Giovanni Miegge's book, *The Virgin Mary: The Roman Catholic Marian Doctrine*, which appeared in English in 1955; and the pamphlet, *The Exaltation of Mary* by Reverend Samuel

Poyntz, now Church of Ireland Bishop of Cork.

If I may be allowed a personal reminiscence – I can remember reading these publications at the time of their appearance and I can remember feeling offended by them. To someone who had grown up and been nourished on the marian enthusiasm of Pope Pius XII they seemed to me to be mean-minded and ungenerous in an area of theology and devotion where largeness of spirit was the demand. And so, as I see now, my marian sensibilities prevented me from seeing the point of these works and my immersion in the *total* Catholic marian atmosphere in which we lived under Pius XII did not encourage me to look outside it for a more rounded understanding of Mary's role. That was to come later with John XXIII and the Second Vatican Council.

Both these publications, which I believe are representative of their time, can fairly be taken as expressing the rather negative position on Mary which characterised most Churches of the Reformation during the time of Pius XII. From their standpoint the Roman marian doctrine and devotion had to be characterised as misleading, false, unevengelical, if not blasphemous.

The basic marian position adopted in these books is theologically minimalist. There is very little positive in it. Essentially it can thus be summed up: Mary is the human mother of Jesus; she is our exemplar of Christian life. I think it is healthy for us to recall these times in order to see how far we have come.

3. The decline of certainties.

The end of the pontificate of Pius XII in 1958 can be seen now to have marked a turning point in the way the blessed Virgin Mary was presented to Catholics and to the world. It was not that his successor Pope John XXIII was any less personally devoted to Mary. It was more a question of style, the style of the pontificate. The new Pope seemed from the beginning to be a man of a different mould, and he presided over the re-emergence of a more sober marian approach, both in terms of doctrine and of devotion. This significant shift in the theological presentation of Mary can be seen taking shape particularly in Chapter 8 of the Constitution on the Church, *Lumen Gentium* – which while it does not represent a complete turn around, at least admits to significant Church documents marian insights which served to relativise Mary and to complement the one-sided mariology of power and glory whch had characterised the previous pontificate. These were those insights which related Mary clearly to the Church as its model and principal member and which located her clearly among the children of Adam and placed her definitively with all those redeemed in Jesus Christ.

These insights were themselves not new, they were very traditional but their recovery was a very necessary step towards a Roman Catholic marian position that would be balanced even in terms of its own past. They also served to bridge the chasm which had grown between the pre-conciliar Catholic presentation of Mary and the position of many Christians of the Reformation tradition.

It is from this change of direction and emphasis that I would date the emergence of an ambivalence about Mary both within the Catholic Church and in some Churches of the Reformation.

Certainty, be it positive as in Catholicism or negative as in many Churches springing from the Reformation, is not easily abandoned. The emergence of these new insights called into question the certainties of both – but did not replace them with a new certainty. As a result we find ambivalence both *inside* the various Churches and *between* the various Churches.

4. *The challenge of ambivalence*

The ambivalence we find about Mary within individual Churches at the present time is thus rooted in earlier certainties, which are now in the process of being questioned. This is true whether we look at the large and positive certainty which characterised Roman Catholicism or the smaller and, may I call it, negative certainty which characterised Roman Catholicism or the smaller and, may I call it, negative certainty which marked some Churches related to the Reformation. This ambivalence may be painful for us, but it represents a significant ecumenical challenge and we need to look at some ways in which it might possibly be overcome.

It is clear that it would be of benefit to all Churches if they were to carry through a doctrinal cum devotional critique of their own present position on Mary in the light of their own past. A devotional tradition waxes and wanes. Things of value may disappear. Balance may be lost. Emphasis on one aspect of devotion may obscure other aspects so that a certain one-sidedness develops. The part may be taken for the whole. Things may be imported into a devotional tradition which has lost balance which would sit ill with the same tradition if it had preserved its earlier wholeness.

Roman Catholicism, at Vatican II and thereafter has demonstrated that a new richness and depth is attainable when a tradition struggles with imbalance and seeks to recover and reintegrate insights which have fallen from view or been obscured. It seems reasonable to suggest that the marian traditions of other Churches might follow the same road and from a critical and *loving* examination of their own past might recover and reintegrate insights of their own marian traditions which may have become lost to view.

There is a duty on all of us to look at our past critically in order to gain a standpoint from which we can clearly perceive any imbalance or narrowing. In this way we may hope to move towards one another by striving for a broader and more balanced marian devotional tradition in each of our Churches. I stress again, this is an ecumenical task we carry out within our own Churches and traditions. It is a possible pathway along which we can move towards overcoming ambivalence within our own Churches.

We need in all the Churches to criticise our present in the light of our past. And we need to strive for a broader and more balanced devotional tradition. But we need more – we need to become acutely aware of the characteristic sensibilities or feelings which reside in our own devotional traditions in both their positive and negative aspects.

Any Church's attitude to Mary, even the most negative one, is not a purely doctrinal matter. It is compounded of doctrine and sensibility or feeling. But we should in fact note that there is no necessary correlation between these two. A Church with a highly developed doctrinal position on Mary will likely have a highly developed marian devotional tradition and marian sensibilities. It does not follow, however, that a church with a minimal doctrinal position on Mary and a slim or non-existent devotional posture will *ipso facto* lack a developed sensibility in regard to her, though in this case it will be a negative sensibility. And this negative sensibility can be and it seems to me often is in inverse ratio to the minimal doctrinal devotional position.

I do hope I have not laboured the question of sensibility overmuch. But I do feel it is a key to much of our differences in what concerns the blessed Virgin Mary. It is for this reason that I would insist on the need for us all to be fully aware of the sensibilities or feelings which are deeply lodged in our own traditions today. It is for this reason also that I would insist even more on the need for us to become aware of the historical roots and causes of these precise sensibilities.

None of our churches today is unmarked by its own past. No Christian can escape our inheritance of conflict. No Western Christian tradition exists today that does not embody feelings and sensibilities generated in deeply divisive conflicts in the sixteenth and seventeenth centuries.

The fact that we have become civilised, even courteous to one another, by the grace of God even after so long a time, does not magically obliterate our burdens of inherited prejudice or redeem immediately our long-possessed partisan sensibilities.

This is a matter in which we need to be frank with one another, and kind and gentle. There is no point in trying to pretend that we are all at one in issues of sensibility or even indeed that we are sufficiently aware of the gaps which divide us at this point. It is a difficult area. It would have been so much simpler if our forefathers had conducted a calm doctrinal debate *in abstracto*, like we sometimes do at Ecumenical Conferences. But they didn't! They used the secular arm, they disenfranchised, they exiled, they invaded churches, they broke statues, appropriated church ornaments, burnt relics and killed each other all for the truth of the Gospel. It was not a cold intellectual debate apart from life. It was waged with feeling and passion and it gave birth to passions and feelings which are still there below the surface even or maybe particularly in what concerns the blessed Virgin Mary.

The reason we need to be keenly aware of the sensibilities or feelings embodied in our own traditions in regard to Mary and of the historical roots of these sensibilities is because they are part and parcel of the ecumenical divide we are attempting to bridge. This truth was brought home to me with extreme forcefulness due to ecumenical discussions on Mary in which I took part in Ireland. These discussions were extremely friendly and produced a statement clarifying agreements and differences about the Virgin Mary in regard to doctrine and devotion. Looking back on them now, I realise, they did not go deep enough. We never got into a straight forward examination of the sensibilites of each tradition, positive or negative. It is in examining these sensibilites in mutual Christian frankness, even if this involves hurt and pain, that real ecumenical dialogue about Mary begins. Simple exchanges about doctrines and devotion may correct errors of fact in the understanding of each others positions. They do not by themselves bring us closer in true mutual understanding and sympathy while our sensibilities remain contrary and unexamined.

There are inherent difficulties in direct Roman/Reformation comparisons today about positions on Mary because of the often unacknowledged burdens of the past. It is precisely these unacknowledged burdens that make a knowledge and awareness of our own sensibilities in this area a *sine qua non* for ecumenical progress. To cultivate the suggested frankness of exchange is an extremely difficult task and to make this exchange effective calls for not just awareness of our own and others sensibilities but also for a clearly critical stance vis-à-vis our own positions.

We need to feel as well as to know the 'what' and the 'why' of the decline of marian devotion within some Reformation Churches and of the growth of a negative marian sensibility. We need to feel as well as to know the 'what' and the 'why' of the overgrowth of marian devotion within Roman Catholicism and of the development of a marian hyper-sensibility within this particular tradition.

I am not talking here about the normal dessicated dialogue of theologians but of the need to talk freely and frankly about how we feel about each other's devotional stances. These things are difficult to express without causing offence, but the need is great and the task is urgent and there is always the grace of God to help the awkwardness of our words.

It is my belief that we can always learn from the past. And in the case of Reformation divisions about Mary which are the remote origin of our diverse marian sensibilities, I think we can certainly do so. I say this with more certainty now since I recently read a book called *War against the Idols* by Carlos Eire, which is subtitled *The Reformation of Worship from Erasmus to Calvin*. In this book one is brought face to face with the seriousness of the Reformers and of the charges they brought against late medieval Catholic piety. In this book equally we are brought face to face with the theory and practice of iconoclasm or statue smashing. That Reformation-inspired movement certainly caused a clearing up and purifying of medieval devotional practices, but it also led in the same Reformation Churches to the abandonment of the theoretical foundation on which devotion to Mary and the saints was based. To the extreme iconoclasts this whole system appeared as a piety of superstition, unevangelical, a creation of irreligion. To the Catholic reformers like Peter Canisius, who published a classic study of Mary towards the end of the sixteenth century, the problem appeared as one of some reformable abuses. Indeed, from the few words that Peter devotes to abuses at the start of his classic *De Beata Maria Virgine Incomparabili* and in the absence of other evidence one woud be hard pressed to conclude that the late medieval situation was as bad as it was made out. These, then, were the two poles of the argument.

But there was another voice, somewhat earlier than Canisius, who gave his attention to the matter and I think his approach is worth some attention. Desiderius Erasmus (1469-1536), scholar, humanist and near-contemporary of Luther and Zwingli turned his attention to the problem of marian devotion more than once, perhaps most interestingly in his *Letter to Glaucoplutus*. In this letter Erasmus (through the mouth of the Virgin Mary) makes very severe criticisms of contemporary devotion. 'How many there are,' he writes, 'who put more trust in the safeguard of the Virgin Mary or St Christopher than of Christ himself. They worship the mother with images, candles and songs and offend Christ grievously by their evil living.'

Some requests made to Mary are downright evil: she is made to say:

> Nay, and they ask such things from me a Virgin, that a modest young man scarce dare to ask of a bawd, and which I am ashamed to commit to writing. A merchant that is going a voyage to Spain

to make money recommends to me the chastity of his kept mistress; and a professed nun, having thrown away her veil in order to make her escape, recommends to me the care of her reputation which she at the same time intends to prostitute. The wicked soldier, who butchers men for money, bawls out to me: 'O blessed Virgin, send me rich plunder!' The gamester calls out to me to give him good luck, and promises I shall go snips with him in what he shall win; and if the dice don't favour, I am rail'd at and curs'd, because I would not be a confederate in his wickedness. The usurer prays, 'Help me to large interest for my money', and if I deny 'em anything, they cry out, 'I am no Mother of Mercy'.

Other requests are not so much evil, as quite simply selfish and silly: The Virgin is made to say:

And there is another sort of people, whose prayers are not properly so wicked, as they are vain and empty: the maid prays, 'Mary, give me a handsome, rich husband'; . . . and the doting old man, 'Send that I may grow young again'; the Philosopher says, 'Give me the faculty of starting difficulties never to be resolv'd'; the priest says, 'Give me a fat benefice.'

And yet, in spite of the savageness of the Erasmian critique of contemporary Catholic devotion, where he finds it corrupted, the last words of the *Letter*, which Erasmus puts into the mouth of the Virgin Mary are these:

And as for myself, although I wear no weapons, you shall not turn me out, unless you turn my Son out too, whom I hold in my arms. I won't be pulled away from him. You shall either throw us both out, or leave us both, unless you have a mind to have a Church without a Christ. . .

But alas the wisdom of Erasmus, the voice of critical reason was lost in the loud savagery of the polemic of the extremes and we are still living with the results.

5. *A feminist postscript.*

The ambivalence occasioned by feminist thinking affects the Christian presentation of woman and specifically, of Mary. I am unable here to do more than outline a few remarks which bear on this critique and on the Christian reponse to date.

I detect the beginnings of that strident polarisation of views, which calls my mind back to the sixteenth century divide. I see an arena of confrontation full of blind beasts of genus hippopotamus – both male and female, hippopotamus versus hippopotama so to speak. I perceive large and awkward manoeuvrings, loud bellowings and a profound inability to move except in a straight line forward towards confrontation. There is so much dust in the air and so much noise that it is probably over-optimistic to imagine one could hear the small Erasmian voice trying to deliver an even-handed critique of both feminism and Christianity.

Are we then doomed to choose between an ecclesiastical Mary unrelated to twentieth century woman and a theory of woman, feminism, which has no place for the greatest woman who ever lived? Or maybe it is that these rock-hard certainties which now clash so destructively will mature slowly towards a constructive ambivalence, and through that stage to a new vision.

Mary's Place in Lumen Gentium, *Vatican II's* Constitution on the Church

Alberic Stacpoole, OSB
Roman Catholic, St Benet's Hall, Oxford

The Second Vatican Council opened with the intention that a complete Constitution or Decree should be accorded to the blessed Virgin, and closed with her assigned to the last chapter of its Dogmatic Constitution on the Church. Even then, this Council had more to say about Mary than any of the previous twenty General Councils. Chapter VIII of *Lumen Gentium*, in its final form, proved a third longer than the proposed separate schema. And yet the Council marked the turning point in what had been a once exuberant Catholic devotion to Our Lady.

Cardinal Josef Frings of Cologne, leader of the Conference of German Bishops, gave a conference in Genoa in November 1961 as a preparation for the Council. He made the point that our Lady is a sign announcing the Church, 'that holy people made one through the common worship of the liturgy'. He then surmised that coming decades would face the task of integrating the marian movement with the liturgical: he saw the marian approach as giving the liturgically minded something of its heart-felt warmth, its fervour and feeling, its readiness for atonement and penance. Equally the marian minded would receive from the liturgy something of its 'sacred sobriety and lucid charity'.

What the Council brought was a deepening sense of Mary as model of the Church. Its early draft documents provided a privilege-centred approach: Mary was unlike others, immune from original sin, excused the general judgment of mankind after the general resurrection. Its final text provided a community-centred approach: Mary was the exemplar of the whole Church, as immaculate bride of Christ and as already joined to him in glory. The document in its changes went through three titles: 'Mother of the Church' (1962), 'Mother of God and Mother of Men' (1963) and 'Mother of God, in the mystery of Christ and the Church' (1964). When completed, it succeeded in balancing two aspects of mariology, viz. the blessed Virgin's unique relationship with Christ the Redeemer, her own Son (nn. 52-9, esp. 55); and her close relationship with Christ's body, the

Church and all the redeemed (nn. 60-5, esp. 63-5 which draw out the theme of Mary as type of the Church). As to the latter, that is why the fathers of the Council eventually decided to place their statement on Mary within their Constitution on the Church.

History of the Marian document through the Council's second session

Lumen Gentium VIII transpired as an amalgam of two equally valid, equally scriptural and equally traditional expressions of an authentic Catholic attitude to Mary: one considering her in herself, another considering her as part of salvation history. It would be well to trace that process.

During the two years before the Council opened a subcommission, headed by Cardinal Alfredo Ottaviani of the Commission *De doctrina fidei et morum* (with S. Tromp SJ as secretary), worked out a draft upon the Church (11 chapters). To it was added a chapter on 'Virgin Mary, Mother of God and Mother of Men'. It was debated in the last week of the stormy first session (1-7 December 1962). Cardinal Ottaviani suggested to the fathers (not officially, but in an impromptu fashion which put them on their guard) that, rather than debate the complex thirty-six-page schema on the Church hurriedly, they should debate the six-page schema on the Blessed Virgin – and so, 'with the assistance of our Lady', the Council could then conclude its first session 'in union and harmony'. But wisely the fathers chose to begin upon the Church: they saw how regrettable it would appear to Protestants (observers and beyond) were a council, ostensibly smoothing a path towards unity, to settle too quickly for marian piety.

The draft submitted on the blessed Virgin in 1982 was more complex than it seemed. It was an expression not only of the views of the members of the Theological Commission (impressive theologians whose convictions were not swayed by popular interest), but also the views of other theologians and bishops worldwide. Six hundred bishops had petitioned Pope John XXIII that the Council should produce a clear statement, standing in its own right, of the authentic teaching of the Church on our Lady. This was printed separately from the first draft of the Dogmatic Constitution on the Church. It distinguished two approaches to marian doctrine: a *Christo-typica* (Mary as a type of Christ) and an *Ecclesio-typica* (Mary as a type of the Church). It left many mariologists dissatisfied: among them there were 'maximalists' who followed St Bernard's advice, *De Maria numquam satis*; 'minimalists' who asked for irrefutable proof of every doctrine and devotion; and 'middle-of-the-roaders' who claimed to belong eclectically to both views. Before the second session a special schema was provisionally allotted to Mary.

During the first half of 1963 the Fulda Group (the Austro-German bishops and theologians) judged that the marian text as it stood would do 'unimaginable harm' to oriental and Protestant church relations. Fr Karl Rahner, in particular, urged that the blessed Virgin should be dealt with as an epilogue of the schema on the Church. He argued that, in the title 'Mediatrix of all graces', that teaching was not a dogma but a commonly-held doctrine; and that if the word 'Mediatrix' was to be used at all, it had to be most carefully defined. The Fulda Conference accepted all this, declaring that it was not absolutely opposed to the retention of the words 'Mediatrix' and 'mediation' in the schema provided that the phrase 'Mediatrix of all graces' was not used. It gave close scrutiny as well to contrary views.

When the second session opened in September 1963 with a debate upon the Church, Cardinal Frings spoke first in the name of the German and Scandinavian fathers. He said that he wished the Church's relationship to the blessed Virgin and the saints had been set out more clearly. Supporting him, the Cardinal of Chile acknowledged that 'in Latin American countries devotion to our Lady is sometimes too far removed from the proper devotional life of the Church' – a judgment echoing John XXIII's earlier warning to the clergy of Rome against their tendency 'to cultivate certain excessive devotional practices, even with respect to the devotion to the Madonna'. If it were proposed in a separate treatise, the theology of Mary would not be easy to relate to the whole doctrine of Christian salvation: so the schema on Mary should be incorporated into the schema on the Church. Cardinal Frings had made the same judgment, on the grounds that it would foster dialogue with separated brethren better; and Cardinal Silva Henriquez of Chile accepted this, saying that devotional excess sometimes gave non-Catholics wrong notions: 'Devotion to Mary and the saints, especially in our countries, at times obscures devotion to Christ.' In the early stages the only dissenting voice came from the Cardinal of Tarragona, speaking for fifty-six Spanish bishops, who put in a strong plea for keeping Mary separate from the Church, as he said, 'because the mystery of Mary is greater than the mystery of the Church. There is danger that she would be seen in a merely passive role as representing the Church, as the Church's elder daughter, and not as the Mother of the Church by her vivifying influence'. He said that if the Marian schema was to be included in the main one, then it should appear as chapter II and in its content should be as profound and extensive as the subject deserved.

October 1963 proved a month of marian activity. Firstly, Abbot B. C. Butler (President of the English Benedictine Congregation) published his own proposed marian schema, worked up with a brother monk from Downside whose doctoral thesis had been upon St John Damascene; it drew for its evidence upon the pre-schismatic period. Then a pamphlet was issued of Servite provenance, suggesting that Our Lady's titles should be listed and should include both 'Mediatrix' and 'Co-redemptrix' (the 'co-' being diminutive, as in 'collaborator'). Then a *peritus* from the Theological Commission used the Vatican Press imprint and official document style (even including the classification *'sub secreto'*) to run off a leaflet that deceived the fathers as to its provenance, strongly advocating a separate schema: this was the Yugoslav mariologist Carlo Balic, a Franciscan consultor at the Holy Office and principal drafter, playing politics. Then the Chilians issued their own substitute schema (on 17 October) before offering a conflation of three texts: those of themselves, Abbot Butler and Abbé Réné Laurentin of Tours, a great mariologist *peritus* (20 October). The Moderators called for a debate on 24 October; and the next day five Eastern Rite bishops – in communion with the Holy See – argued for a separate schema, as did the Servite Bishop Giocondo Grotti of Brazil. On 29 October the main issue was put to the vote by the Moderators. Cardinal Rufino Santos of Manila and Cardinal Franz König of Vienna, both members of the Theological Commission, were required to argue respectively for and against a separate schema, texts of their speeches were circulated for study overnight, and the vote was then taken. As a procedural matter, it required only a straight majority. The result was received in stunned silence because it proved so inconclusive. The fathers had voted 1074 for a separate schema, and 1114 for incorporating it in the Church: the curialist representatives of 'The Age of Mary' had lost by a slim margin of forty votes (only 20 being required to go the other way) to the European alliance. This was the only vote of its kind during the course of the Council.

The vote proved embarrassing. The desire for unanimity and justice among the fathers placed both the Theological Commission and the Council itself in a difficult situation. Changes had to be made in the so far agreed text. But unexpectedly the controversy was happily resolved the following year.

At the closure of the second session on 4 December Paul VI told the fathers of the Council: 'For the schema on the blessed Virgin Mary we hope for the solution most in keeping with the nature of this Council, i.e. the unanimous and loving acknowledgement of the place, privileged above all others, which the Mother of God occupies in the Holy Church. . . after Christ, her place in the Church is the most exalted, and also the one closest to us; and so we can honour her with the title *Mater Ecclesiae* to her glory and to our benefit.' It was to become especially interesting that Paul VI should so strongly and indeed serenely presume that title for the Mother of God. His own spirituality and conviction in this regard was to prevail above that of so many of the fathers, in the last instant.

History of the Marian document through the Council's third session

On 15 September 1964, early in the third session, Chapter VIII on the Church was again taken up. A compromise text, the work of two theologians, was presented. Of these, one was the Yugoslav Fr Carlo Balic and the other Mgr Gerard Philips of Louvain, a Belgian regarded as Cardinal Suenens' theologian. The latter's text had dropped the words 'Mediatrix' and 'Mother of the Church'; but he was told that such austerity would not produce the votes needed from the Council fathers. During the next three days the major debate upon the marian chapter of *Lumen Gentium* was undertaken, thirty-three fathers speaking in all.

The essential documents were these: a *textus prior* from the second session; published in parallel, a *textus emendatus*, which took in the amending process; a set of *modi* generated from the debate; a final synthesis presented for voting. The *textus emendatus* was composed of five chapters: *prooem – De munere B. Virginis in œconomia salutis – De B. Virgine et ecclesia – De cultu B. Virginis in ecclesia – Maria, signum certae spei et solatii peregrinanti populo Dei.*

The debate was opened by a statement from the *relator*, Archbishop Roy of Quebec. Cardinal Ruffini of Palermo began by commenting on the title 'Mediator', which had to be further explained so that 'non-Catholics will come to realise that the use of this title implies no lessening of the dignity of Christ who is the one absolutely necessary Mediator'. Speaking on behalf of seventy Polish bishops, the fiercely marian Cardinal of Poland, Stefan Wyszynski refered to Paul VI's very recent encyclical *Ecclesiam suam*, in which the Pope had called attention to the fundamental importance of the blessed Virgin in the life of the Church. That had prompted the Polish bishops to send the Pope a memorandum (and similar ones had followed from other episcopal groups) requesting that Mary should be proclaimed 'Mother of the Church', and that her chapter should be promoted from last to second in the schema, so that it would better illustrate the role of Mary in relation to Christ and his Church.

He was followed by Cardinal Léger of Montreal, another Canadian, who thought it necessary 'to renew the marian doctrine and cult': such a reform, already begun among theologians, 'must also reach the pastors and the faithful, and this final chapter of the Constitution on the Church offers the best opportunity for promoting it'. Emphasising the need for precise and sober terms, the Cardinal questioned the use of such titles as 'Mother of men', 'Handmaid of the Lord Redeemer', 'Generous companion' and 'Mediatrix'. The origin and the meaning of them all should be scrutinised in the light of the best theological research before their use was endorsed by the fathers in a conciliar text. He was followed by Cardinal Julius Döpfner on behalf of the ninety German-speaking and Scandinavian bishops, who affirmed that the chapter on Our Lady contained solid doctrine and should be left essentially as it was – without additions upon the role of Mary as Mediator. Cardinal Bea (President of the Secretariat for Promoting Christian Unity) added that that title was still disputed by theologians, and so should not be included in a conciliar text at all. Such a text was not a manual for private devotion; it required the highest theological proof. Then Cardinal Corrado Mingo of Monreale (Italy) gave an emotional speech in favour of the title 'Mediatrix' being amplified to read 'Mediatrix of all graces'. He complained that the title *Mater Ecclesiae* had been deleted from the 1963 *textus prior* without justification and contrary to the wishes of the Pope expressed on 11 October in the Basilica of St Mary Major and again at the closure of the second session on 4 December. There, in St Peter's, Paul VI had spoken of 'the unanimous and loving acknowledgement of the place, privileged above all others, which the Mother of God occupies in the Holy Church.'

In his turn, Bishop Hervás y Benet of Ciudad Real (Spain) complained that the new *textus emendatus* was too severe an adaptation from the *textus prior*, not corresponding to the wishes of the fathers. It had reduced the doctrine of Mary to an absolute minimum, despite the fact that the fathers had been assured that 'by inserting the schema on the Virgin Mary into the schema on the Church, no such diminution was intended or would be carried out'. Speaking the next morning, Cardinal Léon-Josef Suenens of Malines (Belgium), agreed upon the danger of minimising the importance of Mary. He said that the new text did not place the spiritual maternity 'which Mary continues to exercise in the Church even today', in its proper light. He described the text as defective in expressing what the faithful believed as to the co-operation of the Virgin in Christ's work of redemption. He felt that the schema should bring the faithful to realise that they were associated with the maternal action of Mary in carrying out their apostolate. It was a valuable and independent contribution.

On behalf of the eighty-two bishops of Portugal, Bishop Francisco Rendeíro of Faro asked that the title 'Mediator' should be retained. Among the faithful who knew that the matter had already been discussed publicly by the fathers, its omission would generate scandal. Taking up this issue, Bishop Ancel of Lyon commended that the title 'Mediator', brought into the text but not endorsed therein (and thus left open for further study), should be listed with other such titles to avoid the impression that it was a privileged one: indeed that was so done.

Speaking on behalf of the eighty-two bishops of Spain, Archbishop García y García de Castro of Granada took to task the Theological Commission for their radical revision of the *textus prior*, rather than adaptation according to the mind of the fathers. He asked that the original title of the chapter, 'Mother of the Church', should be restored, since it corresponded to pontifical documents, issued by six popes from Benedict XIV to Paul VI as well as the writings of Irenaeus, Augustine and Pope Leo the Great. To omit the doctrine implied in that title would undermine the devotion so far shown to the Virgin by Christians. Thus the debate progressed: there were fourteen speakers on 16 September, sixteen the next day and three on the last day including Cardinals Frings of Cologne and Alfrink of Utrecht. At one stage the Ordinary of the Poles in exile, Archbishop Guiseppe Gawlina spoke of devotion to Mary as no obstacle to ecumenism: he quoted Luther's dissertation on *The Magnificat*: 'Come to God through Mary; from her you learn to believe and hope in God. . . Mary wishes that you come not to her, but through her to God.' Last words: four days later, the same director of the Polish hospice in Rome was dead!

Cardinal Frings' speech was a summary piece of advocacy. On the previous night one of the two drafters of the compromise text for the Theological Commission, Fr Carlo Balic, had gone to the German Cardinal and persuaded him that the unresolved controversy over the two titles, 'Mediator' and *Mater Ecclesiae*, could nullify all that had been achieved. The German Cardinal was to urge acceptance of the compromise text as it stood; and to this he agreed. He said in his address that Chapter VIII contained nothing contrary to Catholic faith or to the rights of the separated brethren. It offered a middle road between diverse opinions 'and in a certain way may be considered a compromise'. At that state, it would need an improbable two-thirds majority to make major changes to the text: so, he asked, let each father 'sacrifice some personal ideas, even very right ones', and – when detailed points have been corrected – approve the schema. He said: 'Theologians can then take this text for a starting point to make more profound studies of those doctrines which are not yet clear, and can better develop those which are still in dispute.' He was supported in this by Cardinal Alfrink; and the text was then referred back to the Theological Commission for further revision, which was to include written interventions and comments submitted before the third session began.

Cardinal Frings' speech proved crucial, not to say decisive. Archbishop Roy of Quebec, as *relator*, presented the further conclusions of the Theological Commission. The new text spoke of Mary's motherly affection for the Church while not explicitly using the title *Mater Ecclesiae* (which lacked attestation in tradition). Her motherhood in the order of grace was expressed with precision: the word 'Mediatrix' was to be used on the same footing as such as 'Intercessor' or 'Adiutrix', i.e. without being given a technical meaning. At the same time the context was to contain a declaration upon the transcendence of Christ's mediatorship. Pastoral comments were filled out to be more extensive, showing how all apostolic activity in the Church has a perfect exemplar in the Mother of God, who is also Mother of Men. The vote upon the *textus emendatus* (an amendment re-amended) was taken on 29 October 1964: 1559 voted affirmative, 10 voted negative, 521 voted affirmative *juxta modum* (i.e. offering further qualifications). So the necessary two-thirds majority had been achieved.

In the last stage, the Theological Commission again examined the text, in the light of the 521 *modi*. Archbishop Roy was able to explain that though the title *Mater Ecclesiae* was omitted from the final text, it was equivalently expressed in Article 53 where it states: 'Taught by the Holy Spirit, the Catholic Church honours [Mary] with filial affection as a most beloved mother' *(tamquam matrem amantissimam)*. As to the title 'Mediatrix', the suggestion of Bishop Ancel of Lyons was taken up, being adopted in Article 62: 'The Blessed Virgin is invoked by the Church under the titles of Advocate, Auxiliatrix, Adjutrix and Mediatrix. These however are to be so understood that they neither take away from nor add anything to the dignity and efficacy of Christ the one Mediator. For no creature could ever be classed with the Incarnate Word and Redeemer. . . The Church does not hesitate to profess this subordinate role of Mary' *(tale munus subordinatum Mariae)*. 'Christ the one Mediator' has already been established as Article 8, with due references; and was again established in Article 60 (within Chapter VIII): it appeared six times in all, in three Decrees.

The final vote upon *Luman Gentium* VIII, after the *modi* had been dealt with, was taken on 18 November: of the 2120 fathers present, 2096 voted affirmative *(placet)*, 23 voted negative *(non placet)* with a single invalidity. The following day, for the record, a final vote was taken upon the whole of the Dogmatic Constitution *Lumen Gentium* on the Church: of the 2145 fathers present, 2134 voted *placet*, 10 voted *non placet* with one invalidity. A solemn vote and promulgation was taken on 21 November 1964, the last day of the Council's third session: of the 2156 fathers present, 2151 voted *placet*, 5 voted *non placet*. Thus the mariological text moved into the Church's historical record.

There were, throughout the Second Vatican Council, particular inter-ventions of the Pope – either John XXIII or Paul VI – into the working of the commmissions or plenary decisions. One such, and a strong one, concerned the title *Mater Ecclesiae*. On the day when the final vote was being taken upon *Lumen Gentium* VIII, the text that only implicitly included that title, Paul VI made a statement at a public audience which bade well to overturn the process. He said on 18 November: 'We are happy to announce to you that we shall close this session. . . by joyfully bestowing on our Lady the title due to her, Mother of the Church.'

This he did on the last day of the 1964 third session, in his closing address. Gérard Philips – with Fr Carlo Balic, one of the two principal drafters of the marian chapter (as we have seen) – in his history of the Constitution summed it up by saying that the Pope took an affirmation of tradition a step further, with the help of a vocabulary that had come into use only in recent times. He said that this lively session 'ended with a peaceful gesture, which makes it impossible to speak of winners and losers, terms which are in any case quite out of place in speaking of a council. This will be clearer to future generations than it is to us.'

Almost a half of Pope Paul's closing address on 21 November 1964 was taken up with the Virgin Mary, 'sentiments of sincere and filial gratitude to the holy Virgin' who had been protectress, patron and counsellor from the outset. For him by the promulgation of the Constitution *Lumen Gentium*, 'which has as its crown and summit a whole chapter dedicated to our Lady, we can rightly affirm that the present session ends as an incomparable hymn of praise in honour of Mary.' Never before had a Council presented such a vast synthesis of Catholic doctrine as to the place Mary occupies in the mystery of Christ and his Church – 'to which she is closely linked as *portio maxima, portio optima, portio praecipua, portia electissima*'.

Because so many fathers from various parts of the Catholic world had pressed him for an explicit declaration of 'the motherly role of the Virgin among the Christian people', and because it seemed so fitting, the Pope decided to proclaim Mary *Mater Ecclesiae* 'for the glory of the Virgin and for our own consolation'. She was to be 'Mother of all the people of God, of the faithful as well as of the pastors. . . honoured and invoked by the entire Christian people with this most sweet title'. Paul VI went on at length about this, calling Mary 'the model of faith and of the full response of any call from God, the model of the full assimilation of the teaching of Christ and of his charity; so that all the faithful, united in the name of the common mother, may feel themselves ever more rooted in the faith and in union with Jesus Christ. . . The humble handmaid of the Lord, exists only in relation to God and to Christ, our sole Mediator and Redeemer. . . (And thus) those not part of the Catholic community may understand that devotion to Mary is not an end in itself but a means essentially ordained to orient souls to Christ and so unite them with the Father in the love of the Holy Ghost.'

At this stage, and with a promise to visit the Portuguese shrine of Fatima, the Pope resorted to prayer to 'the Virgin Mother of the Church. . . *auxilium episcoporum*. . .' He went on: 'look with benign eyes on our separated brethren and condescend to unite us, you who brought forth Christ as a bridge of unity between God and men. . .' The day had begun in dark humour, as the Pope came into St Peter's to concelebrate a last solemn Mass with twenty-four fathers from sees with national shrines in honour of the Blessed Virgin. The mood had changed; Pope Paul was interrupted seven times during his last address, applause increasing throughout. A standing ovation greeted the announcement of the title *Mater Ecclesiae*, signifying the assent of the Council fathers – but not all of them, for some voiced their criticism of the Pope's independent action later when they had returned home. Cardinal Bea of the Secretariat for Promoting Christian Unity, pointing out that the issue had never been put to a plenary vote, asked: 'By what right then can one pretend to know something about the presumed majority opinion of the Council?'

Paul VI was perfectly correct, and in no way overriding, in the sequence of his actions – a twofold exercise of his own supreme authority, and that of the Church. He first conformed himself to his College of Bishops by promulgating the Dogmatic Constitution on the Church, which included the new marian title in an 'equivalent' manner (as we saw). Afterwards, the first action completed, the Pope then invoked his own personal authority to state explicitly what he and the College had just stated implicitly or 'equivalently'. Thus it is that a Pope may guide a Council, rather than surrender to it. It is interesting to recall in this context that so far back as during the debates of the first session on the Church, two Cardinals had been wont to employ the phrase *Mater Ecclesiae*, Suenens of Malines and Montini of Milan! At so early a stage these far-sighted Cardinals were sensing the vital importance of integrating mariology with ecclesiology.

What development of mariology has there been between 1960 and 1965?

In the period of the Council there occurred a clear re-orientation of the way our Lady was perceived, and following that of the ways of marian devotion. Pio Nono in the nineteenth century had given a strong impetus to marian thought. Movements had grown up: for instance Pius XI had approved the Legion of Mary, and then the feast 'Mary, mediatrix of all graces'. Devotion to the rosary had been fostered since the time of Leo XIII (who had given eleven of his forty-two encyclicals to the subject of Mary); but it was during the reign of Pius XII that an astonishing upsurge of devotional practice occurred. The years of the 1950s have been called 'the age of Mary': the recorded statements of Pius XII on the blessed Virgin add up to more than those of his five predecessors – encyclicals, addresses, sermons. Our Lady became more prominent in the minds of theologians and lay folk alike, and the magisterium became clearly engaged with this marian movement, this rising enthusiasm whose momentum carried through into the reign of a Pope with a much cooler approach to mariology, John XXIII. The preparatory phase of the Council's first marian document belonged in that atmosphere.

When the Catholic bishops of the world were consulted during the ante-preparatory phase (before 14 November 1960) 2000 episcopal *vota* were received in Rome. Some 300 asked for a new definition on mediation, 50 each on spiritual maternity and on co-redemption, and 20 on marian royalty. Some 200 asked that something be said about Mary at the Council, while half that number asked that nothing be said. Some 1400 *vota* were silent upon the subject. With this in view the Theological Commission constructed its first schema, which was approved as such in March 1962, being given its *nihil obstat* by the Central Commission on 10 November. On 23 November it was presented to the fathers of the Council as two schemata within one volume, upon the Church and on Mary. The marian schema, drawing overmuch on recent papal statements, remained unaltered into the second session, though gathering its new title *Mater Ecclesia*. The great change came in the period before the third session; and that was the reason why some of the fathers grew so angry in their speeches in 1964, confronted as they were by a newer mariology, more rooted in scripture and tradition, for which they were unprepared. It was Mgr Gérard Philips of Louvain who was most directly responsible for the changes. Up to 7 March 1964 five successive drafts had been prepared, and the last was then put before the Theological Commission for final ammendment and – with a further amending process in early June – publication to the fathers.

Some of the fathers asked to have old phrases and formulas worked into the new schema, familiar from papal documents; others wanted new thought to go through, especially uniting the visions of ecclesiology with those of mariology. When in 1943 Pius XII promulgated his encyclical, *Mystici corporis Christi*, he gave 109 sections to the life of the Church, and sections 110-111 to an 'Invocation of the Virgin Mother of God'. The Council fathers, by contrast, gave their longest chapter on the Church to 'The Blessed Virgin Mary, Mother of God, in the mystery of Christ and the Church'.

Marian devotion after Vatican II

Most people who had followed the Council with enthusiasm thought that the Church was due for a period of unqualified expansion, with a strong increase of vocations to the priesthood and religious life alike. Instead the Church moved into a severe unrest, which partially took the form of a challenge to what had hitherto been one of the most flourishing features of the life of the Church: marian devotion. As Fr Eamon R. Carroll O Carm puts it: 'Even when there were no attempts to play down devotion to Mary, there was often embarrassed silence from preachers and teachers. People were used to hearing sermons about the blessed Virgin; all of a sudden there was silence from the pulpit – no homilies about the Mother of God.' The recitation of the rosary became less common, either publicly or privately. Pieties were reduced in the parishes, or were replaced by the new dispensation, evening Masses; and no other devotions were, for a while, offered. The charismatic movement grew up, with its focus on the work of the Spirit of Christ among us; and it took a long time for charismatics to come to know our Lady as the Spirit-filled woman of faith evident in the gospels and the Church's tradition.

With the diminution of marian devotion has disappeared – perhaps as well in our age – the world of marian sacramentals: rosary, scapulars, medals, holy pictures and other badges of religious devotion. Undoubtedly some aspects of marian devotion were overdue for purification, but not surely for elimination. And when all of this was at its most vulnerable, it encountered the hard-fought struggle for women's rights, such as the Equal Rights Amendment (ERA), a vehicle among others of the feminist movement for equality. Women began to see Our Lady as employed by Church authorities to keep women in subjugation; and so they lost interest in her as being a model for the past. Her humility, her obedience, her 'passive' virtues which included a world-ignoring purity, made her – in the words of Marina Warner's book title – *Alone of all her sex* (a phrase indeed from a fifth century Latin poet), in Miss Warner's view at the expense of all other women.

Gradually, through the excellent improvements in the liturgical life of the Church (and one remembers, for instance that from 1 January 1970 New Year's Day had become 'The Solemnity of Mary the Mother of God'); and through steady ecumenical advances (and one remembers not only the work of ESBVM but such as the Lutheran-Roman Catholic Consultations in the United States, with their publications), marian devotion is returning in stronger state, resting upon the true tradition of the Church and its scriptures, to where it might have expected to be after Vatican II. This has been splendidly helped by Paul VI's Apostolic Exhortation, *Marialis Cultus* ('To honour Mary') of 2 February 1974; and by frequent exemplary acts and statements from the present Pope. A more real mariology has come into currency and therefore with it a more real and abiding devotion.

Bibliography

Bernard & Barbara Wall, *Thaw at the Vatican*: session two (Gollancz 1964).

Xavier Rynne, *The Second Session* (Faber 1964).

Xavier Rynne, *The Third Session* (Faber 1965).

Ed. Herbert Vorgrimler, *Commentary on the documents of Vatican II*, Vol 1 (Burns & Oates/Herder & Herder 1967): Gérard Philips, Dogmatic Constitution on the Church: History of the Constitution; Otto Semmelroth, Chapter VIII.

Ralph M. Wiltgen SVD, *The Rhine flows into the Tiber: a history of Vatican II* (Hawthorn 1967).

Ed. Kevin McNamara, *The Church*: a theological and pastoral commentary on the Constitution on the Church (Veritas Publ. 1968/1983); Donal Flanagan, 8. The Blessed Virgin Mary, Mother of God, in the mystery of Christ and the Church.

Guiseppe Alberigo & Franca Magistretti, *Constitutionis dogmaticae Lumen Gentium: Synopsis historica* (Istituto per le Scienze Religiose, Bologna 1975).

Gerard M. Corr OSM, '"Mother of the Church", an ecumenical title?', *Marianum* III (1975), 281-90.

Eamon R. Carroll OCarm, 'Mary after Vatican II', *St Anthony Messenger* (May 1984), 36-40.

I should like to thank Fr Gerard Corr, a former staff member of the Secretariat for Promoting Christian Unity from 1960, for reading this text and advising amendments. A mariologist, he had been directly involved in this Chapter VIII at draft stages during the Vatican Council. At the time of final proofs (March 1987), volume 37 (1986) of *Marian Studies* (University of Dayton, Ohio) had not yet reached this author. It is to include a series of four conference papers on *Lumen Gentium* VIII from the May 1986 National Convention of the Mariological Society of America.

The New Testament Charisms of the Blessed Virgin Mary

Rev Eamon R. Carroll, O. Carm, STD,

Roman Catholic, Professor of Theology, Loyola University of Chicago

Current interest in the New Testament charisms of the blessed Virgin, the holy Mother of the Lord, has been stimulated by three factors: first, the charismatic renewal; second, biblical studies; third, ecumenical efforts of recent years. In common prayer and public witness members of many Christian churches and communities are discovering or rediscovering Mary of the Gospels as the woman filled with the Spirit, from the annunciation to Pentecost, even from her grace-filled origins to her union with the risen Christ in glory. What is truly remarkable and surely the work of the Holy Spirit is that members of mainline Churches, such as Roman Catholicism, have not only been challenged but also encouraged by members of strongly Protestant groups – I speak descriptively – to justify, to deepen, to share their own veneration of the holy Virgin.

In his recent encyclical letter on 'the Holy Spirit in the life of the Church and the World,' Pope John Paul II has some helpful contextual statements about the blessed Virgin, the Church and the Holy Spirit. 'The Church perseveres in prayer with Mary. This union of the praying Church with the Mother of Christ has been part of the mystery of the Church from the beginning: we see her present in this mystery as she is present in the mystery of her Son.'[1] Quoting the Second Vatican Council *(Lumen Gentium*, n. 63) the Pope continued, 'The Virgin Mary through the singular graces and offices of the Holy Spirit is intimately united with the Church, she is a model of the Church.' Indeed, it is in 'contemplating [a word of loving wonder and admiration] the mysterious holiness of Mary, in imitating her charity, that the Church becomes herself a mother, a virgin who in imitation of the Mother of the Lord, and by the power of the Holy Spirit, preserves with virginal purity an integral faith, a firm hope, and a sincere charity.'[2]

'The Holy Spirit, bringing about in Mary *the beginning of her divine Motherhood*, at the same time made her heart perfectly obedient to that self-communication of God which surpassed every human idea and faculty. "Blessed is she who believed" . . . Mary entered the history of the salvation of the world through the obedience of faith. And *faith*, in its deepest essence, is *the openness* of the human heart to the gift: *to God's self-communication in the Holy Spirit*. 'St Paul writes, "The Lord is the Spirit, and where the Spirit of the Lord is, there is freedom".' (2 Cor 3:17)[3]

New Testament Witness

The New Testament supplies strong support for regarding Mary as the perfect charismatic. In her case the charisms are not only compatible with her central vocation of being the Mother of the Son of God, they are also inseparable from her holiness. The biblical evidence comes from both St Luke and St John, with Paul as our guide for the scriptural sense of charisms. For Luke the Virgin Mary is the Spirit-filled woman of Nazareth and of the Cenacle. In his infancy narrative Luke placed pentecostal anticipations. The Spirit is poured out on Mary, on the family of the Baptist – Elizabeth, reluctant Zachary, unborn John.

In John the Mother of Jesus put before her Son the human need of the failing wine and then counselled the puzzled waiters to do whatever Jesus would tell them. In the overflowing supply of rich wine, exegetes have seen the sign of the long-prophesied wine of the Spirit, poured out not in human measure but with divine largesse for the nuptials of Christ and his bride the Church. Mary, inspired by the Spirit, was requesting the messianic fulfilment. In the Acts, the Apostles were intoxicated with the new wine of Pentecost morning. Through her Son's testamentary words to Mary on Calvary John sharpens again our sensitivity to our Lady and the Holy Spirit, as the saviour breathes forth his Spirit and the Church is born from his pierced side in sacramental blood and water.

Charisms are linked to the outpouring of the Holy Spirit, free gifts which are the specific signs of the Spirit, particular manifestations of *agape*, the fundamental gift of love.[4] For Paul a charism is a free gift given for the building up of the body of Christ – a spiritual gift given to some and not to all for the *aedificatio* of the Church. To receive a charism is to be educated in humility, for it is God who is acting.

Before Pentecost the risen Jesus assured his followers, 'The Holy Spirit will come upon you.' That was already realised for Mary in the annunciation. Mary was 'baptised in the Spirit' in order to lay the first foundation of salvation, the conception of the Son of God, who takes his human nature from her. Here also is the secret beginning of the mystical body of Christ. In the power of the Spirit, Mary hastens to Elizabeth – evangelisation has now begun, the missionary dimension of Pentecost is already put before us. Zachary had been promised that his son would be filled with the Holy Spirit from his mother's womb, and now Elizabeth 'filled with the Holy Spirit' prophesies, 'Blessed are you among women and blessed is the fruit of your womb. But who am I that the mother of my Lord should come to me? The moment your greeting sounded in my ears the baby leapt in my womb for joy'. Mary returns Elizabeth's greeting with her prayer of praise, 'My soul magnifies the Lord, and my spirit rejoices in God my saviour.'

Two of the best-known and most powerful charisms in the Church are praise and intercession. No attempt is made here to consider all the New Testament charisms of Mary.[5] We speak first of the gift of praise. 'Praise is a gift that reaches out to eternity. We are to live forever in the praise of God.'[6]

The charism of praise

First, the gift of praise: this charism involves the ability to address God spontaneously and exuberantly. The Spirit give this gift to overcome customary human reserve. We are so often tongue-tied in our praise of God, prisoners of convention and human respect. Adoration, which is primarily inner reverence for God, is a necessary complement to praise. 'Whilst praise is what we do with God's grace to respond to the revelation of his glory or works, adoration carries a further nuance of our being overwhelmed by the holiness of God and our nothingness.'[7]

In word and deed the holy Mother of Jesus shows forth the charism of praise. 'Mary looks to herself only to discover what God has done for her, and gives him praise. . .'[8] Mary's song does more than express her attitude before the birth of Jesus. Its sentiments have a permanent truth that applies to Mary now 'in union with the risen Christ as well as when she walked this earth' in faith.[9] Praise goes beyond emotion or exuberance; it involves the decision here and now to praise God. The charism of praise gives an added facility.

Some years ago the American Benedictine, Kilian McDonnell, wrote of his own rediscovery of Mary of the scriptures and the marian charisms of the Gospels.[10] As he describes it, his ecumenical experience had reinforced his 'native restraint' with respect to our Lady. A French exegete urged him to read Luke's Gospel and the first chapters of the Acts of the Apostles, and to seek light on our Lady as herself a charismatic. When Dom Kilian did so, he made the joyful discovery of the gifts of the Spirit possessed by the Mother of Jesus. According to him Pentecostalism knows two major forces: one is *presence*, the other *praise*. 'Presence' means that God takes the initiative, seizes us totally, claims us completely. The human response to the approach of God's presence is a profoundly personal 'yes', an affirmative answer that usually takes the form of praise. 'The natural response to God at work in his world is praise.'[11]

At the annunciation presence is the capital theme, 'The power of the Most High will overshadow you,' reminiscent of God's protecting presence over the ark of the covenant. How did Mary respond to God's presence within her? The Church has enshrined her response as its evening prayer, 'My soul magnifies the Lord.' When the Spirit comes on the disciples, first in the company of the Mother of Jesus at Pentecost and subsequently through the Acts, their response is similar to Mary's. They too declare the great things of God and magnify the Lord in joy (Acts 2:11; 10:46). As Dom Kilian concludes, we too should pay heed to the witness of Mary in considering the New Testament teaching on presence and praise. The Virgin Mary exemplifies scriptural charisms, for Mary in the bible and in traditional Christian celebration, both in formal liturgy and in popular piety, is the ark of the presence and the singer of praise.[12]

Tongues

Mary's presence at Pentecost shows her charism of 'tongues', or glossolalia, a familiar and much studied phenomenon in the contemporary charismatic renewal. 'Speaking in tongues' is the least of the gifts according to Paul, yet one that he valued and hoped that the Corinthians might have. 'Tongues' seem to be best described as non-rational oral prayer that sounds like language without actually being a true language, so that the complementary charism of 'interpretation' is not translation but rather an explanation of the meaning of these spontaneous and joyful sounds. Paul writes of this gift carefully, almost cautiously, but also approvingly, in 1 Cor 14:14-17. Our Lady shared this experience on Pentecost day, 'They were all filled with the Holy Spirit and began to speak in other tongues as the Spirit gave them utterance' (Acts 2:2-4).

We recall the beautiful word *jubilation* used by St Augustine to describe Paul's teaching on singing in tongues (1 Cor 14; Col 3:16). Jubilation has a community character. 'Singing in jubilation means that words are not enough to express what we are singing in our hearts. . . this jubilation, this exultant song is the melody that means our hearts are bursting with feeling words cannot express.'[13]

Intercession

Along with praise, intercession is another powerful charism in the Church that is illustrated by the New Testament picture of the Virgin Mary. This charism has special ecumenical importance, bound up with the eucharist and the communion of saints. Dr Ross Mackenzie spoke of four biblical women as loving intercessors, forerunners of the Virgin Mary, and he said that to intercede is what Mary did and still does. For Christ is never alone, and so we ask Mary and the saints to pray for us – such is the sense of the Church, as yesterday afternoon in Chichester Cathedral, at the once despoiled and now restored shrine of St Richard I asked the saint of my baptismal name to intercede for my pilgrim self.

A first view of the charism of intercession is the gift of presenting to God in prayer the needs of others. But this initial understanding is only a feeble beginning, for the charism of intercession is not 'a detached recital of the needs of the world which God knows anyhow.'[14] Rather it means, as Paul wrote to the Galatians (2:20), 'I live now, not I but Christ lives in me.' The model of the gift of intercession is the self-giving of Jesus, his supreme intercession on the cross and his everlasting intercession in heaven. This is the meaning also of the much-misunderstood 'entrusting' of the world to our Lady that Pope John Paul II requested for the annunciation weekend, 1984. The point of the Holy Father's recommendation was our intimate association with the consecration of himself that Jesus made to the Father's will (as in John 17:19), with the Mother of Jesus offered as an example and effective encouragement to give ourselves totally to Christ, our supreme intercessor, our unique mediator, even as Mary did by God's gift.[15]

The charism of intercession, so fruitful for the people of God, demands great deeds of its recipients, but empowers them to achieve even heroic works for God's glory, as Moses did, as the great Old Testament women did, as the faithful Virgin Mary did – and indeed still does – in total dependence on the saviour who lives forever to make intercession for us. Some authors describe Mary's intercessor charism as a 'gift of healing', and other studies consider marian intercession in the setting of the eucharist.[16]

Lukas Vischer, in a World Council of Churches brochure on intercession, wrote of the place of intercessions at the eucharist as occurring as early as the Didache, a document from the first decades of the Church. In prayers for other Churches, wrote Vischer, we need to give thanks above all, for thanksgiving in our intercessions is the only safeguard against cynicism in the Church and in the ecumenical movement.[17] Perhaps we brother and sister Christians are approaching before long full inter-communion – in the communion of saints, with Mary, the Mother of Jesus, full of grace and gifts, first of the saved, masterpiece of the Holy Spirit, and we shall share the holy table as well as the holy word. God speed the possibility of our singing together the medieval eucharistic hymn, *Ave verum corpus natum de Maria Virgine* (Hail true body born of the Virgin Mary) as we celebrate the truth that underlies those ancient and beautiful words. Perhaps the Holy Spirit will gift us also with the charism of jubilation!

Notes

1. *Dominum et vivificantem*, May 18, feast of Pentecost, in the translation published by St Paul Editions, Boston, 1986; italics are as in this translation, number 66.
2. *Ibid*, and *Lumen Gentium*, n 64.
3. *Ibid*, n 51.
4. 1 Cor 12:31-33.
5. The full range of the marian charisms in described by a number of authors, e.g., René Laurentin, *Mary the Charismatic; the Charisms of Mary in the New Testament* (an essay commissioned for a meeting of Catholic charismatic leaders held in Milwaukee, September, 1984, translated by Eamon R. Carroll, O Carm, and so far only in manuscript); 'Mary Model of the Charismatic', a chapter in Laurentin's *Catholic Pentecostalism* (Doubleday, Garden City, NY 1977); 'Mary, Model of the Charismatic as seen in Acts 1-2, Luke 1-2, and John', chapter in ed. V. Branick, *Mary, Spirit and the Church* (Paulist, NY 1980); 'Les charismes de Marie: Ecriture, Tradition et Sitz-im-Leben', article in *Ephemerides Mariologicae* (whole number on *Los carismas de Maria*) vol 28 (1978, final fascicle). See also Christopher O'Donnell, O Carm, *Life in the Spirit and Mary* (Glazier, Wilmington, Delaware 1981, also Dominican Publications, Dublin 1981, especially chapter seven, 'Mary and the Gifts of the Holy Spirit'. I would like also to acknowledge my indebtedness to my confrère and colleague at the Rome-based Institute for Carmelite Studies, an expert on the charismatic renewal, Father Louis P. Rogge, O Carm.
6. C. O'Donnell, in *Life in the Spirit and Mary*, 96.
7. C. O'Donnell, 'The Sacred Heart in the Holy Year', in *Carmel in the World* (Rome), 23 (1984:1), 21; section on Charisms of praise, intercession, reparation, 20-24.
8. C. O'Donnell, *Life in the Spirit and Mary*, 99.
9. *Ibid*, 97.
10. K. McDonnell, OSB, 'Protestants, Catholics and Mary: Does Mary Belong Just to Catholics?' in *New Covenant* (March, 1977); see also the chapter, 'The Holy Spirit and the Virgin Mary', in my book *Understanding the Mother of Jesus* (Glazier, Wilmington, Delaware 1979, also Veritas, Dublin 1979)
11. C. O'Donnell, *Life in the Spirit and Mary*, 101.
12. Adapted from McDonnell's article. He is presently working on a study of the Holy Spirit among men.
13. As translated by C. O'Donnell, in *Life in the Spirit and Mary*, 106.
14. C. O'Donnell, in *Carmel in the World*, 23 (1984), 23.
15. The papal letter, 'Entrusted to Mary', dated 8 December 1983, was published in *The Pope Speaks* 29 (1984:2), 142-145, also in the English *L'Osservatore Romano* for 27 February 1984; the annunciation weekend was March 24-25, 1984. See E. R. Carroll, 'A Survey of Recent Mariology', in *Marian Studies* 35 (1984), 167-9, also E. R. Carroll, 'Mary: the Woman Come of Age', in *Marian Studies* 36 (1985), 150-5.
16. See C. O'Donnell's section on 'Mary and the Charism of Healing' in his *Life in the Spirit and Mary*, pages 110-3. See also E. R. Carroll, 'Mary and the Spirit in the Prayer of the Eucharist', in ed. V. Branick, *Mary, the Spirit*

and the Church.

17. L. Vischer's publication was *Faith and Order Paper*, no 95 (WCC, Geneva, 1980); I reviewed it in my annual *Survey of Recent Mariology* in *Marian Studies* 34 (1983) 114f.
Final note: I have found useful also the following: Francis A. Sullivan, SJ, *Charisms and Charismatic Renewal: A Biblical and Theological Study* (Servant Books, Ann Arbor, Michigan 1982), and two further articles by C. O'Donnell, O Carm, 'Mary and the Charismatic Renewal' in *Carmel in the World* 18 (1979), 195-202, and 'Mary and the Charismatic Renewal', paper given at the international conference held in Dublin, April, 1984, the sixth such conference sponsored by the ESBVM, and published as *Communications at the VIth ESBVM International Congress, II, Mariology in Modern Practice* ESBVM, (January, 1985), a paper that appeared also in *One in Christ*, 1985-1, 72-5.

APPENDIX

Amplification of Note 5, referring to an unpublished essay
by Canon René Laurentin (Angers University),
'Mary the Charismatic'. [Ed]

Vatican II, which (as Pope John put it) 'inaugurated a new Pentecost', proved to be the *locus* of a living rediscovery of the Spirit in Mary. Luke, in his infancy narrative, speaks of Mary: 'She kept these things in her heart' (Lk 2:19, 51); and in Acts he brings her experience though to term (1:14): 'Constantly at prayer together; with them a group of women, including Mary the mother of Jesus', immediately before Pentecost. Luke, who came from the most charismatic of communities, Antioch (where they were first called 'Christians'), sought in the infancy of Christ the anticipations of Pentecost: the pouring of the Spirit on Mary and on the family of the Baptist (1:15, 35, 41, 67; 2:25ff). He perceived Mary as prototype of the Church and of the outpourings of the Spirit, i.e. charisms. Her latter-day appearances are charism in ages given to juridicism or the cult of power or cerebral religion. Luke portrays her as characterised by the grace of God.

From Acts 1 we may conclude: that Mary was present in the primitive community of the upper room, all awaiting the Spirit as Jesus had enjoined (1:5, 8), she singularly ready to receive the Spirit; that she was present at the coming of the Spirit, among the first Pentecostal community in prayer; that she was 'baptised in the Spirit' (cf 10:46) as she had been at the annunciation; that she belonged to a graced community endowed with charisms, given by the Spirit (especially 'agape'); that she and they were conscious of the Spirit's gifts e.g. the charism of tongues.

What occurred at Pentecost fulfilled Christ's promise to the twelve: 'The Holy Spirit will come upon you' (Acts 1:8). That had been realised in Mary at the annunciation: 'The Holy Spirit will come upon you' (Lk 1:35). There had begun the Mystical Body: the Son of God made man, announced to Mary in faith, received by her in faith, forms with her a single body both physical and according to the Spirit. Mary then hastens to share her secret with her cousin. Elizabeth is also 'filled with the Spirit' (1:41); and she is first to prophesy: 'Blessed are you among women, and blessed is the fruit of your womb' (1:41-5). This is a rich passage; for the Spirit is present in both mothers, in both of their sons and in their greetings to one another. The passage thus underlines the close connection between the physical and the spiritual, both being essential to the incarnation; and the transition from the Law to grace.

Mary in her turn then prophesied: 'My soul magnifies (*megalunei*) the Lord': Her word was to be used again when pagans were first baptised in the Spirit: 'The circumcised believers accompanying Peter were surprised that the gift of the Spirit should have been poured out also upon the Gentiles, whom they could hear speaking in tongues and *glorifying* God' (Acts 10:46). The word signifies the enlarging of hearts to celebrate the grandeur of God, which exceeds human understanding. And Mary continues: 'The Almighty has done great (*megala*) things for me', then says: 'And my spirit exults in God-who-saves' or 'God-my-Jesus' (for both are as one). To herself she takes no credit, all is given to God in his gifts; for God is source of all grace, charism, salvation and therefore joy.

In the Gospel of John, anticipation is the specific charism of women. His book of signs begins with two episodes where two women anticipate the design of God. At Cana, Mary advances the hour of Jesus; at the well, the Samaritan anticipates the good-news to be brought to the Gentiles. John's book of the passion begins similarly. The sisters of Lazarus obtain his resuscitation as a foretaste of Christ's resurrection; one sister performs an anointing prophetic of the burial of Jesus. John's book of the resurrection begins similarly. Mary of Magdala is first to the empty tomb, becoming evangelist to the evangelists. Again she is first to see the risen Christ, and is given her mission to proclaim him to the twelve.

In the Gospel of John , the 'hour' of Jesus twice involves his mother. At the outset at Cana she uses words redolent of those words from Exodus (19:8): 'Everything the Lord has said, we will do.' At the demise at Calvary, her highest achievement is her communion of Christ, her charism of compassion. She finds herself made mother of the disciples (19:25ff) in place of her Son. (The exact Greek pronouns are vital for the understanding, here). Motherhood dies with the Son, so becoming vacant until it is redeployed or transferred: 'By the cross stood *his* mother and the sister of *his* mother. . . Seeing *the* mother and the disciple whom he loved, Jesus said to *the* mother: Woman, behold *your* son. . . *your* mother.'

By becoming the Mother of the Son of God, the Lord and saviour, Mary allows the first cell of the mystical body to be formed – the *corps communitaire* – to which are to be joined Elizabeth and John. At the hour of the annunciation, the 'kingdom' and the 'reign' secretly begin; and the fundamental charism of Mary, her motherhood, gives rise to all other charisms, which flow as from a single source. Receiving Christ and forming him, she is to give him to others.

Canon Laurentin last addressed the ESBVM at the Canterbury Congress (1981), to the title: 'Pluralism about Mary: biblical and contemporary'. Cf *The Way Supplement* 45 (June 1982), 78-92.

Our Lord's Relationship with his Mother

Rev. William J. Bridcut
Church of Ireland

Does the blessed Virgin Mary have a motherly influence in heaven?[1] If we are to consider the possibility of such an influential position we should start by assuming that it would be an expansion of, or be capable of being deduced from, what we know of the relationship and influence which Mary had with our Lord during his earthly ministry. For this reason we shall look at all that the Gospels have to say about our Lord's mother during Christ's ministry. The idea of a motherly influence in heaven also assumes that the family relationships of this life with rights and obligations are carried into the next.[2] We shall consider this as well.

What the Gospels say

I. *Mary's last words*

After our Lord's baptism we first meet Mary and Jesus together at a marriage feast. The miracle of turning water into wine is the only one in which Mary has a role: there is no other direct conversation between mother and son recorded during his ministry; and the last known words of Mary are spoken when the public ministry of Jesus has not really begun properly (Jn 2:1-11).

Mary informed Jesus that wine was needed and from our Lord's reply it appears that Jesus understood her to be asking for two things: not merely that the wine problem be solved but also that in doing this he would at least enhance his reputation to all present.[3] In his reply Jesus addressed her as 'woman' which, no matter how respectful, can apply to any woman and so is most unusual for a son to use to his mother.[4] Indeed the contrast in two verses is striking: '*The mother* of Jesus said. . . Jesus said to her *"O woman"*.'

'O woman, what have you to do with me?' Whatever these words mean an objection and refusal are implied, with 'woman' showing a gentle distancing from mere home and family.[5] By the addition of 'My hour has not yet come' Mary felt that he would, at least in part, do as she asked. We have suggested that our Lord's reply shows that he felt that the request involved more that merely solving the wine problem. A miracle was performed but Jesus was careful to show that he was not to be pushed in his work which involved revealing himself to people. Christ did manifest his glory but for the sake of the disciples only. With this we can compare the request to his brothers (Jn 7:1-10) to go to Jerusalem and show himself to the world. Jesus told his brothers that he would not go but later he did go up, not publicly but in private.

The last recorded words of our Lord's mother were spoken to servants, but we should ask, since they were written down for our benefit, why we hear no further advice from her. There could be no better guide for daily life than her words, 'Do whatever he (Jesus) tells you.' But by making her *last* words to be those spoken at the *beginning* of Christ's ministry, the gospel writer makes Mary say in effect: 'My part in preparing Jesus for his great work is over, and now that he has entered upon his ministry you should forget about me and pay attention only to him'.[6]

II. *Who are my relatives?*

Mark in his gospel tells how our Lord's family heard reports that he was in an unhealthy state of mind and that while he was teaching in a house they came and sent in a message asking for him. Jesus was told, 'Your mother and your brothers are outside asking for you': and he replied, 'Who are my mother and my brothers?' And looking at his listeners he said, 'Here are my mother and my brothers. Whoever does the will of God is my brother and sister and mother.'[7] Mark makes it clear that his relatives are not on the outside of a crowd seeking to hear him but outside the house where he was and instead of seeking admission, they send a message asking him to come out. If Jesus were to meet his mother and brothers it would mean discontinuing his teaching, which explains the apparently harsh reply in asking 'Who is my mother. . . ?' and if he were to continue, his words would have to assert his freedom from the restraints of earthly relationships.[8] That Matthew's view of the incident is similar to Mark's is seen in his placing it among illustrations of misunderstanding of and opposition to Christ's ministry.[9] Matthew has also just told us that our Lord's influence and wisdom are greater than those of Jonah or Solomon, so it must have been hurtful to be misunderstood at home and both Matthew and Mark tell us that this was the case.[10] In his reply Jesus does not separate his mother from his brothers, but mentioning her gives his words greater emphasis. His followers will have to learn that there are closer bonds than those of blood relationship. This is not to suggest that Jesus thought little of his relatives; indeed the fact that he compared the relationship between himself and those who do God's will to the connection between himself and his mother and brothers and sisters, implies that his blood relatives held a high place in his mind. But calling him away from his teaching ministry gives the impression that there is more urgent business, or people with superior claims, to be attended to. Jesus is anxious to correct this possible interpretation of his relatives' action.

What light does this incident throw on the thought that Mary now has great intercessory power? It is natural to assume that Mary and the brothers saw Jesus when he finished speaking, but the fact is that the gospels do not tell us this. If Jesus did grant the requested interview the silence about it is remarkable when compared with encouragement to seek her intercession. Instead of hearing of an influential motherly relationship, we are told that the favourable relationship is determined not by ties of blood but by readiness to do the Father's will: a believer is a mother of Jesus.

III. *Blessed rather are those who hear and keep*
In the context where Mark has the relatives seeking to speak to Jesus, Luke[11] has a woman calling out, 'Blessed is the womb that bore you and the breasts that you sucked!' to which Jesus replied, 'Blessed rather are those who hear the word of God and keep it!'

By her words this woman intended to praise Christ for she had probably never even met his mother. Her words may have been a common expression but Christ felt he had to respond in the same way that he did when told that his mother and brothers were looking for him. In both cases Jesus points away from his mere person and human relationships to his work and mission. Through this woman Jesus says to us: 'Blessed are those who rightly hear, so concentrate on what was spoken, not on the mother of him who spoke.' In speaking like this Jesus is not rejecting his mother but showing that being mother would have been of no avail 'had she not been very good and faithful'.[12]

In her *Magnificat* the Blessed Virgin said that all generations would call her blessed and the praise of this woman is the first direct fulfilment of Mary's prophecy. The reply of Jesus saying that there is an even greater blessing, contains a thought similar to one seen in words spoken of John the Baptist: 'Among those born of women there has arisen no one greater than John the Baptist: yet he who is least in the kingdom of heaven is greater than he.'[13] Because of John's connection with Jesus he was the greatest of the prophets and yet, according to Jesus, that close, external and official connection paled into insignificance when compared with the connection open to all through faith. There was only one prophet immediately before Jesus and only one woman could be his mother, but a superior blessedness is open to all who fulfil the spiritual qualifications.

IV. *At the Cross*
When Jesus saw his mother and the apostle John standing near his cross he said to his mother, 'Woman, behold, your son!' and to John,

'Behold, your mother!' And from that hour the disciple took her to his own home.

Mary, who was about fifty years of age, might have had a hope that Jesus could be saved from dying, but his last words to her would indicate that she was to lose him. A chief element in the suffering of death can be concern for those left behind. Jesus was not worried about the strong youthful John: his concern was for his mother about to be bereaved. He asked John to look after her, at least until the crisis was over,[14], for it is our Lord's brothers who are with her on the day of Pentecost. It is sometimes said that Jesus by his words made Mary mother of the Church (represented by John). But Jesus was not asking Mary to look after John; he was asking John to take care of her – to mother her. It was John who led her away from the cross, not vice versa.[15]

When Jesus spoke to John he said 'mother' but when speaking directly to his mother he said 'woman'. Various reasons are put forward as to why he said 'woman' such as: it would have hurt Mary more to say 'mother'; it would have marked her out as related to him and so exposed her to ill treatment to say 'mother'; to say 'mother' would have caused a flood of emotions within himself. But the view of Westcott is worthy of consideration: Jesus said 'woman' because the special earthly relationships were now at an end.[16]

The possibility of Mary having a motherly influence in heaven needs to be considered when examining Christ's final words. There is nothing in his words about the relationship between mother and son being continued or reknit in the heavenly realms. When speaking to the disciples who were about to be bereaved Jesus said, 'I go to prepare a place. . . and I will come again and will take you to myself, that where I am you may be also.'[17] Why are the parting words to his mother so very different if in the next life she is to be with him in a place of influence? If she were to continue being his mother in the next life and to be bodily assumed into that position, would it not have been a comfort to say so just as he spoke about the future to the disciples? The last words of Jesus to his mother directed her attention, as regards family relationships, away from himself and by carrying out our Lord's wishes in taking her away, John was underlining this and perhaps his action made Mary consider that when the crucifixion had done its worst Jesus would be her son no more. Death ends all earthly relationships and this is hardly less true in the case of one with extra eternal relationships such as Son of God and husband of the Church.

We have looked at every recorded incident during our Lord's ministry where Jesus speaks to or about his mother and we did not see Mary having a special influence which would lead us to think that she should occupy an influential place in heaven. But we did see that whenever emphasis was laid upon the natural family relationship that Jesus did not encourage this but took the opportunity to emphasise the spiritual relationship open to all his true followers.

Are family rights and obligations eternal?

The clearest teaching about relationships in heaven was given when Sadducees asked what husband a woman would have in the next life if she had had seven in this life.[18] Jesus replied saying that in the resurrection there is no marriage and no death, for those who take part in that age are like angels. 'They are God's children, since they are children of the resurrection.' So, according to Jesus, the risen dead, as regards the rights and obligations of relationship, are like angels who are separate creations of God with no partners or parents or children. Earthly relationships are necessary because of death, but the children of the resurrection are God's children. The first human relationship spoken of in the bible and the strongest and closest, from which all others spring, is that of husband and wife. If, as Jesus makes clear, there is no husband and wife in heaven, there is, as regards continuing relationships, no mother and son either.

That Augustine was of this opinion is seen when commenting on the instruction to hate relatives. 'Whoever wishes here and now to aim after the life of that kingdom, should hate not the persons themselves, but those temporal relationships by which this life of our is upheld; because he who does not hate them, does not yet love that life where there is no condition of being born and dying, which unites parties in earthly wedlock. . . this is to be understood both of father and of mother and the other ties of blood, that we hate in them what has fallen to the lot of the human race by being born and dying, but that we love what can be carried along with us to those realms where no one says, my father; but all say to God, our Father and no one says, my mother, but all say to that other Jerusalem, our mother.'[19]

Has Mary a motherly influence in heaven? In the absence of scriptural teaching making that relationship an exception to what we have just considered, the answer would appear to be in the negative.

The words of a former archbishop of Armagh[20] can be regarded as expressing the conclusion of this paper. 'We owe her reverence and gratitude. But that is in return for what she was, not for what she is – for what she once did, not for what she does. . . The obvious teaching of the bible is that the office of mother to the Lord carried with it no permanent prerogatives. It is not without reason that scripture is silent about her later life and its close. We are led to see that once her special work is done, nothing more of importance hinges upon her personality. . . We affirm that, putting aside the honour and gratitude due to the blessed Virgin, there is no authoritative teaching anywhere to show that she stands today in any relation towards God in heaven and man on earth different from that in which any other departed saint stands.'

Notes

1. For statements about Mary's influence in heaven see: Second Vatican Council, Dogmatic Constitution on the Church *Luman Gentium* sec 62; Apostolic Exhortation of Pope Paul VI *Marialis Cultus* nn. 6 and 57. Pope John Paul II has said that Mary is *omnipotentia supplex* (the omnipotence of intercession) which, says Archbishop Kevin McNamara, (The teaching of Pope John Paul II *Mary, the Mother of God* CTS Do 540 [London 1982], p.11) emphasises 'the unfailing efficacy with her divine Son of her Mother's prayers.'
2. Mary is united to her Son 'by a close and indissoluble tie, she is endowed with the high office and dignity of being the Mother of the Son of God. . .' *Lumen Gentium* n. 53.
3. Chrysostom sees more than a mere request to do something about the wine shortage and his words give us an insight into his views about our Lord's mother. 'She desired both to do them a favour, and through her Son to render herself more conspicuous; perhaps too she had some human feeling like his brethren, when they said, "Show yourself to the world", desiring to gain credit from his miracles. Therefore he answered somewhat vehemently.' Alfred Plummer, in *The Humanity of Christ*, says that Christ's reply 'implies that she has taken too much upon her; that she has interfered without sufficient reason and without right.' (p. 135).
4. The note in the Jerusalem Bible says that woman is an unusual address from son to mother. 'There is no precedent in Hebrew or, to the best of our knowledge, in Greek for a son to address his mother thus', *Mary in the New Testament* A collaborative assessment by Protestant and Roman Catholic scholars edited by Raymond E. Brown, Karl P. Donfried, Joseph A. Fitzmyer, and John Reumann (London 1978), 188. John McHugh *The Mother of Jesus in the New Testament* (London 1975): 'When a Jew addressed his mother he said *imma* ('mother'). Jesus was therefore drawing attention away from Mary's blood-relationship with him by addressing her as "Woman".'
5. 'What have you to do with me?' shows that 'what Mary is asking, or the aspect under which she is speaking to Jesus does not belong to Jesus' understanding of the work his Father has given him to do.' *Mary in the New Testament*, 191. 'Jesus dissociates himself from his mother, who does not realise that the work which the Father has given him takes precedence over the claims and interests of his natural family.' *Ibid*, 287.
6. This point is made by Alfred Plummer in *The Humanity of Christ*, 139.
7. Mark 3:31-35; Matthew 12:46-50; Luke 8:19-21.
8. Commenting on the verb 'to seek' in Mark, R. P. Martin *Mark: Evangelist and Theologian* (Exeter 1972) points out that it is always used with either a hostile reference or in the bad sense of distracting from his mission. Calvin

says that the words 'Who is my mother?' were unquestionably intended to reprove Mary's eagerness, and she certainly acted improperly in attempting to interrupt the progress of his discourse.' Chrysostom says that Jesus did not insult Mary by asking 'Who is my mother?' for he wanted her, as others, to have a proper opinion of himself and that he spoke to her through others in order to be more convincing. 'She expected that she should always be honoured by him as a son, and not that he should come as her master.'

9. Matthew 11:2-12, 50. Luke places the incident after our Lord's first parables and is not interested in the relatives themselves but merely uses the story to press home the teaching about hearing the word of God and doing it.

10. Matthew 13:57; Mark 6:4.

11. Luke 11:27,28.

12. Chrysostom on John 2:4.

13. Matthew 11:11; Luke 7:28, cf Luke 10:19 where a place in heaven is worth more than authority over demons.

14. The fourth gospel does not say (cf John Wenham, *Easter Enigma* [Exeter 1964], 138) that John looked after Mary for the rest of her life. Our Lord's chief aim may simply have been to have his mother taken away from the cross to spare her and himself.

15. There is no evidence that Mary had any influence in the early Church which could have given rise to belief in a spiritual motherhood in relation to the Church. The impression given by the only subsequent reference to her (Acts 1:14) is that of a modest praying believer. If Mary had been given such a position it would be hard to explain how Luke does not even mention her presence at the cross if he knew she were there (Luke 23:49).

16. *Speaker's Commentary* (London 1880).

17. John 14:3.

18. Matthew 22; Mark 12; Luke 20.

19. *On our Lord's sermon on the mount*, book 1, chapter 15.

20. J. A. F. Gregg *The Primitive Faith and Roman Catholic Developments* (Dublin 1928).

Our Lady of Sorrows –
a devotion within a tradition

Rev. William M. McLoughlin, OSM
Roman Catholic

This offering is a reflection on the Mater Dolorosa or Most Sorrowful Mother, under which title the devotion has found expression in more than one form both in the life of the Catholic Church and specifically in the life of the Order of Servants of Mary (Servites). There has been an interplay between the Church and this religious order in regard to this devotion and while there have been, from time to time, variations in expression of and interest in the devotion, it seems to have proved enduring and receives attention even in these times.

The sorrows of Mary, standing under the cross of Christ, has had a prominent, not to say dominating place in the spirituality of the Servite Order. In the post Vatican II reform of religious life, Servite historians clearly felt the need to express that spirituality as free of a restricting traditional devotionalism by the phrases that, while referring directly to the order's traditional veneration of Mary under the title of 'Mother of Sorrows', reflect more the christological and ecclesial orientation of the teaching of Vatican II. Mary is described in relation to the entire mission of her Son and the reference is not limited to the one moment of the passion.

While by no means all would have a direct interest in or great awareness of the history of the devotion to the blessed Virgin under the title under discussion, almost everyone will have some acquaintance with the themes of the devotion expressed so often in art, music and literature. The mystery of the sorrowing Virgin Mother's share in the passion and death of her Son as described in the gospels accounts are not private experiences. In fact, there is no episode relating to Mary in the gospels which cannot be read in terms of the mystery of the passion of Mary's Son. Since the Virgin Mary 'everything is relative to Christ and dependent on him' (Paul IV, *Marialis Cultus,* n. 25). The sufferings of Christ define the Marian sorrows and give them their significance and salvific value in the life of the Church and individual Christians.

Devotion to the blessed Virgin under the title of the sorrows has found expression, as I said, over the centuries both within the life of the Church and very particularly in the Servite Order which sees itself as '. . . a community of men reunited in the name of the Lord

Jesus. Moved by the Spirit, we engage ourselves, like the first Fathers, in giving witness to the Gospel in fraternal communion and in being at the service of God and man, taking constant inspiration from Mary, Mother and Servant of the Lord' (OSM Constitutions, art 1). The text goes on to say '. . . In this bond of service, let the figure of Mary at the foot of the Cross be our guiding image. . .' (art 290).

Almost to state the obvious, the devotion to the Sorrowful Mother had a gradual development. Popular traditions of devotion to Mary's sorrows, from the very beginnings, have always seen her as 'the Mother dressed in black'. Full documentation for a description of popular devotion to Our Lady of Sorrows is not available. Even before this veneration found its way into the Divine Office in the fourteenth century and the Mass-Liturgy in the early fifteenth century, it was already popular among the people. The eminent marian biblio-grapher, Fr Besutti notes the existence of an oratory at Herford, Paderborn, bearing the dedication of our Lady at the foot of the cross as early as 1011. The influence of the Cistercians in the twelfth century and of the Franciscans in the thirteenth century has been very import-ant in regard to popularising this devotion. These began and com-pleted a remarkable transformation of European consciousness, reflected in writings and the arts: the sheer *humanity* of Jesus and the sufferings of the humanity came more and more to the fore. Naturally, this implied a similar renaissance of awareness of the human dimen-sion of Mary's sorrows. It gave rise to popular forms of verse and song, verging on drama, such as the *Laudi*, the *Passioni* and the *Lamenti*, and our Lady as 'sorrowful', features in the English mysteries of these times. St Anselm of Canterbury (d. 1109), St Bernard of Clairvaux (d. 1153), St Bonaventure (d. 1274) and Jacopone da Todi (d. 1306) of *Stabat Mater* fame, were among its most prominent supporters. The devotion also inspired numerous *Planctus Mariae*, which was a very popular literary form from the thirteenth to the fifteenth centuries, first in Latin and then in the vernacular and though they differ among themselves, the various *planctus* (lamentations) pre-sent the Sorrowful Mother as the 'highest model of Christian suffer-ing'.

The middle ages saw a parallel development of devotion to the joys of Mary and to the sorrows of Mary. Before the settled convention of seven sorrows was arrived at, we know that there are occasional references to five sorrows to complement five joys, but also of nine joys, fifteen sorrows or twenty-seven sorrows. Over and above histori-cal considerations, the choice of the number seven was related to its symbolic value. In the biblical symbolism so widely accepted during the middle ages, seven was seen as suggesting fullness, completeness and abundance. Medieval writers, therefore, did not, in listing seven sorrows, intend a limit of the sufferings of the mother of Christ to seven particular episodes but rather wanted to assert that she was truly 'full of sorrows' as was often written in the devotional literature of the time. As the symbolic value of the number seven became less obvious, it came to be seen as a limit and authors often had to specify that these were only the 'principal sorrows'.

The sorrow of the Virgin found its first and ultimate meaning in the mystery of the cross of Christ, but it was also extended back from Calvary to embrace the other events of the life of the Son in which the mother took part personally according to explicit mention or where tradition has deemed it likely that she did.

From the first half of the fourteenth century, when the number of the sorrows was already firmly established, there were two ways of beginning the series of sorrows:

— in those devotions in which the seven sorrows of the blessed Virgin were strictly tied to the events of Christ's passion, the first sorrow was the arrest of Jesus in the Garden of Olives.

— in other devotions in which the sorrows of Mary were extended to include episodes of the Lord's infancy, the first sorrow was the prophecy of Simeon.

— very rarely is found a list of seven sorrows beginning with the circumcision of Jesus (as in that issued at the General Dieta OSM at Reggio Aemelia of May 1660) and as yet no pontifical document has been produced which prescribes beginning the series of sorrows with that suffered by Mary at the circumcision of her Son.

The pastoral advantage of uniformity of method in the devotion had by 1678 influenced the OSM writers to stand by a list proposed by Fra Arcangelo Ballottini in 1612. This Servite friar was primarily responsible for the emphasis on devotion to the sorrowing mother in Servite spirituality. He advocated 'meditation on the blessed Mother at the foot of the cross *with* her dead Son, our Saviour, Jesus Christ *in her arms*'. To facilitate this reflection, Ballottini himself composed 'meditations on the sacred mysteries of the passion of Jesus Christ and the compassion of his most sorrowful mother divided into seven points, for the seven days of the week, so that varying the meditation each day the soul will experience greater devotion and the body greater consolation.'

The teasing out of the themes of the sorrows, therefore, resulted in the fixed set of sorrows set in the responsories of matins in the feast granted to the Servite Order in 1668, which then became the popular form of the devotion. It seems helpful to set them forth here with the texts which either explicitly referred to the event of the sorrow or from which tradition has inferred it:

1. The visit to the temple by Joseph and Mary to present Jesus

there forty days after his birth, and the prophecy uttered by Simeon: 'He is set for the fall and rise of many in Israel, and for a sign that is spoken against (and a sword will pierce through your own soul also), that thoughts out of many hearts may be revealed' (Lk 2:34ff). This sword is understood as the progressive revelation that God makes of the destiny of his Son and brings suffering – a symbol of the sorrowful journey of our Lady, which, in later tradition, will be used as the material symbol of the sorrows suffered by the mother of the redeemer and often be shown as seven blades fixed in the heart of representations of Mary, especially in baroque art.

2. Our Lady's journey of faith was soon marked by a fresh sorrowful event: the flight into Egypt with Jesus and Joseph: 'An angel of the Lord appeared to Joseph in a dream and said to him; "Arise and take the babe and his mother and escape into Egypt, for Herod is seeking the child in order to kill him!" Joseph arose and, taking the child and his mother with him, fled by night to Egypt' (Mt 2:13ff).

3. Again during the infancy of Jesus, we have the loss in Jerusalem and the troubled, sorrowful search of Mary and Joseph which ends in finding Jesus in the temple – a new motif for meditation and interpretation of God's will in the heart of the mother: ' . . . and when the feast (Passover) was ended, as they were returning, the boy Jesus stayed behind in Jerusalem. His parents did not know it, but supposing him to be in the company they went a day's journey, and they sought him among their kinsfolk and acquaintances; and when they did not find him, they returned to Jerusalem seeking him' (Lk 2:43-45). Three days in the very same city, at the time of the very same feast, when he will return to his Father.

4. Traditional meditation has seen in Jesus' journey to Calvary with the cross upon his back the experience which synthesises his mother's way of faith. Even though the gospel accounts do not mention it, traditional piety sees the blessed Virgin among the women who meet Christ: 'And as they led him away. . . there followed a great multitude of the people, and of women who bewailed and lamented him' (Lk 23:26f).

5. The crucifixion itself gives the primary and ultimate meaning of the sorrowful mother: 'But standing by the cross of Jesus were his mother and his mother's sister, Mary the wife of Clopas and Mary Magdalene. When Jesus saw his mother and the disciple whom he loved standing near, he said to his mother: "Woman, behold your son." Then he said to the disciple, "Behold your mother!"' (Jn 19: 25-27a).

6. Again, the devotion of the faithful has wished to prolong Mary's loving share in the redemptive death of her Son by recalling Jesus gathered to his mother's breast on his descent from the cross

(Mt 27:57-59 [inferred from] Mk 15:42) – an event which has attracted the special attention of painters and sculptors.

7. Once more an inferred sorrow, from Jn 19:40-42a, has the blessed Virgin place the body of Jesus in the tomb, awaiting the resurrection, for in solid tradition she is the faithful disciple and mother who believed in the words of her Son Jesus (cf Lk 9:22 and Lk 11:27).

Present day doctrinal and liturgical position

Over the centuries the blessed Virgin's sorrowful mysteries were divided up, as it were, and venerated singly, but in today's theological scene and in the piety of the faithful, the ancient and the contemporary distinction between aspects of the sorrow of Mary of Nazareth is not perceived as a sharp distinction between water-tight compartments. Rather, even in specifying distinct episodes, the sorrows are all referred back harmoniously to the mystery of a faith-journey which knew suffering in utter communion with the Man of Sorrows and in total openness to the will of God the Father. Vatican II's *Lumen Gentium* (n. 58) tells us 'The blessed Virgin, too, moved on in her pilgrimage of faith and preserved her union with her Son faithfully right up to the cross where, in God's plan, she stood (Jn 19:25) suffering deeply with her Son and uniting herself in a motherly spirit in his sacrifice, consenting in love to the immolation of the victim born of her.' It is this profound communion – which in some sense becomes conscious – between Mother and Son, a communion that is not linked merely with parenthood but with personal faith, that leads Mary to play her part in the whole work of Jesus, right up to Calvary. René Laurentin says: 'Mary's co-operation in what happened on Calvary is, in fact, the prolongation of her active, irreversible, unconditional consent, first given at the annunciation and persisting, culminating on Calvary.' Vatican II also make explicit the dimension of communion which extended throughout Mary's life and penetrated the very quality of her being – she was before all others uniquely the companion of the Redeemer: 'She conceived, brought forth, and nourished Christ, she presented him to the Father in the Temple, shared her Son's sufferings as he died on the Cross. Thus in a wholly singular way she co-operated by her obedience, faith , hope and burning charity in the work of the Saviour in restoring supernatural life to souls. For this reason she is a mother to us in the order of grace' (*Lumen Gentium*, n. 62).

The sorrows discerned in the lives of Jesus Christ and of his blessed mother are the consummation of the sorrow which has weighed down humanity since the original mysterious 'break' between God and mankind (cf Gen 3:1-17) expressed in repeated acts of infidelity to the covenant. Christ is the suffering servant who bore our infirmities and endured our sufferings, (cf Is 53:4; Mt 8:17); because of his incarnation and role as head of all mankind, he participates in the suffering of every person, past, present and future. Mary is the woman of sorrow according to the tradition of the Church: liturgical offices and popular devotions place on her lips the words of the daughter of Sion: 'Come, all you who pass by the way, look and see, if there is any suffering like my suffering?' (Lam 1:12). That same tradition sees in her the fulfillment of certain prophetic images announcing a woman's salvific mission accomplished through suffering and struggle. Mary has been seen as the new Eve who together with Christ, the new Adam, struggles against the ancient serpent (Gen 3:15); as the new Mother Sion who in suffering gives birth to all nations (cf Ps 87:4-7) drawn together by the love of Christ raised upon the cross (cf Jn 12:32; 11:52; 19:25, 27); as the faithful daughter of Sion and the personification of God's beloved Israel, so often oppressed, divided, and overcome by fear and anxiety (cf Lam 1:5) but which places her hope in the Lord (*Lumen Gentium*, n. 55).

In the liturgy of the Roman rite, the feast first corresponding to the sorrowful mother did not originate with the Servite Order but with a local church. It was decreed by a provincial Synod of Cologne on 22 April 1423 to expiate crimes of the iconoclast Hussites against images of the Crucified and Mary at the foot of the cross. The feast was called the 'Commemoration of the agony and sorrows of the blessed Virgin Mary' and the decree states exactly which moment in saving history is being celebrated ' . . . in honour of the anguish and sorrow which she suffered when Jesus, his hands outstretched upon the cross, immolated for our salvation, entrusted his blessed mother to his beloved disciple'. The decree interestingly refers to liturgical texts that may be used whose existence appears to go back to *before* the Synod – perhaps they were from the Missal Proper of the Servite Order which had made a foundation at Cologne in the thirteenth century. What merits an emphasis is that the feast was focussed on the scene of Calvary and on the commendation of his mother to John by Jesus, and the feast was to be kept in the Easter season. In 1482, Pope Sixtus IV composed a Mass which he included in the Roman missal. It was centred on the saving-event of Mary at the foot of the cross and was called 'Our Lady of the Pietà'. This feast then spread through the West under various titles and was kept on various dates. Apart from the title given by the Decree of the Council of Cologne and that used for Pope Sixtus' Mass, it bore the following names: 'The Transfixion of the Martyrdom of the Heart of the Blessed Mary', 'The Co-Passion of the B.V.M.', 'The Spasm and Sorrows of Mary', 'The Mourning of Blessed Mary', 'The Lamentation of Mary', 'The Seven Sorrows of Blessed Mary the Virgin' and so forth. The date of celebration varied. From being called 'The Commendation' it moves to being 'The Seven Sorrows' (i.e. from the scene at the foot of the cross to the different sorrows of Mary's life), from a date at Easter, it goes back to Lent. Naturally all these changes took place slowly, even if we cannot track them. On 9 June 1668 the Servites were granted the Mass of the Seven Sorrows of the Blessed Virgin on the third Sunday of September using a text, which suggests it was like the one of 1482. Since then, many changes have come about in the feast being extended for celebration by the whole Church (1814) and in the style of the feast being reduced to a memoria for the whole Church in 1969. Interestingly, in the new calendar OSM of 1971, the title of the feast reads simply 'Our Lady of Sorrows'. The liturgy requires a separate study but expresses the Johannine themes of exaltation and the hour of Jesus.

Pious marian exercises will greatly depend on their quality and their ability to accept valid forms from the past and, even more, to respond to the new needs which continuously emerge in the life of the Church. They must not merely flourish on the fringes of the sacred liturgy, but must accord with the liturgy, in some way be derived from it, and lead the people to it, since in fact the liturgy, by its very nature, is far superior to any of them. Within the Servite Order three popular devotions honour the sorrowful mother: the Servite or Dolour Rosary, which is used by many without knowing of its association with this particular religious order; the *Via Matris Dolorosae*, similar in form to the Stations of the Cross; and the *Desolata*, being a meditation on the climax of Mary's sorrow as she buried her dead Son on Good Friday. All three devotions had suffered a certain post-council desuetude, but in recent times are gaining new esteem.

Conclusion

The continually developing re-emphasis within the liturgy over the course of the twentieth century – helped along by biblical and patristic thinking – has coincided with a growing quality in meditation on the mystery of the Blessed Virgin's sorrow, so that it has been situated within the more ample context of Saving-History. One no longer contemplates and venerates the *Mater Dolorosa* merely in order to share, consciously and as an individual person in the passion of Christ, so as to live his resurrection. Now, also, one looks to Mary, as the Icon of the Church, to inspire believers to be a presence at the foot of the infinite human crosses to bring support and a co-operation that is redemptive.

The sorrows, therefore, is not merely an added extra devotion, properly understood. In the venerable tradition of the Servite Order, the black habit of Mary's widowhood was given on Good Friday

1239 by the Mother of God to the founders of that order, and this particular Good Friday coincided with the feast of the annunciation (which was to become the dedication of the first Church of the order.) It is worth noting that the blessed Virgin Mary's *fiat* was to conceive the redeemer and not one who was only later to become the redeemer. It is possible to see then that Mary's unique co-operation in what happened at Calvary goes to the heart of the annunciation as a prolongation of her active consent then and at every stage of her life. Far from being an accretion or entrapping kind of traditional devotionalism, when appropriately expressed in harmony with the liturgy etc, the devotion to the sorrows has a worthy and proper place in the tradition within which it emerged.

(The paper has had the benefit of articles and material recently published in Italian and English by various Servite writers, and I acknowledge my indebtedness.)

The place of Mary in the writings of St Francis and St Clare

Rev John Harding, OFM
Roman Catholic

The best English edition of the Writings of St Francis and St Clare is published in the series *The Classics of Western Spirituality* as *Francis and Clare: The Complete Works*, translation and introduction by Regis J. Armstrong, OFM Cap, and Ignatius Brady, OFM, London, SPCK, 1982. All quotations from the *Writings* are from this edition and cited as *AB* with page number. Quotations from Thomas of Celano and St Bonaventure are from Marion A. Habig, ed, *St Francis of Assisi: Writings and Early Biographies. English Omnibus of Sources for the Life of St Francis*, Chicago, Franciscan Herald Press, 1973, cited as *Omnibus* with page number.

Introductory Remarks

In the history of marian doctrine and devotion we would not expect to hear very much of either St Francis or St Clare of Assisi. One of the reasons for this has been the lack of a reliable edition of their writings. This lack has been met.

Clearly it would be too much to number St Francis or St Clare among the most prominent contributors to the Church's growing understanding of the place and role of Mary in salvation history. There are however a number of insights present in their works which show them to have been firmly within the central tradition and to have made a distinctive contribution.

To understand the teachings of St Francis and St Clare on the Virgin Mary we must recognise the intended way by which they sought to parallel in their lives the living relationship between Christ and his mother. This informs the perspectives from which Francis and Clare wrote.

It should be noted that neither wrote any formal treatise on the Mother of God. Their writings are in the form of prayers, letters, rules (or better, spiritual documents) and admonitions, and these fill only a small volume.

Both saints derive their insights into the role of the Virgin Mary not from the schools but from their constant contact with the liturgy, from their prayer and above all from their contemplation of God in the scriptures and in creation.

In this paper I aim to allow the words of Francis and Clare to speak freely and shall offer just a few comments.

1. *Mary and the Trinity*

One of the most exquisite of St Francis's prayers is his *Salutation of the Blessed Virgin Mary*. The opening lines make clear the relationship of Mary to the blessed Trinity:

> Hail, O Lady, holy queen,
> Mary, holy Mother of God:
> you are the virgin made Church
> and the one chosen by the most holy Father
> in heaven
> whom he consecrated
> with his most holy beloved Son
> and with the Holy Spirit the Paraclete,
> in whom there was and is all the fullness
> of grace and every good. . . (*AB* 149).

and in his *Office of the Passion* he writes:

> Holy Virgin Mary, among women,
> there is none like you born into the world:
> you are the daughter and the servant of the most high and supreme King
> and Father of Heaven,
> you are the Mother of our most holy Lord Jesus Christ,
> you are the spouse of the Holy Spirit. . . (*AB* 82).

In these two excerpts we see how St Francis understands the Virgin Mary as the one open to God and receptive of the grace of election. In Mary we see a humanity truly graced and restored to communion with the creator and Father. As Mary is truly the daughter and servant of the Most High so she is receptive of the Word and is sanctified by the Holy Spirit from the beginning of her existence. St Francis never confuses the reality of Mary as creature with the reality of God as creator, redeemer and life-giving Spirit. He instinctively senses that Mary is unique and is the first of the redeemed. He constantly draws us to appreciate the fact of Mary's election by the Father, her consecration by the Spirit and her mission to be the mother of the Word made flesh.

Leaving aside for the moment the phrase from the *Salutation* referring to Mary as 'virgin made church' (see below), we can here note especially the other original appellation: 'spouse of the Holy Spirit'. While this is familiar enough today, few realise that it originates with St Francis of Assisi. Here also he seems instinctively to have grasped that Mary is the pure vessel, totally receptive to the entry of the divine life and especially of the Word made flesh and this by the power of the Holy Spirit.

Being the 'spouse of the Holy Spirit' Mary prefigures the mystical union of the lover with the beloved. Standing for the Church, she symbolises the receptivity of the Church to the divine life, the mystical marriage of the Church to Christ the bridegroom, and the possibility of God and creature being united in a community of life and love. This is nothing less than an extension of the life of the Trinity.

St Francis seems intuitively to have grasped the most apt way of describing the relationship of Mary to the blessed Trinity. Mary is open to the Father as daughter and servant, made holy by her espousal to the Spirit and receives the gift of the Word to whom she give birth in the flesh. Thus she shares in the life of the Trinity as a creature. In Mary we see realised the promise of our own sharing in the trinitarian life of God.

2. *Mary and the Christ*

While being attentive to the relationship of Mary to the blessed Trinity, St Francis and St Clare are both keenly aware of the special relationship of Mary to Jesus Christ. In his *Rule of 1221*, St Francis writes:

> All-powerful, most holy, most high and supreme God
> holy and just Father
> Lord, king of heaven and earth
> we thank you for yourself
> for through your holy will
> and through your holy Son
> with the Holy Spirit
> you have created all things spiritual and corporal
> and, having made us in your own image and likeness,
> you placed us in paradise.
> And through our own fault we have fallen.
> And we thank you
> for as through your Son you created us
> so also, through your holy love, with which you loved us
> you brought about his birth as true God and true man
> by the glorious, ever-virgin, most blessed holy Mary
> and you willed to redeem us captives
> through his cross and blood and death. . .(*AB* 130).

St Francis' love and honour for Mary stems precisely from the fact of her being the Mother of Christ. One of his early biographers, Thomas of Celano writes:

> Towards the Mother of Jesus he was filled with an inexpressible love, because it was she who made the Lord of majesty our brother. He sang special praises to her, and poured out prayers to her, offered her his affections, so many and so great that the tongue of man cannot recount them. . . (*Celano* 198, *Omnibus* 521).

and this is confirmed by St Bonaventure when he says:

> He embraced the Mother of our Lord Jesus Christ with indes

cribable love because, as he said, it was she who made the Lord of majesty our brother, and through her we found mercy. After Christ he put all his trust in her and took her as his patroness for himself and for his friars. In her honour he fasted every year from the feast of Saints Peter and Paul until the assumption. . . (St Bonaventure, *Major Life* IX, 3, *Omnibus* 699).

St Francis was full of gratitude to Mary because she uttered an uninhibited Yes to the wish of the Father that she conceive and bring forth Jesus Christ. By her assent she had made it possible for the Word to enter the world and take upon himself our frail humanity. That a creature could utter so complete a fiat was to St Francis a source of unending joy and gratitude. It showed that it is possible for every creature in imitation of the Virgin to utter their own Yes to God and so also become mothers of Christ.

St Clare, too, saw that the motherhood of Mary was to be imitated by every faithful soul. When she writes to Blessed Agnes of Prague to give encouragement she tells her:

Therefore, as the glorious Virgin of virgins carried [Christ] materially in her body, you, too, by following in his footsteps. . . especially [those] of poverty and humility, can, without any doubt, always carry him spiritually in your chaste and virginal body. . .' (*Third Letter, AB* 201).

Rarely, if ever, does St Francis speak of Christ without also being moved to speak of his Mother. He sees clearly the intimate communion between the Mother and her Son and the unity between the disciple and the master. Thus, in his efforts to honour Christ he would never fail to give due honour to his Mother. The reason, already given, 'she made the Lord of majesty our brother'. He loved especially the feast of the nativity because it showed most profoundly the loving union between Mother and Son:

The birthday of the child Jesus, Francis observed with inexpressible eagerness over all other feasts, saying that it was the feast of feasts, on which God, having become a tiny infant, clung to human breasts. . . (*2 Celano* 199, *Omnibus* 521).

In honouring Mary as Mother of Christ Francis employs the richest imagery he can find:

Hail, His Palace!
Hail, His Tabernacle!
Hail, His Home!
Hail, His Robe!
Hail, His Servant!
Hail, His Mother! (*Salutation, AB* 150).

There is nothing contrived nor misplaced, for we have here the outpourings of a heart and soul filled with wonder and gratitude. To honour Mary is to give honour to God who chose her, sanctified her with his Spirit and enabled her to carry the Word who is Christ:

> Through his angel, Saint Gabriel, the most high Father in heaven announced this Word of the Father – so worthy, so holy and glorious – in the womb of the holy and glorious Virgin Mary, from which he received the flesh of humanity and our frailty. . . . (*Letter to the Faithful*, 2nd Version, *AB* 67).

The doctrine of the divine motherhood is the central marian doctrine in the writings of both Francis and Clare. Coupled with this is the doctrine of Mary as the perfect disciple. Mary exemplifies the poor of Yahweh who are empty before God and open to receive the gift of himself. In their own lives both St Francis and St Clare lived anew this receptivity in their poverty and followed the example of the Virgin Mary. They saw it as their task to bring forth Christ spiritually as Mary had done materially.

3. Mary and the Church

'You are the virgin made church. . .' (*Salutation, AB* 149).

From these few words we can see how perceptive St Francis really was into the place and role of Mary. Here, in so few words he grasps the connection between the image of Mary and the image of the Church. He understands Mary within an ecclesial perspective. As Mary is the Mother of Christ so also is she the mother of his mystical body, the Church. As in her poverty she conceived and brought forth the Word, Jesus Christ, so she becomes the model for all those who, in their poverty, receive God's Word and bring him to birth in their own day.

For both Francis and Clare the Christian life is patterned or mirrored in the life of the Virgin Mary who bears Christ within her. Every Christian is called to imitate her as the first disciple of Christ her Son:

> We are spouses when the faithful soul is joined to Jesus Christ by the Holy Spirit. . . [We are] mothers when we carry him in our heart and body through love and a pure and sincere conscience; we give birth to him through [his] holy manner of working, which should shine before others as an example. (*Letter to the Faithful*, 2nd Version, *AB* 70).

As the first and perfect disciple, Mary followed her Son by choosing the poor and lowly state. This is the condition of the openness to the will of the Father and of dependence on the providential gift of the Spirit. St Francis and St Clare likewise make this conscious choice to be poor and lowly. In his *Last Will for St Clare and her Sisters*, St Francis exhorts them:

> I, brother Francis, the little one, wish to follow the life and poverty of our most high Lord Jesus Christ and of his most holy Mother

and to persevere in this until the end. . . (*AB* 46).

St Clare extols the life of poverty because it affords the opportunity to share in the life of Jesus Christ who emptied himself, and of Mary who imitated his self-emptying:

> If so great and good a Lord, then, on coming into the Virgin's womb, chose to appear despised, needy and poor in this world, so that people who were in utter poverty and want and in absolute need of heavenly nourishment might become rich. . . in him by possessing the kingdom of heaven, then rejoice and be glad. . . Be filled with a remarkable happiness and spiritual joy! Contempt of the world has pleased you more than [its] honours, poverty more than earthly riches, and you have sought to store up greater treasures in heaven rather than on earth. . . And you have truly merited to be called a sister, a spouse, and mother. . . of the Son of the Most High and of the glorious Virgin. . . .' (*First Letter to Bl Agnes of Prague, AB* 192).

The love for this kenotic poverty flowed naturally into the love for the poor:

> . . . in all the poor he [Francis] saw the Son of the poor Lady, and he bore naked in his heart him whom she bore naked in her hands. (*2 Celano* 83, *Omnibus* 432).

St. Francis' deep sensitivity to the constant love of God for the poor led him to appreciate the image of the church as mirrored in the blessed Virgin. His love for the poor Lady was, so to speak, made especially visible in his most preferred place on earth, the little church of St Mary of the Angels (Portiuncula – Little Portion). This small chapel was precious to him because it embodied something of the gospel poverty as lived by Jesus and his Mother. This little chapel symbolised the universal Church betrothed to Jesus Christ as the spotless bride. It was poor and humble as Christ and his Mother were poor and humble. In this little chapel both he and St Clare had begun their new lives: he like Jesus would be moving back and forth from the busy world to the high places of solitude. She, like Mary, would withdraw into silence to support him by her prayers and self-denial. Between them they gave an immense testimony to the relationship between the Lord and his Mother, between Jesus Christ and his bride, the Church.

St Clare chose to imitate the Virgin Mary and by this to become a worthy spouse of Christ. She encouraged her sisters to do likewise and encourages the Church along the same path. In her *Letter to Ermentrude of Bruges*, Clare assures her that to imitate the Virgin Mary is to stand with her at the foot of the cross (cf *AB* 207).

St Francis and St Clare understood that to be worthy of Christ it is necessary to put aside all other interests and to follow him wherever he may lead. They saw in Mary the pattern of how this might be accomplished and thus sought to imitate her poverty and humility as she imitated the poverty and humility of Christ her Son. For Francis this meant placing all his confidence in Mary as queen of heaven. For Clare it meant imitating the womanly virtues of Mary as Mother in the hidden life of San Damiano. If St Francis was a true follower of Christ, then St Clare was a true imitator of Mary. The success of their joint life shows how necessary it is that both the masculine and the feminine combine to make the Church what it is: the Body of Christ.

Concluding Remarks

In this paper it has been possible only to indicate some of the principal thrusts in the marian doctrine of St Francis and St Clare. Theirs is a thoroughly trinitarian, christological and ecclesial understanding of the place and role of Mary in the economy of salvation. Much that can be learnt has to be distilled from their prayers, letters, rules and admonitions for neither has left us a formal treatise on the Virgin Mary. There is, we believe, much of contemporary worth that can be garnered from these two saints. St Francis and St Clare together form a significant if only small link in the long story of the Church's reflection on the Virgin Mary.

Mary in Recent Ecumenical Documents

Fr Kevin McDonald, BA, STL
*Roman Catholic, Staff member,
Secretariat for Promoting Christian Unity, Rome*

I wish to give a general idea of how the figure of Mary tends to figure in ecumenical documents. I will be referring to a selection of reports and agreed statements published over the last fifteen years. These documents are different in kind and in scope but they adequately serve the limited purpose of this talk.

I

As a first general heading I wish to take the word *authority*. Mary frequently occurs in the context of agreements and disagreements about the proper exercise of authority in the Church. In the final report of the Anglican-Roman Catholic International Commission (ARCIC – I) the Catholic dogmas of the immaculate conception and the assumption are referred to in the section of Authority II that deals with infallibility. They are invoked to illustrate Anglican concern about the exercise of an infallible teaching authority. The document says: 'If the definition proposed for assent were not manifestly a legitimate interpretation of biblical faith and in line with orthodox tradition, Anglicans would think it a duty to reserve the reception of the definition for study and discussion.'

We find reference to these dogmas also in the agreed statement on christology which came from the Old Catholic-Orthodox conversations of 1975 and 1977, in which there is confirmation of the teaching of the Council of Ephesus that Mary is the Mother of God – *Theotokos*. But the statement also says, 'The Church does not recognise the recent dogmas of an immaculate conception and bodily assumption of the Mother of God.'

The question of the Church's authority to teach these dogmas is put in sharp focus in the final report of the dialogue between the Secretariat for Promoting Christian Unity and some Classical Pentecostals (1977-82). This report states that as far as the Pentecostals are concerned the Church can never go beyond the clear meaning of the New Testament in its teaching. The Pentecostals see no scriptural grounds for these dogmas and so are unable to accept them.

The question of the Church's authority in relation to scripture also comes up in the report of the Evangelical-Roman Catholic Dialogue on Mission (1977-1984) (ERCDOM). Agreement is reported on the principle that scriptural texts can have a 'spiritual' meaning as well as a literal one, a *sensus plenior*. But differences are reported between Catholics and Evangelicals on the extent to which the literal meaning can be separated from the spiritual. The following quotation from this report effectively pinpoints the question that still requires further ecumenical study in view of the differences I have outlined: 'Roman Catholics say that scripture must be read in the light of the living, developing tradition of the Church, and that the Church has the authority to indicate what the true meaning of scripture is.'

II

My second general heading is *content of dogma* and I will indicate now some of the reported agreements and disagreements on marian doctrine. ARCIC reports agreement on much that the doctrines of immaculate conception and assumption are designed to affirm: Mary is inseparably linked with the doctrine of Christ and the Church; she is *Theotokos*; she was prepared by divine grace to be the mother of our redeemer, by whom she was herself redeemed and received into glory; she is a model of obedience, holiness and faith for all Christians.

The Old-Catholic/Orthodox report, while rejecting the two most recently defined Roman Catholic dogmas on Mary, affirms that the Church 'solemnly celebrates the entry of the Mother of God into eternal life and solemnly observes the festival of her dormition'. Moreover the Church ascribes to her 'a relative sinlessness by grace from the time the Holy Spirit descended upon her, for our saviour Jesus Christ alone is sinless by nature and absolutely'.

In quite different vein, the Catholic-Pentecostal report expresses considerable reservation about the content of several Catholic dogmas on Mary. On the immaculate conception it is reported that Pentecostals see no value for salvation in this doctrine. It is noted that further work on this matter would require a wider discussion by participants of pneumatology, christology and ecclesiology. This particularly because Roman Catholics see a distortion taking place when marian doctrines are considered in isolation from these matters. The report also refers to the doctrine that Mary is *Theotokos*, Mother of God. It is a point of agreement that it was at the moment of the incarnation that Mary became Mother of God; she is not, however, Mother of God in his eternal triune existence, but Mother of the Son in his incarnation. There is also agreement that Mary was a virgin at the conception of Jesus but this statement is followed by the report that

'Pentecostals commonly maintain that scripture records she had other offspring and lived as the wife of Joseph in the full sense'.

In assessing the extent of ecumenical agreement on the content of marian dogmas a fairly clear distinction emerges from the Roman Catholic point of view. On the one hand there are those whose only difficulty with Catholic teaching on Mary is that in the dogmas of immaculate conception and assumption the Catholic church is seen to have given fuller and more precise definition than is either really justified or necessary. On the other hand there are those who would want to limit Christian teaching on Mary to the precise terms of the biblical accounts.

III

As a third and final heading I wish to take *Mary in the order of redemption*, since a particularly sensitive issue seems to be that of Mary's place in God's plan for our salvation, and especially her role as intercessor on our behalf.

The Old-Catholic/Orthodox statement affirms that the Church recognises Mary as intercessor for human beings before God. 'But it distinguishes between the intercession of the Mother of God and the quite unique mediatorship of Jesus Christ.' It adds that 'Although the Mother of God is also called *mediatrix (mesitria)* in the hymns of the Church, this is never anywhere in the sense of co-mediatrix or co-redemptrix, but only in the sense of intercessor.'

The concern that Catholic understanding of the intercessory role of Mary can detract from the unique mediatorial role of Christ is also found in the American Catholic-Lutheran statement *Justification by Faith* (1985). It is said of the Lutherans that 'they wonder whether official teaching on Mary and the cult of the saints, despite protestations to the contrary, do not detract from the principle that Christ alone is to be trusted for salvation because all God's saving gifts come through him alone.'

Likewise the Catholic-Pentecostal report states that the greatest area of practical difficulty lies in the area of Mary's relationship to the Church and her role in the communion of saints. But is is interesting to note that apparently both sides were quite surprised when they actually heard each other's views on this matter.

The Catholic-Evangelical report includes some questions raised by evangelicals about certain formulatons in Pope Paul VI's *Marialis Cultus*. The idea of her 'association ' or 'co-operation in redemption' was clearly a concern for the Evangelicals.

In conclusion: I hope that I have said enough to provide at least a glimpse of the kinds of ways in which Mary is liable to figure in ecumenical discussions. I have no time to draw conclusions and so I will simply make one comment. When Mary does surface in ecumenical dialogue she appears often to be a focus of contention or difficulty. But what is normally happening is that thoughts and attitudes about Mary uncover and pinpoint deep difference about ecclesiology and soteriology. There is good reason to believe that the way to overcome differences about Mary is to work for shared faith in the areas of ecclesiology and soteriology. This could eventually dispel differences about Mary and make her much less a focus of division.

Visions of the Virgin

Mrs Joan Ashton
Anglican

A general rather than a particular interest in visions of the blessed Virgin Mary may have been aroused last year, at least in this country and in France, when the events in Yugoslavia were reported at some length by the *Sunday Times* and *Paris Match* magazines. It seems possible that the current interest in visions and healings may be a means of drawing attention to the Virgin and her message, and I therefore suggest that these visions concern us all and are addressed to us all, as a means of casting light on the mystery and revelation of the incarnation: that Mary's visible presence is a challenging and continuous reminder to all sorts and conditions of men, women and children that God became man by the consent and with the co-operation of an ordinary woman, and that in being for many centuries permitted by God to reveal herself supernatually as part of the natural order, she corroborates the original revelation and shows us its immediacy for successive generations.

Just as the Gospel is itself outside time and still happening, so Mary is perpetually bringing God to us. The apparitions may therefore be said to be more about Christ than his mother: and just as Christ is with us always, so is her fiat.

What I have to say will however be marian rather than mariological; that is to say, devotional rather than theological.

My purpose in this brief statement is to show that there is a thread of continuity bringing together the accounts of these visions, from early legends to the present daily appearances in Yugoslavia. The one constant is Mary's main message, sometimes unspoken; to turn to God, to believe and to pray.

It seems likely that Mary spoke to the visionaries in words with which they were familiar, just as she always appeared comely and in a form which they could recognise: but there are certain other common factors, such as the ordinariness of the chosen visionaries, whatever their age and walk of life; the universality of the appearances and their historical context; the healing consequent on conversion and worship; the maternal concern, always implicit and sometimes explicit; and of course the phenomenon of brillant light, uncreated or at the very least inexplicable light. There is also the undeniable shock of certainty experienced by pilgrims on arrival at the places where visions have ocurred: the numinous presence of which I have myself been aware in Walsingham, Mexico, Ephesus, Lourdes, Fatima, Paris, Knock and Medjugorje besides the Holy Land.

'Who are you, Lord?' asked Saul of Tarsus, blinded by the light of Christ. He was told. So too, when the same shock allowed them to speak, were the children who asked the same question of a lady. The reply was no less clearly understood by them than by St Paul.

Dr David Doyle, in a communication of the sixth ESBVM International Congress in Dublin, notes that 210 such apparitions were reported between 1928 and 1970;[1] and Marina Warner tells us that besides the several authenticated visions of the nineteenth and twentieth centuries, there were 200 not officially approved by the Catholic Church.[2]

I shall touch on a mere twelve events, selected as having occurred in every continent;[3] experienced by Eastern Orthodox, Coptic, Roman Catholic and Anglican Christians; and to children and adults of both sexes.

Two saints of the Eastern Orthodox Church, both Russian, recorded visits from Mary; Sergius of Radonezh in the fourteenth century and Seraphim of Sarov in the eighteenth. Both visits were witnessed by others. Sergius described the light surrounding her as 'greater than the shining sun' and Seraphim that his cell 'was lit up as though with the blaze of a thousand candles'. There have been supernatural healings at a shrine on the Greek island of Tinos, where an icon of the Virgin and Child was found under a ruined church in 1832. I believe a vision was associated with this discovery, but I lack further information in English of this or any other appearance in Greece or Turkey.

The Virgin appeared in what is now called Guadalupe in Mexico in the winter of 1531, ten years after the Spanish conquest. An American Indian, who had been christened Juan Diego, was walking over the hill of Tepeyac in darkness to attend early Mass, when a cloud of brilliant light disclosed a girl, with a complexion like his own, standing amidst rocks and grass which shone like gems. On the derelict site of a temple that had been dedicated by the Aztecs to their mother-goddess, in tender words of his own language, this girl told Juan Diego that she was the Virgin Mary, Mother of the true God, and asked him to request the bishop to build a church there. But the bishop wanted more than a peasant's word for it, and he asked for proof of the vision. Returning for the third time, Juan dropped from his folded cloak the roses which Mary had told him to pick that morning on the mountain-top, where nothing flowered in winter; and he was agreeably surprised when the bishop and his attendants sank slowly to their knees. They were overawed not by the roses, but by something of which Juan was quite unaware; a coloured representation on the inside of his cloak, depicting Mary exactly as he had twice descibed her. There are two further surprises. The cloak hung for 116 years above the high altar of the church, where it neither deteriorated nor became discoloured, in spite of damp air and candle smoke; and in 1921, when considerable damage was caused by the explosion of a bomb concealed among altar flowers, the glass frame protecting the cloak remained intact.

The symbolism of Revelation 12:1, 'a woman adorned with the sun, standing on the moon', may have awed the Christians, but for the Aztecs who wrote by pictograph the vision was equally significant. Mary was standing in light greater than their sun-god; the moon beneath her feet meant defeat of the feathered serpent, their greatest god; the blue of her mantle was their royal colour; and her head was bowed over a brooch in the shape of a cross, emblem of the victorious Spaniards. Mary's appearance in Mexico encouraged the Indians to come forward in their thousands for Christian baptism.

I have told this story at some length since it seems to illustrate the common factors I spoke of earlier; for example the historical relevance of the message of conversion, in maternal words, to a typical layman, in a hitherto pagan continent: the vision heralded by light and followed by healings.

Mary announced herself to Juan Diego: but in 1830 a sleeping nun named Catherine Labouré was woken by a child angel, who told her that the Virgin awaited her in the chapel. A very improbable tale, one tends to think; yet it has the ring of truth when considered with a sequel, that of the silent appearance of Mary twelve years later in Rome to an unbelieving Jew, who was instantly converted to Christianity. This is the story of the Miraculous Medal and Alphonse Ratisbonne, about which Father René Laurentin has written so convincingly, as he has of the events at Lourdes and Medjugorje.

René Laurentin has also contributed an encouraging preface to a more recent book about the visions at Kibeho in the Republic of Rwanda, Central Africa.

In Yugoslavia, where Mary is still appearing, two boys and four girls claim to have seen and spoken to her daily since 24 June 1981.

In Rwanda the first of six girls and one boy first saw her on 28 November 1981, the visions continuing until 1984. These girls were all Christians, but a pagan and illiterate Rwandan boy was converted by a vision of Christ himself.

Then there are records of three places where Mary has appeared as a tableau or living picture. First, the familiar story of Knock, in Ireland where, on a wet August evening in 1979 fifteen people saw the exterior wall of the east end of the church bathed in golden light. In front of this wall stood three white figures recognisable as Mary, with on her right St Joseph and on her left St John the Evangelist. To the left of these three was a plain cross above a plain table on which stood a lamb, and round the table flew what looked like angels. Again there were two further surprises. Despite the rain driving towards it, the outer church wall and the ground below it were perfectly dry: and a farmer on a hill a mile away thought the church was on fire, decided there were enough people in the village to put it out, and so went to bed. Secondly, a British soldier on sentry duty in Northern Ireland on a cold dark night in 1969, who was cursing the Pope and Catholicism while pacing the grounds of a Catholic school in Belfast, was suddenly aware of a sense of warmth and peace; and turning to look at the dark shape of a church he saw above it a white light which gradualy assumed the form of the Virgin. He was converted immediately whereas his mate, who also saw the vision, nearly died of fright. A third tableau was seen almost nightly in Cairo between April 1968 and May 1971 when Mary appeared in the sky above the Coptic Orthodox church of St Mary, believed to be on the route of the flight into Egypt. The visions were watched by a vast crowd of Christians, Jews, Moslems and others estimated as 250,000 a night, and there were many conversions and healings. Formations of what looked like white doves, believed to be the souls of the dead, flew round Mary who knelt or stood by the cross on the dome of the church.

A final example concerns a married Anglican priest who emigrated to Australia in 1963. The influence of his Catholic mother as well as his Protestant father seem relevant to the story. He had worked in Australia for fifteen years when in 1978 at the age of fifty-four he had a stroke. Lying in hospital he was conscious of the Catholic nursing sisters praying for his recovery; but he was ready to die, aware of 'the great cloud of witnesses' and of God as suffusing light awaiting him, when he heard Christ's voice, as an interior locution perhaps, calling him to return. He later recognised this as the tunnel or near-death experience about which Dr Kubler-Ross and others have written; accounts which he *afterwards* read. Following four months' convalescence he returned to work but he then had a second stroke and found himself on the top floor of the same hospital, where the nurses gave him a rosary, to which he had been accustomed since childhood. The greatest event of his life occurred as he gazed idly out of the window from his hospital bed. Pondering on his future he was amazed to see the Virgin regarding him from the top of a fir tree level with his window, her arms outstretched. His response was joyful recogition rather than awe, the vision remaining until he had understood her message. Again as an interior voice, Mary told him that his recovery would be complete, but she asked two gifts: that he would help to bring about unity, tolerance and love between Christians and that he would find how to honour her.

Through an unlikely chain of events he later founded what is now the International Anglican Marian Movement, with the blessing and encouragement of the Roman Catholic Marian Movement of Priests. This was in turn founded by Father Stefano Gobbi as the result of an inspiration at Fatima in 1972, followed by interior locutions in July 1973.

Perhaps it is not unfair to conclude with a quotation from the Anglican Marian Movement's journal of Advent 1984: 'But something which worries us is that our Roman Catholic brothers still feel that Mary is their province, and that by some strange and exciting coincidence which they find hard to work out, she has strayed into Anglican minds and experience.'

Notes

1. David N. Doyle, 'Marian apparitions', in ESBVM publication: 'Mariology in modern practice'; reprinted in *One in Christ*, 1985-1, 78-83.
2. Mariana Warner, *Alone of all her Sex* (Quartet Books 1978).
3. Mariologists at the 41st seminar on Marian studies, Saragossa (September 1986) estimate that the blessed Virgin has appeared 21,000 times during the past ten centuries. Of 210 visions reported during 1928-71, ten per cent have been judged false, while the remainder are still under investigation. *Tablet* 27 September 1986, 2024.

The meaning of contemporary apparitions of our Lady

Rev. Robert Faricy, SJ, STD
Roman Catholic, Professor of Spiritual Theology,
Pontifical Gregorian University, Rome

In the contemporary explosion of alleged apparitions of our Lady, some apparitions clearly appear false, others have serious ambiguities, and a few present themelves as worthy of belief. Three series of apparitions, all going on at the present time, seem to me authentic and of great importance: those at Medjugorje, in a Croatian part of Hercegovina, Yugoslavia;[1] those at Kibeho in southern Ruanda;[2] and the apparitions at Oliveto Citra in south western Italy.[3] This paper briefly reports and reflects on these apparitions.

At Medjugorje, in Yugoslavia, our Lady has appeared to and spoken with a small group of young boys and girls every day since 24 June 1981. The apparitions take place at about six o'clock every evening, sometimes for ten or twenty minutes but more often for only a few minutes. The young people see Mary as a young woman of that area, and hear her speak Croation in the local manner and with their own regional accent. She gives them advice, answers their questions, and prays with them. She gives them messages for the parish and for the world.

Our Lady has initiated and continued to guide three prayer groups in the parish. She speaks to the groups and leads them either by appearing to some of the same young people who see her every evening, or through prophecy. For several years, Mary has personally formed a small group of people, teaching them how to pray and in general how to lead Christian lives. She has been forming her three prayer groups. And she teaches and forms the whole parish mainly through a weekly message given to one of the small group who meet her daily. The message comes on Thursday evening, and one of the priests reads it to the parish at the daily evening Mass.

What is our Lady's message to the local parish and to the world? First of all, conversion. Conversion to God the Father and to Jesus Christ, a new and lived-out continuous turning to the Lord through faith, prayer, and fasting. Mary urges faith in the traditional New Testament sense of the word, belief in God, trust and hope in his love and his providence, personal loving adherence to God in everyday life. She recommends personal prayer and family prayer, emphasizing Mass, the sacrament of penance, and the rosary. And she asks for fasting. Most people in the parish fast on bread and water on Wednesdays and Fridays. Our Lady speaks often of the suffering coming to the world because of its sins, and she asks our prayers for peace.

In May 1986, the Vatican Congregation for the Doctrine of the Faith, headed by Cardinal Joseph Ratzinger, took the matter of Medjugorje out of the hands of the local bishop. The commission appointed by the bishop was dissolved without ever having completed its investigation or preparing a report for the bishop. The Vatican gave no reason for this completely unprecedented and startling action. The bishop, however, had spoken out, unofficially but forcefully, against the authenticity of the Medjugorje apparitions, and had threatened officially to pronounce them false and to close Medjugorje to pilgrims.

The Congregation for the Doctrine of the Faith has requested the Yugoslav Bishops' Conference to set up a national commission to continue the study of the apparitions, reporting back to the Congregation when judgment would be made (i.e. in Rome rather than Mostar).

The Kibeho, Ruanda, apparitions began on 28 November 1981, just a few months after the beginning of the events at Medjugorje. They have been given to six young women, at the beginning all students in a Catholic boarding school, and one young man. Six of these young people, now all about twenty years old or a little older, have stopped seeing our Lady. The seventh, Alphonsine, who saw her first in 1981, will have at least one more visit from the Blessed Virgin, perhaps the last one, on 28 November 1986.

Our Lady has appeared at Kibeho about once a week or less frequently, to only one person at a time, always at some length, for an hour or longer. The young person who sees Our Lady has spoken not only to Mary but also to the crowd present for the apparition, sometimes not only speaking prophetically the words Mary has spoken, but also acting them out by dancing and singing. The young persons who see her report that our Lady appears as an African from that region and speaks as they do.

Mary's aim has been clear from the beginning: to speak to and to help the boarding-school students, and through them the world. Her message is basically the same as at Medjugorje: continuous turning to God in conversión, faith, and prayer – especially personal prayer, the sacraments, and the rosary; and fasting and penance. Our Lady often speaks apocalyptically, encouraging us to accept and to carry the cross in our lives, referring to imminent calamities in the world, and saying that Jesus Christ is coming a second time.

The bishops of Ruanda have spoken out favourably regarding the Kibeho apparitions. The local bishop has appointed both a medical commission and a theological commission to study the apparitions so as to arrive at a judgement as to their authenticity.

The apparitions at Oliveto Citra, a small Italian town south of Naples, began more recently, just after midnight on 25 May 1985. Our Lady appeared to twelve boys, all about eleven or twelve years old, who were playing games near the gate to a ruined and abandoned castle. Since then, she has appeared frequently, even daily, to numerous people. I have spoken to nine local people, seven of whom see the blessed Virgin often, and I am convinced they are telling the truth. It seems unlikely, however, that everyone who goes to the castle gate in Oliveto Citra and who claims to have seen her has really seen her.

The seven people I interviewed, who seem to compose the main group to whom our Lady appears, have little in common, and see our Lady separately at different times, usually but not always at the castle gate. They include two middle-aged fathers of families: an automobile mechanic and a road construction worker; and a housewife, a waitress, a fourteen-year-old schoolgirl and two children: a girl of eleven and a boy of eight.

At Oliveto Citra, our Lady's message is for the town and for the world. It is a message encouraging us to be converted, to have faith, to pray and do penance. The Oliveto Citra events have the same apocalyptic quality as do the events at Medjugorje and at Kibeho. As she does in the other two places, Mary speaks of coming suffering for the world, and calls us to pray for peace.

The vicar for the diocese, who also acts as parish priest at Oliveto Citra, believes firmly that our Lady truly appears and speaks there. The Archbishop of Salerno, who has jurisdiction, seems quite open to whatever recommendations will come from the small commission he has appointed to investigate the matter.

What do these three series of apparitions have in common? (1) Positive spiritual fruits: greater fervour and conversion of heart on the part of those people in the three localities, and a remarkable effect on pilgrims. (2) Healings, conversions, unusual signs seen in the sky (such as the sun spinning), and an acceptance of the truth of the apparitions by the local Catholics as well as by the priests of the parishes involved. (3) Our Lady appears in all three places as a local person, completely 'inculturated', and as a caring mother. (4) In all three places, our Lady calls us to respond to her message of conversion, faith, prayer, penance and fasting in the light of coming catastrophes for the world, and she asks us to pray for peace.

What is the meaning of these apparitions for us? First, God calls us through our Lady to continuous conversion and to greater faith. Mary calls us to pray and to fast and do penance. And she brings us a message of the need for peace and of prayer for peace. Secondly, that call takes on serious urgency in the light of coming calamities and sufferings due to sin in the world. The apocalyptic style and content of much of the material of the three series of apparitions impresses us with the power of God as the Lord of history and with the urgency of Mary's message.

Finally, our Lady presents herself and conducts herself as caring mother. She carefully nurtures and guides the persons to whom she appears. And she nurtures and guides the communities; the parish in Medjugorje, the school student body in Kibeho, the town of Oliveto Citra. Moreover she acts as mother to the world, concerned and caring about where she sees it going.

Mary acts the mother in the order of grace for each of us and for all of us. Her mediation of graces for each one and for all creates for us the possibility on our part of turning to her as our mother in heaven.

After thought

Why do I, however tentatively, hold these series of marian apparitions to be genuine? Granted that Christians remain free to believe while remaining open to the conclusions of official ecclesiastical investigations, what are my reasons for believing them? Because all three seem to be genuine when examined according to the criteria set forth by the Holy See's Congregation for the Doctrine of the Faith, in a reserved document sent to all bishops in whose dioceses apparitions are reported to take place: *Norms of the Sacred Congregation for the Doctrine of the Faith about How to Proceed in Judging Alleged Apparitions and Revelations* (1986).

Notes

1. A large body of literature in several languages exists on the Medjugorje apparitions. See especially R. Laurentin, *Is the Blessed Virgin Mary Appearing at Medjugorje?* (Washington, DC 1984); L. Rooney and R. Faricy, *Our Lady of Peace* (Dublin and New York 1984); *ibid, Medjugorje Unfolds* (London 1985), published in USA as *Medjugorje Up Close* (Chicago 1986). [Cf also Michael O'Carroll, *Medjugorje* (Dublin 1986). Ed.]
2. See Gabriel Maindron, *Les apparitions à Kibeho* (Paris 1984).
3. See R. Faricy, *Maria in mezzo a noi: le apparizioni a Oliveto Citra* (Padua 1986).

Mary in the theology of Hans Urs von Balthasar

Rev. Charles Smith

Formerly an Anglican priest, now a Roman Catholic priest in Oxford

> At the point where all roads meet which lead from the Old Testa-
> ment to the New we encounter the marian experience of God, at
> once so rich and so secret, that it almost escapes description. But
> it is also so important that time and again it shines through as the
> background for what is manifest. In Mary, Zion passes over into
> the Church; in her, the Word passes over into flesh; in her, the
> head passes over into the body. She is the place of superabundant
> fruitfulness (*GL* 338).

I read you that passage from *The Glory of the Lord* to justify this
communication, for such papers should surely be concerned with
original theological contributions. It is somewhat presumptuous,
therefore to burden you with a paper, however brief, on one contemporary theologian, however eminent. That Hans Urs von Balthasar
is difficult to understand is no excuse, for I have no reason to believe
I have understood him better than anyone else has, and his writings
are gradually becoming known as his great work is translated into
English.

No; the reason for making this contribution to our discussions
is that, as the opening quotation will have shown, in the theology of
Balthasar, Mary has a central and integral place. For him, the fundamental orientation of Mary is the fundamental orientation of the
whole Church. It is not an optional extra, nor merely a peculiarity
which appeals to particular people. It is the same as the Church's
spirituality prior to all differentiations into more specific spiritualities
(J. Heft, 'Marian themes', quoting from *Concilium* 9 (1965), 20). To
be Christian, in fact, is to be also marian. He complains that not only
had popular devotion before the Council gone astray, but in the past,
theologians have been too concerned with the privileges of Mary
rather than with her essential place in the divine scheme of salvation
and revelation

In this, as in much else, Balthasar acknowledges his debt to the
great nineteenth-century theologian Matthias Joseph Scheeben, who
had directed him to the Greek Fathers. 'Our wonderment,' wrote
Scheeben, 'should be directed to the creature which has been transfigured by grace, above all to Christ and Mary' (*GL* 108). God is 'an

interior fruitfulness which pours itself out into the creation. . . Made ready by Christ's grace, moreover, creation reaches its epitome in Mary's bridal motherhood. This is the centre from which every aspect of the Church and of Christianity must be interpreted, down to the very nature of the world and of formal ontology' (*GL* 109). From Scheeben comes, too, the emphasis on the bridegroom/bride relationship which is essential to any understanding of the relation between God and Mary, God and the Church; the bridegroom seeks the bride and pours himself out in her; she responds fully and completely. This outpouring is the great example (but the word is too weak) of the outpouring of the divine life which characterises the divine Trinity. 'Grace and faith are thus but forms of the expression of God's central connubium with mankind (and, through it, with the whole world) in the incarnation, which has among its conditions the mystery of Mary's maternal womb' (*GL* 114). So, Mary is the key not only to a right understanding of the Church, but also to a right understanding of the relationship between God and his creation. Balthasar is concerned entirely with the revelation of God the holy Trinity, and for a right understanding of that central mystery, a right understanding of Mary is essential: that is 'the marian question'.

It is not a mere matter of certain beliefs and devotions peculiar to some Christians which must be explained, examined and justified. It is *the* great question at the heart of the approach to God. In the work which, probably, first brought his name to English readers, published under the title *Prayer* in 1961, and translated from the German of 1957, Balthasar writes as follows of contemplation:

> The object of contemplation is God and God is trinitarian life, but for us he is 'life in the incarnation of the Son from which we may never withdraw our gaze in contemplating God. . . the archetype of such contemplation of the Trinity is Mary, who was directly addressed by God. . . in a trinitarian form. It is significant that the three words of the angel of which the first manifests the Father, the second the Son, the third the Holy Spirit, provoke three corresponding reactions on the part of Mary, none of which is mere speculation about God, but each the outcome of her reflection on the right way of answering the message and the responsibility entailed (*Prayer* 154f.).

But such contemplation need not be *explicitly* trinitarian: 'From then on, [Mary] in nurturing her Son and following him, keeping all his words in her heart and reflecting on them, penetrates more and more deeply into the understanding of the Trinity' (*GL* 155):

> That is precisely what the Church as a whole is, and Mary is thus her archetype. . . She is the woman in whom the life of the Trinity

is fulfilled, the woman who, through her existence, compels the divine mystery. . . to shine forth and be manifest. The obedience of Christians is, too, and in contemplation especially, the medium in which God reveals himself as three in one (*GL* 156).

Balthasar has written no single treatise on Mary, nor, on his own principles, is he likely to do so. There is the small work, *The Threefold Garland* (published by the Ignatius Press, San Francisco (1982) after the German *Der Dreifache Kranz* 1978). It is on the rosary, but, as the subtitle tells us, it is concerned with the scheme for the world's salvation in Mary's prayer, and in that scheme, Mary and Church are inseparable. He often writes of Mary/Church or of Mary the Church:

> the Church is what was created on the cross: the gathering of believers around those who have been established in hierarchical offices, with Mary in their midst. Without any doubt, it was to her, as the very core of the Church, that the Son first appeared. . . Crowding around Mary, the Church prays that the same thing might happen to her as happened in Mary her archetype. And Mary herself prays anew for this event; now she prays *as* the Church, as the central point in the community of saints (*Threefold Garland* 112).

Mary is *the* contemplative par excellence; and the contemplative nature of the Church seen in her is repeated over and over again. In her contemplation, Mary is above all a hearer of the word, not only at the annunciation, but at all times: 'Even after she had given him birth, she continues to carrry him within her; she only needs to look into her heart to find him' (*Prayer* 24).

As the essential element in the Church, this contemplation finds its fullest expression in a famous passage in *The Glory of the Lord* where von Balthasar speaks of the four essential elements in the Church; that is, the Petrine tradition (the hierarchical); the Pauline (the missionary and evangelistic); the Johannine (the visionary and apocalyptic), which is closely related to the marian or contemplative:

> The threefold archetypal experience of Christ which is conferred by the Apostles on the Church for its use, remains permanently sustained and undergirded by the marian experience of Christ. . . But the marian experience existed prior to the apostolic experience, and it thus wholly conditions it, for Mary as Mother of the head is also Mother of the body (*GL* 362).

Mariology is, as we have realised in recent years and are continually saying, part of ecclesiology; and it is the neglect of the marian element in it over the past centuries which has been the weak point in our understanding of the Church. The Petrine, i.e. the ecclesiastical, hierarchical element, has replaced it as being of supreme importance. Whereas the marian element shows what the Church essentially is, the Petrine element is a means to an end, important of course, indispensable, but not the final end. In an article entitled 'Who is the Church?' (published by Herder, New York (1967) from the English translation of *Verbum Caro*), Balthasar writes:

> What never falls away is the nuptial encounter between God and the creature for whose sake the framework of the structures is now set up and will later be dismantled. This encounter therefore must be the real core of the Church. The structures and the graces they impart are what raise up the created subjects to what they should be in God's design, a humanity formed as a bride to the Son, become the Church (*op. cit.* 128).

It is this encounter between God as person and man as person that constitutes the Church. It was realised in Mary, the spotless bride, the fulfilment of all the prophecies of the Old Testament, who therefore is the beginning and Mother of the Church. Since Vatican II, this title has been widely used, but it is given to Mary in much more than the metaphorical sense in which, one feels, it is sometimes uncomprehendingly applied to her. Balthasar makes it clear that it is much, much more than metaphor. The Church comes into existence in Mary as an existential reality. Her *fiat* is the human response, the response of the Church, to the word of God; but the Church came into being at her conception. She is the Idea (in the Platonic sense) of the Church, without spot or wrinkle. This is not merely an aspiration of the future: the Church already exists, without spot or wrinkle, in her. So, the immaculate conception – 'that necessary piece of the logic of revelation', as he calls it (*Man in History* 74) – was inevitable. It could be described as the instant in which the Church was created. Mary's identification with the Church involves, too, her standing beneath the cross, for there alone can she (and the Church) enter into the full self-giving of love. The cross is, as it were, the birth-pangs of the Church:

> The crucified utters a word whereby he entrusts Mary to the disciple as his mother, and the disciple to his mother as her son, and this word in a way, constitutes the Church's foundation document, flowing out of the midst of the suffering which gives birth to the Church as such. Mary, who is the Immaculate Ecclesia (Eph 5:27), the heavenly Church who is perfected in advance, is infused into the form of the earthly, organised Church, and to this latter there are entrusted the care and protection of the purity and sanctity of the original – the ideal – Church (*Threefold Garland* 103).

Perhaps that passage helps to clarify the relationship between the Church originating in Mary at her conception, at the annunciation, and the Church which sprang, as the Fathers taught, from the side of the saviour on the cross. And no writer could be closer to the Fathers, or more clearly recognise the origin of the Church on Calvary than Balthasar:

> [Mary] remains to the end of the world. . . *mater dolorosissima*, as is revealed not only by the vision in the Apocalypse, but also by reflection on her union (founded in the 'overshadowing' and never sensed) with the Holy Spirit which groans in suffering hearts. She stands, both as an individual person (Mary) and as a creaturely 'total person' (*ecclesia*) under the cross. She is 'under' the cross because she is together with all sinners, in anonymous solidarity with them, and thus she is not in the least in competition with the unique crucified one. But she is truly under 'the cross' (and not under sin) because only in the figure and the experience of the cross was sin transformed and continues to be transformed into pure love (*Man in History* 74).

Elsewhere Balthasar writes that we may speak of Mary as 'co-operating', provided we are clear that her role and co-operation are entirely passive: she receives, she does not give.

Mary's virginity is essential to her motherhood: it is her faith which makes it possible. She is totally given over to the divine lover in faith and trust, and this response is essential in the relationship between God and humanity. It is the woman's, the female, response. 'The bride is essentially woman, that is, receptive; . . . one who through acceptance of the seed. . . is made competent to bring forth and to bear fruit' (*Who is the Church?* 128). Balthasar's thoughts concerning Mary are his thoughts concerning the Church. God gives; humanity responds and receives, the essentially feminine contribution which is made by and in Mary, and which the Christian experiences through her: '. . . in Mary, believers possess experiences which they have not enjoyed personally, but which have been communicated to them by grace' (*GL* 341). This sharing in Mary's experiences by the individual Christian is not a purely spiritual one; it is not a matter of example to be followed on a different level. 'The experience of the *thou* both among men and between God and man grows out of the realm of the body and the senses into the sphere of the spirit; but in such a way that the original relationship of spirit (man-wife relationship in marriage, or, in virginity, the assent of the virgin to God) is the prerequisite for this growth' (*GL* 339f.).

It would be difficult to over-emphasise the importance of this giving and responding in Balthasar's theology. It is essential in his understanding of humanity – 'Man', 'humanity', is the giving and the response, and that reflects the giving of God in his creation, and the creation responds to him in Mary and in the Church. It lies, if I may say so in passing, at the root of his well-known opposition to women in the priesthood, for that would obscure and contradict the essentially female, marian, nature of the Church.

The physical aspect of Mary's motherhood is essential; because of it, fresh problems arise concerning the relationship between the experience of Mary, the experience of the Church, and the experience of each individual member of the Church. Balthasar goes on, in an important passage (*GL* 340) to make it quite clear that Mary is not only – not, if I may use the pejorative expression – a *mere* archetype. I must quote here at length:

> The Platonic relationship between the archetype (in the heaven of ideas) and a copy, clearly distinguished from it, becomes questionable. There is now a fluid transition from archetypal experiences to imitative experience. This is so, first of all, because Mary's faith, which is the basis for her experience of motherhood, remains the same as the faith of Abraham and the faith of all Christians. In the second place, this is so also because Mary, by bearing and giving birth to her Son, the head of the Church, encloses all Christians within herself and brings them forth from herself along with their experience of faith, and this is a relationship with them which is somehow physical. . . Mary's physico-personal experience of the child who is her God and her redeemer is unreservedly open to Christianity. Mary's whole experience as it develops from its earliest beginnings, is an experience for others, for all.

'Her physical motherhood,' Balthasar says in one place, 'is her personal motherhood, but as this becomes the spiritual motherhood of the whole Church, it becomes universal.' There is a 'mysterious continuity' (*GL* 421) between Mary's physical experiences in the body and the Church's maternal experience. He writes: 'The terrible havoc which the historical critical method is today wreaking in the world of faith is possible only in a spiritual sphere from which the Church's marian dimension has been banished, and which has, therefore, forsaken all spiritual senses and their ecclesial communication' (*loc. cit.*). Where this is preserved, there is a real entering into the experiences of the saints. Balthasar writes of a certain 'spoiling of the saints' among Catholics (*GL* 342). It is not a matter of exterior imitation, but a real entry into life. So that sharing in Mary's experiences is a sharing in her virgin motherhood; he seems to say that it opens a real experience of motherhood to those who are called to the virgin life. Time will not allow this theme to be developed; but you will find it in *The Glory of the Lord* (*GL* 341 *et al*).

Let it not be thought that Balthasar's mariology is entirely concerned with remote theological speculation, with the contemplative (in a restrictive sense) or the mystical life. Where the marian dimension is lacking, he says in a popular and an often-quoted passage from the essay on 'The Marian Principle', in *Elucidations*, 'Christianity threatens imperceptibly to become inhuman. The Church becomes functionalistic, soulless, a hectic enterprise without any point of rest, estranged from its true nature by the planner. And because, in this masculine world, all that we have is one ideology replacing another, everything becomes polemical, critical, bitter, humourless, and ultimately boring, and people in their masses run away from such a Church' (p. 72).

In the same essay Balthasar complains of the Church since the Council, and it is a complaint heard in many Christian communions: it has

> to a large extent put off its mystical characteristics, it has become a Church of permanent conversations, organisations, advisory commissions, congresses, synods, commissions, academies, parties, pressure groups, functions, structures and restructurings, sociological experiments, statistics, that is to say, more than ever a male Church, if perhaps one should not say a sexless entity. . .

Do we think the theologians do not know what is happening in the Church?

Bibliography

Writings of Hans Urs von Balthasar in English translation:
The Glory of the Lord: a theological Aesthetics I. Seeing the Form, T. & T. Clark, 1982 (*Herrlichkeit*: Eine Theologische Aesthetik – GL).
Man in History, Sheed & Ward 1968, 2 ed. 1982.
Prayer, SPCK 1961 (*Das Betrachtende Gebet*, 1957).
Elucidations, SPCK 1975 (*Klarstellungen zur Prufung der Geister*, 1971).
The Threefold Garland, Ignatius Press, San Francisco 1982 (*Der Dreifache Kranz*, 1978).
'Who is the Church?' from *Church and World*, Herder, New York 1967 (*Verbum Caro*).
James Heft: 'Marian Themes in the writings of Hans Urs von Balthasar' (in *Communio*, 1980).

The legends of the unicorn: an approach to the theology of creation

Sarah Jane Boss
Roman Catholic theologian at St Stephen's House, Oxford

To the mediaeval mind – and, I would contend, to the authentically Christian mind – everything within the natural world has religious significance. Everything points to that which is sacred; and a particularly widespread example of this way of thinking can be found in the legends of the unicorn, and the allegorical significance attached to them.

In this communication, I hope to examine the symbols contained in those legends, and hence to tease out the theological meaning inherent in them.

There are two images of the unicorn which predominate, and those are the two that I shall deal with here.

The first of these images is that of the unicorn and the virgin, and the story runs as follows:

The unicorn is a swift animal who runs alone in the forest, and huntsmen are never able to capture him. However, there is one ruse by which the unicorn may be caught: namely, to tempt him with a virgin. The woman must be led out into the woods and seated there; when the unicorn appears he cannot resist the attraction he experiences towards her. He therefore goes straight towards the virgin and, according to some versions, places his head upon her lap, or else – in other versions – rests his head upon her bosom or suckles at her breast. He then falls asleep, and the huntsmen are able to come and capture him.

The allegorical meaning of the legend is this: the unicorn is Christ; the single horn on his forehead stands for the unity of the Godhead ('The Father and I are all one'); the virgin is Mary, and the animal's seduction by her represents the incarnation.

The second story of the unicorn is the following:

The animals of the forest assemble beside the great water in order to drink, but find that a serpent has left its venom floating upon the surface of the water. They dare not drink for fear of being poisoned, but instead, they wait for the unicorn. When he arrives, he steps into the water, makes the sign of the cross over it with his horn and thereby renders the water harmless.

In the allegorical interpretation of the story, the unicorn is again said to stand for Christ, the horn for the holy rood, the serpent for the devil, and the poisoned water for the sinful world. The image of the unicorn at the lake thus signifies Christ's purification or renewal of the world by means of the cross.

It is also worth noting here that the abbey church of St Denis, near Paris, had a horn which was said to be that of a unicorn, and which was kept with one end resting in water in order to bestow the water with magical properties.

I now wish to argue that these two legends – that of the virgin and the unicorn and that of the unicorn at the lake – are, in a radical sense, telling the same story.

Water is everywhere a symbol of maternity: the waters of the womb are called to mind in many mythological images. The clearest Christian example of this can be seen in the blessing of the baptismal waters at the Easter vigil. In this rite, the font is explicitly stated to be the womb of the Church, from which the faithful will be reborn. The imagery of baptism itself is, of course, one of rebirth from water, and one can call to mind many similar images, such as the birth of the nation of Israel from the waters of the Red Sea, for example.

Looking now at the legend of the unicorn with the virgin, we see that the virgin also is a mother, since the unicorn suckles at her breasts. And in the story for which the legend is an allegory, that is, the annunciation, Mary is also a mother. Moreover, one can further enhance this association of images by noting that Mary herself is directly associated with water: she bears the title *Stella Maris*, she is widely invoked as the patroness of springs and wells (as at Lourdes or Walsingham), and she is typically dressed in blue.

Furthermore, in addition to the imagery of motherhood, we also find in both legends imagery suggestive of sexual activity.

When the unicorn's horn acts upon the waters of the lake and *regenerates* them, this again is reminiscent of the rite of the blessing of the font, when the paschal candle is dipped into the waters with the aim of infusing them with new life. Then, when we come again to the picture of the virgin and the unicorn, the sexual innuendo implied in the image of the unicorn placing his head in the lap of the virgin is so explicit that one can hardly fail to notice it (the Council of Trent certainly did not, since they banned the use of this motif in sacred art!).

So here again, the virgin and the lake respectively each hold the same relationship to the unicorn. And likewise at the annunciation Mary is truly the bride of the Holy Spirit.

To sum up, my contention is that the virgin who represents Mary in the one legend is, in a certain sense, identical with the water of the lake in the other legend.

Now, it is important to understand that these legends are stories about *creation* and *recreation*. Think again of the blessing of the font at the Easter vigil. The liturgy explicitly compares the waters of the font with the waters of chaos at the beginning of creation; and the action of the Holy Spirit over the waters in Genesis 1 is replicated in the action of the priest with the candle. But, in addition to the submersion of the candle, the priest also divides the waters cross-wise with his hand. Similarly, in Genesis 1, creation is brought about through the division of the waters. (This is a motif which occurs in many mythologies – perhaps by analogy with the breaking of the waters of the womb at birth?)

Now, the unicorn makes the sign of the cross over the waters of the lake in order to recreate *them*, and there is a marian image which is exactly parallel to this: Simeon's prophecy, 'A sword shall pierce through thine own soul also', is traditionally interpreted as referring to our Lady's suffering at the foot of the cross. So we have here a picture of Mary suffering an act of piercing or division at the very moment of the new creation – at the crucifixion.

All this implies that Mary stands in the same relationship to God's creative activity as do the waters of the lake in the unicorn legend or the primal waters in the Genesis creation narrative. What I am arguing is that implicit in these images is the idea that Mary is a figure for the waters of chaos, or *prime matter*, out of which God forms his creation. (*Matter*, incidentally, is etymologically related to *mater* and *mother*.) It is as if, in the first place, God makes his creation with this prime matter; and then, when he comes to redeem creation, he returns to that prime matter, personified in Mary, and of her flesh makes the new creation in Christ.

The view that I have outlined above probably begs as many questions as it answers! But I would just like to comment on one thing that follows from it.

Traditional Christian philosophy, especially as manifested in Augustine and Aquinas, has always understood spiritual beings to be those which are closest to God, and prime matter (pure matter), by contrast, to be that in the universe which is least godlike – the least like its creator. It is seen as being passive, inert, or even scarcely existing.

Mary, on the other hand, is active, responsive and very close to God. Therefore, on a traditional understanding, Mary and prime matter are very different beings. However, I want to insist upon their real identity, and, furthermore, to say that it is necessary for us to reformulate our understanding of the material world in the light of this association between Mary and matter. We must come to understand the physical universe as active, responsive, and infused with divinity. It is to be co-operated with rather than used, And this is not just an academic point, for if we do not come to this new understanding of the material world, then it will go on being abused, exploited, wasted – until Mother Earth (and Mother Water!) cannot give birth or support her children any longer.

Psychological aspects of Mary as model of the Church

Bronwen Astor
Roman Catholic

Psychotherapy, psychology, psychiatry are the latest tools for religion. But it is necessary for the churches when using them to remember that the Christian objective for every person is not to conform to this world but to the next. Christianity as it is preached so often seems to have little understanding of the kingdom beyond a set of moral rules and to have relegated the sermon on the mount as so much pie in the sky. However, the three chapters of St Matthew accurately describe the state of mind of higher consciousness, of enlightenment, a glimpse of which is sometimes the immediate cause of the patient ending up on the psychiatrist's couch. Breakdown or breakthrough? The person in trouble has come to a point of the conflict of contradiction and is unable any longer to hold opposites together. Often one set of opposites are repressed or suppressed in the unconscious but have surfaced and caused confusion in his or her life.

Beginning with the work of Freud but going well beyond his limited faith we can track to some extent the effect of parents on their children. The effect they have is paramount to the subsequent behaviour of the child and ensuing adult.

The mother's love, attitude and behaviour are more fundamental to the child's formation than that of the father. But the mother's behaviour will be conditioned by the father's maturity and love for her and the child. His influence becomes more direct, less indirect through the mother, after the first two years of the child's life.

The psychological influence of the mother on the child begins at its conception, continuing through every day of the nine months' pregnancy, and especially in the trauma of birth which for the foetus is a death experience, passing, as it has to, through a dark tunnel into the light. In decreasing measure she influences the first few years of the child's life.

The important point we have learnt from the study of the working of the unconscious is the difficulty of holding together in our conscious mind whatever we term 'good' and 'bad'. A mother appears to her child at one moment all good, sole provider, nourisher and comforter. The next minute she is the opposite. She is not there, or not providing, or even stuffing too much milk down our throats, or misunderstanding our cries to be picked up and comforted from our inner nightmares of isolation, rejection, non-survival.

Everything in our earliest perception is in bits and pieces and if a mother cannot bear to hold the emotion engendered by her child's rages, anger and inner turmoil she is going to damage in small or big ways her child's psyche. The tiny vulnerable ego, fighting to survive outside the womb wherein everything had been laid on, so to speak, begins to split and parts of the psyche retreat back into the womb, the unconscious, sometimes never to emerge. Parts of us just never get born again!

If we are afraid of the disapproval of our provider, our mother or mother substitute, we soon devise means of retaining their love by acceptable behaviour; by developing a false self that covers up the real self. We can see this sometimes in highly successful people in the world who have suddenly in middle-age found life meaningless. They have spent their whole life doing what they 'ought' to do to please their provider.

Unfortunately the parts of themselves they found were early on disapproved of, their rages, fears, anger, frustrations, have been repressed and projected on to other people. We all do this. What we dislike in other people are the very bits of ourselves which we have disowned, yet unconsciously recognise in them. If we can own these feelings in ourselves, our attitude to others becomes *com*-passionate, feeling with, alongside.

But the mother who loves her child unconditionally allows the ego to develop with the minimum of this splitting. A strong ego has the capacity to repair and to transform bad experiences such as getting hungry, feeling neglected, into good experiences. Contentment is precisely that: *content*-ment, the ability to contain opposites, bad and good, love and hate. Psychologically healthy parents then have adequately contained the range of emotions of their child and are able spontaneously and freely to communicate their own feelings with which they are themselves in touch. The child of such parents is enabled to hold everything together with a minimum of splitting and repression and has no fear of his deepest self being found and exposed.

One other point I want to mention is the importance of the gradual separation between mother and child. Assuming the child is wanted from the moment of conception – and many of us are not – and is the right gender – again many of us are not – separation begins with the birth experience, followed by the weaning experience until the child becomes a totally separate individual: separate yet relating. This again is very difficult to achieve successfully. The absences of the mother must keep pace with the baby's capacity to feel still with her when she is not there, and later on to be alone while in her presence. A non-possessive, non-intruding, truly loving mother allows her child the respect of individuality so that the child's ego develops in strength and capability. We cannot give up our ego, that is 'die to self', unless it has first reached its potential.

A glance then at the Gospels to see how this is borne out by Jesus's behaviour.

Taking the end first we see the total exposure of his real self. He was naked on the cross. By his own volition he laid down his life and symbolised on the cross the holding together of the opposites. The good thief on one side, the bad thief on the other; he let go of neither. The power of this exposure is a shock and one that many people cannot bear to contemplate. Because their real selves are so buried the crucifixion becomes an affront to their senses and sensibilities. They are not in sufficient touch with their own suffering, their own buried hurts and humiliations which at the time of their infancy they were not enabled to share. Manifestly not true of Jesus, we conclude he received none of the damage an ordinary mother unwittingly and inevitably inflicts on her child.

Jesus had tested himself in the wilderness. There he had come to terms with all parts of himself, owning his life, his self, his soul. He could only have reached such maturity through being honoured and respected by his parents when a small child. He himself has such respect. 'Anyone who welcomes a little child in my name welcomes me' (Mt 18:5). We extend to others the treatment we ourselves have received. We can only truly love to the extent that we feel ourselves to be loved and lovable. Mary's unconditional love resulted in her child having no fear of losing that love no matter what he did. He could relate to everyone in intimacy as his mother/brother/sister. Nor is he at a loss in the face of madness and the psychotic. He speaks to the Gadarene madman or to the epileptic with a familiarity and lack of fear that immediately has results. He *inhabits his own unconscious* where these demons and archetypes hold sway.

He is equally at home with the feminine. It is bewildering to try and define what we mean by the particularly feminine or the particularly masculine and I am not going to attempt it here. A revolutionary Rabbi, Jesus taught women. Mary of Bethany 'sat at his feet', a phrase meaning she was as a student. He nurtured and gave meaning to a woman's *spiritual* fertility, her potential, as in Martha, or the Samarian at the well. He leads them into the awakened state of higher consciousness which is tuned in to matter, mater, matrix, and through going into the depths the soul reaches the heights. Not only does he analyse and differentiate but he unites and transforms as a woman transforms a seed into the image of God. In activity he is passive and in passivity active. His nature a perfect combination of the yin and the yang.

Mary's fearless acceptance of her own conceiving in such an unusual manner that left her wide open to divorce, or even stoning to death, is crucial to the developing foetus. Martin Buber in 'I and Thou' says, 'The ante-natal life of the child is one of purely natural combination, bodily interaction and flowing from one to the other. . . (there is a mythical) saying of the Jews, "in the Mother's body man knows the universe, in birth he forgets it. . ." it remains indeed in man as a secret image of desire. . . the yearning for the cosmic connexion.'

Then comes the separation of birth.

'Between this Alpha and Omega, Eden and Jerusalem, there lies a wilderness in which complete separation must be made from the first as *sine qua non* of entry into the second. And this wilderness is life, conscious and active life – overhung by the shadow of death; in which the loneliness of the path of personal individuation is either shirked because the spiritual umbilical cord keeping a man tied to his earthly mother is never wholly cut, resulting in every kind of negative projection, or else his task is accepted to the best of his ability whereby the union with the internal anima or positive mother-image is gradually formed, leading in turn to the soul's brideship with God to whom the anima herself acts as a bridge, thus leaving the individual free to conduct life without negative projections due to undue and unrealistic dependance on human love.' That from John Layard, *The Incest Taboo and the Virgin Archetype*.

Our Lady through her love does not hang on to her Son but allows him to separate from her. When after three agonising days she and Joseph find him in the temple, no word of recrimination escapes her that would have turned him into a sinner; instead she imparts her own feelings and, as she had masculine-like quizzed the angel Gabriel, asks for an explanation. I wonder if his words to her are accurately translated. I seem to hear his first painful realisation of his utter aloneness, his separateness: 'Did you not know', or, 'Surely *you* know I must be about my Father's business?'

Childlike in his attitude to the Father he also remains childlike to Mary going back home after this episode to live under her and Joseph's authority, growing in his teenage years in wisdom and stature, separate but intimately relating.

And perhaps this is Mary's greatest attribute; her ability to teach us a childlike attitude. Uncontrolling, trusting, yet in tune and in touch with the spiritual power contained in the material, in the matter. 'They have no wine,' she points out. For those who relate to here, the wonderful opportunity exists of receiving the same upbringing as Jesus received.

And finally after his death it is not necessary for him to appear *first* to his mother. His separation is complete. He may or may not. But in order to give *her* her autonomy and freedom he must reverse the effect of original sin. 'Your yearning shall be for your husband yet he will lord it over you' (Gen 3:16).

So how can we sum up for the Church as the model of Mary in psychological terms.? Her power resides in her suffering, maturing, ever changing, endurance. Like the sea she contains all life. Suffering must never be sought as an ego trip, a spiritual materialism, which uses spiritual techniques to inflate, not develop, the ego, but suffering must be undergone as an opportunity for growth and change. Like the splitting of the atom, a transformation takes place and the seed which has been planted within the Church comes to full stature, nourished in the love which encompasses and does not threaten the real self.

My own parish church is kept permanently locked except for the brief daily Mass time. This is not the way Mary released her Son into the world. On the contrary she never kept him to herself, binding and crippling him into becoming a homosexual, a sadist, masochist, or misogynist (not even a neurotic like all of us!), but childlike and trusting she was vulnerable to the point of being stronger than death. The feminine in men is not a weakness but a strength of endurance and transformation. If we are to be Marys bringing the Word into the world, we have to be, men as well as women, unafraid to be in touch with our deepest emptinesses and feelings, our chaos, within which God, who is beyond all good and evil, all splitting, who is pure goodness is to be found ready to be born as a little child. Not only can Mary bring all Christians together, no doubt she will eventually lead the Jews and Islam also gently to her Son.

Mary as a human person: a psychological enquiry

Rev. Terence O'Brien, SDB, MA
Roman Catholic. Editor of Personal Growth & Development

It cannot be said that there is a Christian psychology – the psychology of the human person is the same whatever the race, colour, creed or no creed of people is, just as the anatomy or physiology is the same.

But it can be said that there is a Christian understanding of the psychology of the human person – this stemming from the fact that we are created in the image and likeness of God. That really is the sum-total of human psychology, although it does not appear to be so at first sight. However, if we reduce it to practical terms, it means two things. Firstly, that we are made to be persons because God is a person, and as persons to be in the unity of ourselves because God is in the unity of himself, and secondly, that as persons to live and move in love, because God is love.

A person is a unique individual not meant to be a copy of anyone, and we are born as such, but we are not born in the unity of ourselves or living and moving through love. This is due to the Fall in whatever way it is understood. Instead, we are split in two, open to a host of negative and destructive movements. We live on two levels, one that we are aware of, one that we are not aware of – the conscious and unconscious levels as we understand them today.

So instead of being in a state of unity we are in a state of conflict so agonisingly expressed by Paul:

I cannot understand my own behaviour.
I fail to carry out the things I want to do,
and I find myself doing the very things I hate. (Rom 7: 21-3)

Instead of living and moving only in love, we can hate ourselves, others, even our own kith and kin and God. We can do this while still being sincere Christians, because as sincere Christians, most of this is not conscious but unconscious.

This is why so many Christians do not get so very far in their life for God because it is a life for God at the conscious level, which is the level of act taken in the widest sense. This can be said to be the problem of Christian life – trying to act as God wants us to act without being as he has created us to be. We regard our failure as a failure in act, but it is first and foremost a failure of being. Only in so far as we become more and more the unique mature persons he created us to be, are we able to accept and use the grace which in his love God, our Father, so abundantly makes available to us.

We are aware of our acts; we are not always aware of the movement in our lives which is in what we do. There are basically only two movements in the human person, as in life in general. These are negative and positive – not good or bad. The movement comes from the deepest level of the person: the unconscious level, where goodness or badness as such do not exist, as reason does not exist at this level. So we can be moved on occasion to anger, bitterness, resentment, anxiety, fear, hatred. . . filled with a sense of inadequacy, inferiority, ill will. . . in so far as these prevail in our lives, we remain immature persons, but still 'good' or even 'very good'. Because of this, we fail to be people of integrity, true to ourselves, and if we are not true to ourselves, we cannot be true to God.

When we turn to consider *Mary*, if it is true that we are all created in the image and likeness of God, it is supremely true of her, who is the ever blessed and immaculate Mother of God. The unsurpassable dignity to which God has destined her as the mother of his only begotten Son and to which she freely consented, is no whit diminished, but only enhanced by her totality as a human person.

Mary is the perfect person as such. Full of grace from the first moment of her conception, she never was subject to the results of the sin of Adam. Therefore she not only and above all others, was born a unique person, but unlike us, she was also in the unity of herself as a person with one living spirit and inner movement of love. All her human powers existed and acted in perfect harmony with each other and in subjection to God. Her intellect was of the highest order, and while active from her earliest years, woud have developed more and more as she grew older. Her immaculate conception was a psychological necessity. Fullness of grace can only exist in a perfect nature.

We are born immature persons and can remain so all our lives in spite of developing very well physically and intellectually, having all the skills necessary to acquit ourselves well in whatever way of life we take up (including theology and scripture study!), but our immaturity comes out in our difficulty or failure in human relations. Mary was mature from her early years. This both resulted from her freedom from the consequence of the Fall and was necessary if she was to receive God's grace in its fullness. An immature person can only receive and accept grace in an immature way. It is also shown in the complete dedication of herself to God from an early age in the temple.

This does *not* mean that Mary could not and did not suffer, experience sorrow, be hurt. She lived in an imperfect world with imperfect people. Her experience of suffering and hurt would be greater than that of any other human being. Most of all she suffered in sharing to the full in the passion and death of Jesus. But true sorrow is a positive dynamic – it does not weaken but strengthen. However unlike us, Mary's hurt and suffering did not set up negative and destructive states at the unconscious level, her only response in all such situations was love – that love which is a movement of the whole being, the supreme way of returning good for evil. With us, being hurt, especially in our early years, establishes negative and destructive states as a result of which, resentment, bitterness, distress, anger and anxiety can build up in us and make us respond to succeeding experiences of the same kind with an intensity which belongs to the earliest experiences and not to the present one.

Mary was sinless, but she was free to sin, she had perfect freedom, but she chose to use her freedom to accept in all things the will of the Father. She *chose* to do so, it was a personal act in the fullest sense of the word. She did not act blindly, automatically or even just spiritually.

It is not possible in the time available to examine in detail every aspect of the human person – but it might be asked: did Mary dream? We now know that dreaming is a normal and necessary part of sleep and that everyone dreams every night, although many, if not most people, are not aware this is so. Mary would undoubtedly have dreamed every night and been aware of it as this awareness is what is normal. There would be this difference that in us the dream process is a good deal concerned with the psyche working through the negative and destructive states at the unconscious level, this in Mary's case would not have been so. The psyche would have done its work in maintaining and increasing the unity of the person and the equilibrium and balance of the positive movements from the unconscious level to the conscious level.

If we look at the occasions when she appears in the Gospel narrative, we can see that they are all key points in the unfolding of the redemption. In all of them she acts and decides as a fully mature person in her own right. She does not understand and so asks Gabriel for an explanation; when she sees clearly what God's plan is, she gives an unhesitating yes. And so there results that wonderful moment in the history of the human race. As Aquinas puts it: 'The Word spoke and all things were created – Mary spoke and the Word was made flesh'. Mary does not then go into retreat to ponder the wonder of what she has just experienced and how the Old Law has been fulfilled in her, but decides to go and help her cousin Elizabeth. Luke tells us 'she went as quickly as she could.' It was a personal decision and results in what can be called the first miracle of grace in the New Testament.

As soon as Elizabeth heard Mary's greeting, the child leaped in her womb and Elizabeth was filled with the Holy Spirit. She gave a loud cry and said: . . . For the moment your greeting reached my ear, the child in my womb leapt for joy. . .' (Lk 1: 40)

It has been the tradition in the Church that at that moment John the Baptist was sanctified in his mother's womb. Mary spoke, she who now carried the Incarnate God within her, John was sanctified in his mother's womb, and Elizabeth was filled with the Holy Spirit.

During the period of her pregnancy Mary would have been in touch with the child in her womb, loving him with all her being and expressing it in talking to him, singing to him. . . it would have come natural to her to do so. It makes quite a difference to a baby today when it is accepted in this way, both while still in the womb and in the process of being born. If a baby does not feel after being born, 'it is good to be here', the chances are that it will go all through life without ever having been convinced that this is so.

If we take the period from the birth of Jesus to the beginning of his public life, Mary had the ineffable joy of a mother in holding her child in her arms and having him at her breast. This would have been increased immeasureably with the realisation of who this child was. She would have devoted herself to caring for Jesus, able, as many mothers are not able to do, to let him develop independently of her so that he grew to maturity filled with wisdom.

The family life of Jesus, Mary and Joseph must have been very wonderful also for their neighbours. It would have been very practical because the human person in unity and moving in love is open in love and friendship to all without exception, and therefore very keenly aware of their needs. Mary was not moving on an astral plane divorced from the practicalities of life, because the more she was in the fullness of herself as a person, the more she was living completely in the present and open to the will of the Father in that present.

Luke tells us that Mary stood there wondering at the things being said about Jesus at the presentation in the temple, certainly a very human act as also the expressing of Joseph's and her own concern when they lost Jesus. He concludes his account of Mary's part in the hidden life at Nazareth with the words: 'His mother stored up all these things in her heart'. In this way Mary again was acting in the fulness of herself. The heart spoken of in scripture in this way corresponds to the deeper level of the human person where what is heard is worked upon unconsciously and assimilated gradually, thereby creating a mentality and outlook. In Mary this would have happened without hindrance – with us unfortunately, not so easily.

In the space of a communication it is not possible to enlarge on the place Mary played in the development of Jesus through his boyhood and adolescence to manhood. I suggest the incident related by John in his gospel of the wedding feast at Cana, can help us to realise how complete it was.

Jesus had begun his preparation for his public life by calling his first disciples including John, and John tells us that three days later there was a wedding at Cana in Galilee. The mother of Jesus was there and Jesus and his disciples had also been invited. I think it is Calvin who says, 'Jesus is here represented as accompanying his mother.' The quiet assurance of Mary in saying to the servants – do whatever he tells you – abundantly epitomises the relationship built up over the years between mother and son and the part she had played as a mother in his development to manhood. She had no need to beg and cajole her son to do something to relieve the embarrassment of the young couple – she knew his concern was as great as her own and that he would act on it, although his time had not yet come. So with the assurance arising out of the deep understanding that existed between them she quietly points out the need and leaves it at that. But she understands human nature and knowing that the servants might well be annoyed at being told by someone who was just a guest – to do something they considered totally unnecessary – she says to them 'do whatever he tells you'.

Again it was a personal decision of Mary to do so, and as a result of it we have what in effect is the first miracle of nature in the New Testament, and also the disciples taking the first step in believing in Jesus and accepting his mission.

After Cana Mary fades into the background until she takes her place at the feet of the Cross, except for two brief indirect references. In Matthew Jesus says:

Anyone who does the will of my Father in Heaven is my brother and sister and mother. (Mt 12: 50)

In Luke he says when the woman in 'the crowd' proclaims the blessedness of his mother:

Still happier are those who hear the Word of God and keep it. (Mt 11: 28)

I think it can be said that Jesus is here emphasing that there is little merit before God without a fully personal act and in doing so helps us to understand that it is not the great privileges given to Mary that place her above all other human beings, but her free total response to God as a person-created in his image and likeness.

All through the ages and in our own time, through the second Vatican Council and following on that by Pope John XXIII, Paul VI and John Paul II, Mary is put before us as a model to imitate and have devotion to. I should like to suggest that the words 'imitation' and 'devotion' are now misleading and not helpful for our own generation.

Imitation normally means imitation of acts. One human being imitating another, however admirable, blocks development to maturity and their own uniqueness. Mary is the model of how we should *be* – acts follow from being. The more perfect the being, the more perfect the acts.

Devotion as we understand it, falls far short of what is necessary. With devotion we are only united with Mary through piety on the conscious level – not in the fullness of ourselves as persons. What we need is personal relationship. Relationship is the movement of love which unites us with each other. We need to be united with – one with – Mary in love. We need her to have the place in our lives which only love can give. If we can succeed in that, all the rest will follow. In this way we will be open to the abundant help God has made possible for her to give us in all our needs. She is the Mother of the Church and of each of us. The office of mother is supremely shown in helping freely, lovingly, in all circumstances and in all needs. Most of all, she will help us to live as she lived, in the fullness of ourselves as human persons, totally responding to God as the person created us to be and doing the work he gave us to do.

This I suggest is the greatest need of our generation. It is a generation in which we are more and more substituting feeling for judgement and knowledge for love, with an over-riding basic principle that the end justifies the means.

This results in a fixation in immaturity which leaves us unable to become the unique, wonderful persons God created us to be – able to act with inner freedom and respond to him as person to person. She who is 'the woman clothed with the sun with a crown of stars on her head and the moon under her feet' says to our generation that it is a total personal life for God which is needed, not just a spiritual life.

Theological difficulties loom largest on the ecumenical scene – but no less important, although more neglected, are the psychological difficulties. Antagonism, prejudices, unwillingness, insecurity can be there deep down and working in unrecognised ways at the conscious level. Very often hidden behind a theological difficulty is a personal difficulty. The only real answer is love – *Amor vincit omnia* – love always succeeds – love is never defeated. But only a mature person can love – to be good or even full of theology is not enough.

De Lachrimae Rerum: the Tears of Things or 'On the necessity of tears'

Rev. David H. Clark
Anglican Rector of St Peter's, Oadby, Leicester

> By the waters of Babylon we sat down and wept:
> when we remembered thee, O Zion (Psalm 137,1)

I have had forty-seven years of experiencing. In that time, amidst all the deeper events – courtship, childbirth, the death of my father, a religious retreat, the restoration of my adopted son – I have been conscious of the closeness of joy and tears. Together. As I reflect on that truth, the strange phenomenon of my long fascination with and attraction to the music of John Dowland falls into place.

Seemingly by chance, my music teacher at school, Charles Cleall,[1] suggested I try Dowland's 'Now, O now, I needs must part', when I was seventeen. I waded through the other songs in the First Book of Airs, revelling in their words and the fresh spirit of the late Renaissance which they breathed. I only ever sang these songs privately or for a singing lesson. Later, when I met a lutanist (David Capp) with considerable gifts of accompaniment, I performed them with The Elizabethans, Sheila Graham's troupe of entertainers, who regularly promoted recitals at stately homes and in the Purcell Room. It was then I discovered the immense poewer of the 'big' melancholy songs. I realised they demanded a total performance, just as one would perform lieder. The song not only 'took me over'; performed thus, it had the power of concentrating the attention of an audience wholly on the work of art which was Dowland's. I was surprised by this power, and felt it most strongly present when singing 'I saw my lady weep', 'Sorrow, stay', and 'Flow my tears'. I suppose I performed these songs regularly over a period of seven or eight years from the mid-seventies, often wondering why they spoke so deeply to me.

I began to realise why these songs were so important in 1978. I attended a 'Person Centred Approach Workshop' for a fortnight at Nottingham University as part of a four month sabbatical in the midst of an increasingly busy professional life as an Industrial Chaplain in Norwich. The break came at just the right time, not only to reassess my work, but also to do some personal work, and through that, to become aware of a very great sadness within me. I also knew that I had a strong tendency to refuse to acknowledge the sadness which I had been carrying. I suspect that large numbers of people brought up with the emotional controls typical of Britain, and typical of the British male, are unable to acknowledge their deep sadness.

Sadness, like the tears which express it, may be accumulated and stored within, in the deep recesses of the self. It requires a 'trigger' to release it. That trigger may take some time to be discovered, and it usually comes as a surprise. Having kept a stiff upper lip at my father's funeral, I grieved for him ten years later, during a co-counselling session, which immeasurably enhanced my appreciation of him and all that he had done for me. The 'very great sadness', to which I refer, emerged gradually, in bursts of tears, over a period of years, during which the Dowland songs acted as a kind of background counterpoint, reminding me of the reality of my interior. When I finally acknowledged fully the 'great sadness' in a mini-breakdown lasting some six months, I realised what the songs were saying and wondered why I had not heard it before. The detailed causes of my 'great sadness' need not concern us here: the main causes were twofold – to do with my private life (now much healed), and to do with my professional life. The latter involved counselling and caring for all sorts of people, those made redundant, the unemployed, and a great struggle to establish a new hostel for homeless people in Norwich using disabled long-term unemployed workers under a Government scheme.

All this intense activity brought great stress which I could not handle. I suppose I had not reached the maturity so beautifully described as seeing 'the contradiction between what we hope for and what we really are'. This phrase comes from Alan Jones' great chapter 'The Gift of Tears' in his book 'Soul-Making',[2] and it is worth giving the whole passage in this context,

> When do tears come for the attentive believer? They begin to flow at the moment when we see the contradiction between what we hope for and what we really are; when we see the deep gulf between the Love that calls us and our response to it.

The acknowledgement of the great sadness was facilitated not only by my previous involvement in Dowland, but also by the discovery of certain truths about the inner life. As James Hillman writes,

> But then a man reaches thirty-five or forty, or sometimes not until near fifty, and he feels sad; there is a weight on the heart and no matter what he does it does not go away. This is typical of an anima state, an anima mood, the steady accompaniment of the soul which has become a burden, because it has not been give what it needs. . . the other aspect faces us now: the inner femininity.[3]

This feminine was externalised strongly for me by the discovery of the significance of the Blessed Virgin Mary. Drawn first to the reconstructed cell of Julian of Norwich in St Julian's church, Rouen Road, Norwich, during my enforced break, I discovered an unused rosary I had kept in a drawer for years since finding it in a redundant church. There I used it, having read Neville Ward's book[4] to find out the correct method. Then the reaction began. Invariably, as the pictures of the joyful, sorrowful and glorious mysteries arose before my mind, the tears were released. And I wondered why. I soon found out.

It was the great sadness being released by one who knew the depths of sorrow: one who had watched her son all along the Via Dolorosa, falling exhausted, raised by the kindness of a stranger, then nailed to the cross, jolted upright and left to die. Our Lady of Sorrows knew. Looking back upon it from the distance of three years, it seems like an answer to the whispered invocations,

> Holy Mary, mother of God, pray for us now and at the hour of our death. . .

or more particularly, an answer to the concluding prayer of the rosary, the 'Salve Regina',

> Ad te clamamus exsules filii Evae: ad te suspiramus, gementes et flentes in hac lacrimarum valle. . .
> (. . . to thee do we cry poor banished children of Eve; to thee do we lift up our sighs, mourning and weeping in this vale of tears.)

When the tears first began, I too was exhausted, spiritually, mentally and emotionally. And at that low ebb, all I could do was to be alone, meditate, weep and be with my family, who were most understanding. Later, I realised that my so-called 'great sadness' was but a part of the tears of things, the Lachrimae Rerum, which are the tears for the tragic dimension of nature, for the unfulfilled possibilities, the broken egg, for lost innocence, for the child dying with the diseased brain, for the victim of Huntington's Chorea.

Yet, the paradox is there:

Qui seminant in lacrimis: in exultatione metent.
They that sow in tears shall reap in joy. (Ps 125/6, 9)

I think this profound truth, especially dear to the Christian, is the reason why the unrelieved gloom of despair in 'Sorry, stay', and 'Flow my tears' evokes slightly less of a response in me. Yes, I love both songs: they are incomparably crafted. 'Flow my tears' could so easily be the expression of the voluntarily exiled Dowland; 'Sorrow, stay' is indescribably profound, and never fails to command total commitment. But, 'I saw my lady weep' in words and music is *the* masterpiece.

I saw my Lady weep,
   And sorrow proud to be advanced so;
In those fair eyes where all perfections keep,
   Her Face was full of woe,
But such a woe (believe me) as wins more hearts,
Than mirth can do with her enticing parts.

   Sorrow was there made fair,
   And passion wise, tears a delightful thing,
Silence beyond all speech a wisdom rare,
   She made her sighs to sing,
And all things with so sweet a sadness move,
As made my heart at once both grieve and love.
(Verses 1 & 2 only[6])

Although this is ostensibly a secular song, and the lady could be
any noble (or not so noble) court attendant, yet the words allow a
marian interpretation, although we have absolutely no grounds for
thinking Dowland could have considered this possible. He became a
Catholic briefly during a period he spent in France at seventeen years
of age in 1580. But it is unlikely he remained so, since he became
court lutanist to the King of Denmark, and, for a shorter period, to
the Landgrave of Hessen – both more Protestant than Elizabeth,
under whom he failed to gain employment.[7]

   I venture, nevertheless, this paraphrase of the sentiments of verses
1 & 2 above,

Our Lady stands at the foot of the cross and weeps, proud to be
so 'advanced' in her sorrow for her Son. The sadness of her face
draws more hearts to her, than even attractive laughter.
   In our Lady, ugly sorrow is transformed, passion is made wise,
and tears delightful. In her silent sorrow is deep wisdom (Sophia?),
and everything is given a deep movement of sweet sadness, so that
our hearts grieve and love at the same time.

   Fortunately, the fifteen mysteries of the rosary remind us that
though there are five sorrowful mysteries, the enormous gravity of
these is placed in perspective by the five Joyful and five Glorious
Mysteries. Maybe this is why the shifting major and minor chords of
Monteverdi's 'Salve Regina', and, more than a hundred years previ-
ously written, Josquin's 'Stabat Mater', are so stunning, so life-affirm-
ing.
   Alan Jones has so many treasures in the chapter on tears,
including,

The gift of tears is a sign of the mending of creation.

   We hardly need psychotherapists to tell us of the healing power of tears, for they are reiterating Jesus' well-known beatitude,

Blessed are ye that weep now: for ye shall laugh (Luke 6:21)

Notes

1. Charles Cleall: see his interesting book, *Music and Holiness*, as well as the little *Novello Primer in Choral Technique*.
2. Alan Jones, *Soul Making, the Desert Way of Spirituality* (SCM 1985).
3. James Hillman: *Insearch*, Spring Publications (Texas 1967; 1979 ed.), 104f.
4. Neville Ward's, *Five for Sorrow, Ten for Joy* – the best book on the rosary; and appropriately enough in this ecumenical age, by a Methodist.
5. Mary Kirk, 'the Savage Gene: Huntington's Chorea', in *Good Housekeeping*, June 1986.
6. Dowland's *First Book of Airs* was published in 1597. It is available, as are the other three, in a modern edition (ed Fellowes, revised Dart, published by Stainer and Bell). The second Book begins with the three 'big' melancholy songs discussed above.
7. See Diana Poulton, *John Dowland*, 26+40−2 (Faber & Faber 1982 ed.).

Marian devotion in the United States today

Rev. Donald G. Dawe

Presbyterian, Professor of Theology in Union Theological Seminary, Virginia

A report by a minister from a Reformed church on marian devotion should be brief to the point of almost disappearing. Let me hasten to add that this is a report on research done by Monsignor John J. Murphy through the members of the United States branch of the ESBVM. Because he was unable to attend this Congress, he asked me to interpret the data. The communication is indeed an ecumenical one, because it represents a report by a Presbyterian minister on research done by a Roman Catholic priest on the marian devotion in Catholic, Orthodox, and Protestant traditions represented in our American Society.

In interpreting marian devotion in the United States to a British or European audience, it is important to note differences in cultural tradition and religious heritage. In Britain there are many places associated with marian devotion that go back to the early beginnings of Christianity here. They are churches, places of pilgrimage, and tiny shrines that link people together because they go back to a time before the divisions of Christianity had taken place. During our Fifth International Congress at Canterbury (1981), we met in the tiny Lady Chapel on the crypt level of the cathedral for a prayer service. Here was a site associated with marian devotion that goes back to the founding of the Cathedral itself. Similarly, in Scotland each year, a pilgrimage is held at Haddington-Whitkirk under the sponsorship of the Earl of Lauderdale. It brings together Anglican, Orthodox, Roman Catholic and Free Church traditions, along with a host of people who have no regular ties to the Church. Great marian sites are part of a cultural heritage that binds people to one another.

In the United States, we have no such sites. Where there are great marian shrines, they are ones that have been brought up by immigrants from Europe or Latin America. There are no common traditions or common sites to which Roman Catholics, Orthodox, Episcopalians, and Protestants can look. Even the Catholicism of Lord Baltimore and the Roman Catholics of the eighteenth and early nineteenth century in the United States did not have great emphasis on marian devotion. Marian devotion came to the United States beginning in the middle of the nineteenth century down to the present with the large ethnic groups of Roman Catholics that emigrated from Italy, Poland, central Europe, and now in the twentieth century from Puerto Rico, Mexico, and Central America. Many of the shrines to the blessed Virgin erected in the United States were remembrances of appearances of the Virgin in Italy, Spain, Portugal, Mexico, or some other spot now translated to American soil. Christians of the Anglican, Reformed, Lutheran tradition, as well as Orthodox Christians, had no sense of attachment to these shrines. Marian shrines tended to be looked upon as one of the idiosyncrasies of ethnic Catholicism. It has only been since the development of such places of pilgrimage as the shrine of Our Lady of the Snows in Illinois or the great shrine of the Immaculate Conception in Washington, DC that we have the growth of distinctively American sites of marian devotion.

Marian piety among Roman Catholics has been a vernacular piety. Rosaries, novenas, and marian prayers were offered in a variety of languages while the liturgy of pre-Vatican II worship was carried on in Latin. The growth of this marian piety reached its height in the immediate post-World War II period and found its confirmation in the promulgation of the dogma of the assumption of the blessed Virgin. Two things have affected it since then. The first has been the dispersal of the great ethnic communities in American cities to the suburbs. Second has been the emergence of a fully vernacular liturgy since Vatican II. The centre of popular piety has shifted from the more individualised forms of marian devotion to the corporate participation of the congregation in the vernacular mass. While there are still glorious marian festivals in the ethnic neighbourhoods of the great cities, these forms of popular religion are much less influential in the new suburban developments of American urban life.

However, the heightened crisis in the world – deep divisions reflected in the nuclear war threat – have found Roman Catholics reaching for prayerful solutions. The movement of charismatic renewal has helped to re-emphasise devotion to the blessed Virgin for many. A concern for marian apparitions is a recurrent theme in much of popular piety in the United States.

Among Byzantine rite Catholics, marian devotion has remained central and strong. The annual pilgrimage of Byzantine rite Catholics to the marian shrine at Uniontown, Pennsylvania has brought together as many as fifty thousand worshipers. The shrine of the Immaculate Conception in Washington continues to be a focal point of pilgrimage and devotion.

In the Orthodox Church, Marian piety is beautifully integrated into the liturgical life of this people. Orthodox churches have never had the tradition of a separate vernacular of piety focussed on Mary. Devotion to the blessed Virgin is a theme reinforced in its liturgical life at every step. The significant development has been the emergence in the United States of Orthodox churches in which the liturgy is now celebrated in English. This gives a clear and focussed devotion to Mary in a way accessible to all of the worshipers. Replies to our inquiries about marian devotion to the Orthodox members of our Society did not speak of separate marian devotions. Rather, their replies to our inquiries provided them a chance to explicate the integral role of Mary to the spirituality of Orthodox Christians.

The Anglo-Catholic traditions in American Episcopalianism are strong and clear. They provide a focus for devotion to the blessed Virgin that is not found in many Episcopal parishes. Similarly, some Lutherans have reinvestigated the rich heritage of liturgy, hymnody and preaching of Luther and early Lutheranism as a witness to devotion to the blessed Virgin. The great marian feasts are observed in many Episcopal and some Lutheran churches in the United States.

The feast of the assumption has always been a difficult one for Protestants for theological as well as liturgical reasons. The resolution of this in the Episcopal Book of Common Prayer has been the designation of 15 August as 'The feast day of St Mary the Virgin, Mother of our Lord Jesus Christ'. Liturgists in other Protestant traditions are investigating the possibility of designating a day during the liturgical year as a special day for honouring Mary. Among Reformed, Methodists, Baptists, and other Protestants, the approach to honouring the blessed Virgin has remained cautious. But through the American Society there has continued a vigorous and creative attempt to study the question of marian devotion theologically, biblically, and liturgically from the perspective of a variety of traditions. In private devotion, however, faithful people are celebrating Mary as the person of faith and the bearer of Christ. In this there is the beginning of a piety that points to a new and open future in faith.

Can we learn from Mary about attitudes and manners?

Rev. Mrs Angela Robinson
Congregationalist Minister, Seaton, Devon

Mary and ecumenism and manners – from these, what can we learn? The manners of a servant who puts her master's concerns before her own; of a welcoming hostess to Christ; of one who understood when Jesus had time only for the lost members of the family; of her who insisted on being at Calvary when others were not – or dare not. What light do Mary's manners throw on our ecumenical relationships? One remembers, at the Coloma Congress of 1971 (the first of our Society), Cardinal Suenens' picture of all Christians converging at the home of the Lord, his mother on the doorstep to welcome us to help us create a place of united purpose, mutual dignity, joyful harmony and creative discipleship.

It is my joy to have been minister of a little Congregational church in the Yorkshire Dales, in which people often said: 'I feel as though I've come home.' It is one of the images of salvation. Looking at Mary, we are helped to behave as though we are 'at home', members of the Lord's family. We have yet a lot to learn about relating across the frontiers of our traditions. Relations between churches and Christians need to be worked upon: when things go wrong, it is often not a matter of theology but of manners! It is human feelings, not doctrinal differences, that do the damage; and in particular that insensitivity which not only fails to see how something looks from another standpoint, but is blithely unaware that there is another standpoint. The handmaid of the Lord tries always to see things from the master's standpoint, to see how she can support or join in. We should do the same, listening as to the Lord – otherwise it is secular listening. If we do not learn to love and listen to one another as fellow servants, then we become vulnerable to that pseudo-unity which is the death of real unity. If our 'listening' is only to humour or patronise each other, then we shall return from our occasional ecumenical excursions without having learned a single thing of what the Lord has been trying to say to us through others! Only the kind of humble loving that Mary exemplifies will release us – and the world – into full salvation.

Mary is the model of that obedience which risks the loss of security for the sake of the joy and terror of falling into the hands of the living God. Mary did that, holding on in faith to promises and visions. You and I may say we recognise that: especially those who fought for years against ordination, and then gave up – we know about obeying where we do not understand! When did our congregations take such risks, or in the name of local ecumenism show such vulnerability? Most ecumenical services are so formally organised that no risk is offered. I am on the Standing Conference for Unity in Prayer which helps to produce the texts for the Week of Prayer for Christian Unity; and I attend the Women's World Day of Prayer service. Both services are carefully prepared, but both can be victims of formalism. 'Come in, pick up your piece of paper, read it through, go home – that is your dose of ecumenism for the year!' Nothing handmaidenly about that! No risk, no pain!

It is a far cry from the Graduate School of Ecumenical Study, Bossey (Geneva). I was of the class of 1966 – Catholics and Protestants and Orthodox; priests and ministers and theological students and even lay students. We were welcomed by Fr Paul Verghese of the Syrian Orthodox Church: 'You have come here with your images – of yourself and of others – and here these images will be broken. You will all become iconoclasts!' Neither in ecumenism nor in religious life is guaranteed short-term security; nor was there for Mary. She accepted Jesus as child and authority and is seen, along with him, as friend of sinners. We too are meant to be gracious receivers, but the message we convey in what we say and do is quite other than what we intend. My own eyes were opened at a Grassington Festival held in my church. There I said, 'I don't like the word "visitor": this is your Father's house, and you have every right to be here.' One of our members later told me that her non-church-going father had repeated those words with tears in his eyes. I realised the Lord was saying, 'Don't you dare give anyone entering your church the impression that he is temporarily visiting it at *your* invitation. It is not your club-room but my house; all are there as of right, of my grace, to feel at home there.' In the Lord's house there is no distinction between 'visitors' and 'owners': there are only potential and actual members of the Lord's family. No good hostess divides those present into 'them' and 'us', so why should we?

But what of Mary's manner at Cana? Note, she does not blame whoever was responsible for mis-ordering the wine and nor disclaiming her own responsibility because it would 'cause a fuss and draw attention to herself'! For us, too, 'good manners' can including owning up to the mess the Church is in and working with the servants or little people who are so often in touch with what's going on under the veneer of 'everything is fine' in order to plead for divine intervention before it gets serious. We may be snubbed and told our timing is wrong but no scripture directs us to pretend things are fine when they are not. For instance, if inter-Church events are poor, let us look to the Lord for better wine for he is dishonoured when the occasions for our coming together are not true feasts.

There are ways of following Mary by standing at the cross. The Lord is suffering in his churches. Clergy and laity are suffering the consequences of our failure to become The Church. We have to weep with those who weep as helpless in the face of structures that are far from liberating. Like her we should ponder in our hearts the traditions of others instead of dismissing them unexamined. And there are ways of being, like Mary, *recipients* of good manners. When Mary visited Elizabeth her cousin, who might have envied her her youth or resented her new privilege, Elizabeth showed herself the perfect model of how the older generation in the Church should treat the younger. Younger people come great with gifts, doubtful whether they possess them and nervous about how to deploy them. Elizabeth perceived Mary not through jealous eyes, or resentful or self-concerned; but through eyes that saw God's design and her own and Mary's place therein. What she said in greeting was, in effect: 'You are blessed. We are both pregnant. I am honoured that you are here. Trust God and be joyful!' What was its effect upon Mary, then? The cork flew off, so to say, and out poured the Magnificat: the Spirit working in and through Elizabeth, released Mary into confident praise. God's Church will be released into just such praise by the affirmation of its older members, filled as they are with the Spirit and confident of their own fruitfulness in the Lord, so that they do not need to suppress new life bubbling up in the churches, as being 'unconventional'. What might Mary have thought if after uttering her *Magnificat*, if Elizabeth had replied, 'That is a new song, isn't it? I prefer the Song of Hannah – it's the Authorised Version in our tradition, you know!'

Those of us who have received an ecumenical vocation within our vocation should learn step by step what it is to move with God through this veritable minefield. It is so easy to make churches became ecclesiastical institutions instead of homes for God. It is easy to be exclusive, rather than inclusive. It is easy for office holders to play their own power games rather than the power game of the Spirit. It is easy to have little time to hear, to share, to weep, to grieve. It is easy to forget that we are servants in the Lord's house, and so to forget our manners, Indeed I find it hard: how about you?

NOTE: A tape of the full communication of Rev Mrs Angela Robinson (below) is available on request to 6 Newlands Park, Seaton, East Devon, EX12 2SF (0297-20336).

Thoughts on the future development of ESBVM

Mrs Margaret Kneebone
Anglican

I feel strongly that our Society must begin to make more impact on
the outside world. For twenty years or so we have been getting to
know each other, to trust each other, to understand our differing
theological points of view; and in this process some wonderful and
highly valuable new insights have been gained. But now this understanding should be consolidated, and we should be able, together, to
present a more united front to the world, strong in our basic understanding of the importance of Mary and ready to go forward to the
next stage in our ecumenical pilgrimage.

The question before us is what should that next stage be? The
theological ground has been pretty well covered in the talks and lectures, which have reached a very high standard of scholarship and
erudition; the devotional side of our life has been enriched and
deepened by our sharing in each other's liturgies and our praying
together; and always there has been the good fellowship – the eating
and drinking together, and the emphasis on hospitality. All this has
been very valuable, and for many, both clergy and lay people, the
ESBVM provides a much needed oasis of goodwill, friendlinesss and
renewed inspiration amidst much that is dreary, divisive and sometimes downright destructive in contemporary church life.

But we cannot go on forever taking in each other's washing,
laundering it, ironing it beautifully and then looking in smug self-satis-
faction at the perfectly folded piles of dogmas, doctrines and devotions. Clean linen must be used, or it quickly becomes creased and
dusty again in the cupboard; and surely now, as a Society, we need
to become more of a force in the world at large, and to make some
impact upon it.

But before any such impact can be effective, we must be clearer
in our own minds as to how in fact we view the Virgin. What exactly
does devotion to and understanding of Mary contribute to our life
in the world? What is that extra 'Mary-dimension', beyond our basic
Christian understanding, which becomes of compelling significance
in the conduct of our everyday lives? My personal view is that, while
in our Lord we see divinity realised in humanity, in our Lady we see
humanity so exalted as to become the perfect realisation of purely

human possibility.

I wrote in 1985 (ESBVM May Newsletter) that I felt there was an urgent need for us to look at Mary as the supreme example of motherhood, and to see where she could inspire us in discovering a new concept of the value of family life – in harmony with the ethos of our century, though not slavishly following it. This is particularly urgent at the present time when, on all sides, we see the family threatened.

This leads on to the whole question of the place of women in present-day society, and the good and the evil that are coming in, thick and fast, on the heels of women's emancipation. Let me declare at once that, as far as the role of women in the Church is concerned, I myself am against the ordination of women, but I welcome the greater share women now have in most aspects of affairs, both in the Church and in the world. I also feel, however, that women may have won their freedom but that children are paying the price. Surely it ought to be possible to arrive at some satisfactory compromise, whereby women can continue to enjoy their hard-won new freedom and independence, sharing in the running of the world, yet at the same time not neglecting their responsibilities as mothers.

To me a rather sad fact is that so many women in the traditionally faithful Catholic countries, such as Spain, Italy, or Portugal, who show most devotion to Mary the blessed Mother of God and who still seem content to carry on their age-old roles of wife and mother without agitating unduly for more liberation – these same women perpetuate an image of submissive docility which, I believe, is very far removed from a true understanding of Mary the Mother of our Lord.

How can we in our Society contribute to a new, more invigorating concept of Mary, based on our understanding of the way in which she exemplified true motherhood? I think we might turn first to the Orthodox Church for inspiration. There, in those austere, other-worldly, regal icons of our Lady, we see no hint of the vapid, plaster-doll debased representation of the Mother and Child image which so tragically often appears to be the accepted picture of Mary in many western churches. It is this over-sentimentalised, over-adulated figure which becomes anathema to Protestants – and quite rightly so, as it bears no resemblance at all to the person of Mary as revealed in the New Testament.

Mary appears very briefly in the Gospels, and is only mentioned once again early in Acts; yet, for me, her presence in the Gospel narrative is very real. Without her, none of it could have happened. The incarnation is the heart of the matter: the Word made flesh – of Mary's flesh; the divine child growing in her womb, in exactly the same way as any other human baby grows and develops, except that Mary knew the divine secret, and pondered all these things in her heart.

So much about Mary has to be deduced – to be extracted from behind a veil of silence – yet what emerges is consistent and very strong. She was certainly no submissive village maiden, meekly acquiescing in mysteries beyond her comprehension. Her full acceptance and agreement were sought by God himself before she became the instrument of the incarnation. 'Let it be done to me according to thy word' is not the response of an ignorant or simple-minded person. It is the humble, and at the same time proud, rejoinder of one fully conscious of a great honour, offered and accepted. Her responsibility from then on was to be tremendous. With the help of her husband Joseph, Mary had to undertake the upbringing and nurture of her son, Jesus. To the outward world she and Joseph were the ordinary parents of this extraordinary boy. To them was entrusted responsibility for his safety during the desperately dangerous early years, and it was their task to provide a secure home in which the holy child could grow and develop to his full maturity. And then the 'parents' had to step back – Joseph into total obscurity, and Mary into the background, emerging briefly at the marriage of Cana and once or twice during the years of Jesus' ministry, when crowds prevented her getting near her Son. The full light of publicity glares down on her again at the foot of the cross. That is almost all, but it is enough. The almost total absence of details about Mary must surely be like that because Mary herself wished it to be so.

The evangelists later must have had to enquire and learn from those who had known her about the early days of Jesus' life and it is likely that he, Jesus, would have told his mother about the events in the wilderness during the temptation, and again about things happening when he was similarly alone, with no bystanders to catch the words. But Mary, in sharing, say with Luke, the precious secrets of the annunciation or of the visit to Jerusalem when Jesus was twelve, could very well have insisted that her part in it all was to be played down. She wanted people to listen to her son, 'Whatever he tells you to do, do it' (Jn 2:5). She wanted no credit for herself; yet she must have been totally identified with Jesus' mission of healing and teaching and proclaiming the kingdom of heaven. At the very end of his life Jesus acknowledged this publicly by entrusting his mother to John, and John in turn to Mary.

And so Mary – to me – does not come across at all as a passive person, but as one endowed with great hidden powers. How can this century recapture the full understanding of the strength of Mary, evidenced for example in the liturgy and iconography of the Eastern churches, without necessarily adhering to the tenets of Orthodoxy?

In our ecumenical pilgrimage under the guidance of Mary, might we not make a serious attempt to invite her far more into our daily lives, perhaps along the lines of the ancient traditional prayers used in the Outer Hebrides, and collected so painstakingly from oral tradition by Alexander Carmichael in the late nineteenth century and published under the title *Carmina Gadelica*. In her most valuable booklet, *God under my Roof*, Esther de Waal has selected some of these Gaelic prayers and hymns and written sensitive and moving commentaries on them. Prayers to Mary, to Christ or the saints, are used with total naturalness to precede or accompany the most ordinary activities of daily life, from rising in the morning to going to bed at night. Prayers before baking bread, prayers before going fishing, before milking the cow, before gathering turf for the fire. We could update these by saying, for instance, simple prayers before we drive off in our car or before we start weeding the garden or before writing a letter. I myself have tried this, and find it amazingly helpful and calming, especially when agitated about something. I did it recently when baking a special birthday-cake for my small grand-daughter's second birthday. 'Praying the cake' I called it, exactly as the Orthodox people talk about 'praying an icon', not 'painting an icon'. This simple idea, based on the invocation of Mary's help in our everyday activities, opens up whole new possibilities of a more prayer-filled yet practical attitude to life and its multifarious duties and obligations, and enables one to draw on the strength and prayers of our Lady herself, who knows only too well our human condition.

To help cultivate such prayerful practices, I should like to see our Society encouraging members who may live fairly near one another to take the initiative themselves by arranging to meet together on a regular basis, say once a month, in each other's homes for study, prayer and discussion. These study circles would of course be ecumenical: men and women from different churches , but all agreeing that they want to know more about Mary, and how to draw on her for help. In this connection I would particularly like to see more co-operation between individuals, whether in families or living alone, and members of religious orders. When I was part of one such group I found it especially valuable to have a good mixture of persons – housewives, husbands, career women, nuns – all contributing ideas and sharing attitudes. In a group such as this, much mutual help results, especially in the encouragement of prayer.

To sum up these thoughts on the theme 'Where do we go from here?', I would repeat that I feel the time is now ripe for some new steps to be taken by our Society. The theological foundations have been well and truly laid, and much useful intellectual ground has been covered; but now we should ask Mary to help us go futher in putting into practice the knowledge we have gained. We as members of churches with widely differing traditions, have now learned to trust each other to a much greater degree than would have seemed possible twenty years ago, when it all began. What seemed impossible in 1966 has become almost commonplace in 1986, and I am convinced that our founder Martin Gillett was right to trust the vision of a growing sense of common purpose among those Christians, however widely separated they might be on points of doctrine, who were prepared to ask Mary to be their guide in leading them closer towards her Son.

ALBERIC STACPOOLE, OSB, a monk of Ampleforth Abbey in Yorkshire (England), is at present Senior Tutor at St Benet's Hall, Oxford. He has published numerous articles in the areas of ecumenism, theology and ministry; and edited *Mary's place in Christian dialogue* (1982), *Mary in Christian tradition* (1984), *Charles Lindley Wood, Lord Halifax, 1839-1934* (1984), and *Vatican II by those who were there* (1986).

REV. DR J. A. ROSS MACKENZIE, formerly Professor of Theology in Union Theological Seminary, Virginia, is now in charge of the First Presbyterian Church, Gainesville, Florida (USA). He has contributed full lectures to previous International Congresses of ESBVM as follows: 'The theme of Eve and Mary in Christian thought' (1975), 'Calvin and the Calvinists on Mary' (1979), 'Honouring the Virgin Mary' (1981).

DR ALF HÄRDELIN is Docent at the University of Uppsala (Sweden). He has published works on aspects of nineteenth century Church renewal, notably *The Tractarian understanding of the Eucharist* (Uppsala 1965). His present field of research is the spirituality, liturgy and culture of the early medieval Church. He presented a Communication at the Dublin International Congress (1984).

MRS MARY ANN DE TRANA is married to an Orthodox priest and teacher in Richmond, Virginia (USA); and with him has been involved in founding one of the first parishes in the Southern Diocese of the Orthodox Church in America. She has been a member of the ESBVM in America from its inception (1975). She is a frequent contributor to religious journals, Roman Catholic, Orthodox and Protestant. A lecturer on Orthodoxy, she has delivered the key-note address at the Women's Conference of VI All-American Council of the Orthodox Church in America (1980). At the Dublin International Congress (1984) she contributed a full lecture entitled 'The Theotokos, creation and the modern world'.

RT REV. EDWARD KNAPP-FISHER, former Bishop of Pretoria and member of ARCIC I, recent Archdeacon and Sub-Dean of Westminster Abbey (England), has been until his retirement to Chichester (1987) Chairman of the London branch of ESBVM. Author of *Where the truth is found* (1975) and a study of modern eucharistic teaching, he has given several lectures to the Society, notably 'Prospects for unity: an Anglican view' (*One in Christ* 1983-3, 269-73).

DR DONAL FLANAGAN, formerly a lecturer at St Patrick's College, Maynooth (Ireland), is now a broadcaster at RTE Dublin specialising in subjects relating to women's rights. He has contributed to the *Irish Theological Quarterly* and other journals, on mariology, with a particular interest in ecumenical discussion on Mary and the impact of feminist thinking on the Christian theology of woman. He contributed the marian chapter to *The Church: a theological and pastoral commentary* (ed. [Archbishop] Kevin McNamara, 1968). He is the author of a selection of marian texts with commentary, *In praise of Mary* (1975); and of *The theology of Mary* (1976).